REPRESENTATIVE BUREAUCRACY AND THE AMERICAN POLITICAL SYSTEM

REPRESENTATIVE BUREAUCRACY AND THE AMERICAN POLITICAL SYSTEM

Samuel Krislov
David H. Rosenbloom

PRAEGER

PRAEGER SPECIAL STUDIES • PRAEGER SCIENTIFIC

Library of Congress Cataloging in Publication Data

Krislov, Samuel.
Representative bureaucracy and the American political system.

Includes index.
1. Bureaucracy—United States. 2. Representative government and representation—United States.
3. United States—Politics and government.
I. Rosenbloom, David H. II. Title.
JK421.K74 353′.01 81-10625
ISBN 0-03-059446-4 AACR2
ISBN 0-03-059447-2 (pbk.)

Published in 1981 by Praeger Publishers
CBS Educational and Professional Publishing
A Division of CBS, Inc.
521 Fifth Avenue, New York, New York 10175 U.S.A.

123456789 145 987654321

Printed in the United States of America

To Jennifer, Gina, and Dvora Dina

PREFACE

"Cogs," "pygmies," "agents of repression"—these are but a few of the derisive labels applied to public bureaucrats by social scientists and others. Bureaucracy conjures up images of dull, routine, impersonal, formalistic paper-shuffling and red tape. Indeed, it seems to suffer world-wide condemnation, regardless of the natures of regimes, ideologies, and levels of development. Yet, at the same time, bureaucracy continues to expand and to engulf political systems. Consequently, the problem is not to denounce bureaucracy or to flail away at it ineffectually, but to address it as a fact of twentieth-century political life and to seek to integrate bureaucratic power with dominant regime norms.

In the United States such an approach requires combining the existence of independent bureaucratic political authority with representative republican government. The 1970s witnessed an anti-bureaucratic mood that sought to limit the bureaucracy's power through various budgetary approaches, reorganizations, reforms, and spending limitations such as California's Proposition 13. Though not without efficacy and utility, overall such approaches are inadequate to the task. They must be augmented by an effort to maximize the political representativeness of public bureaucracy. That is the fundamental problem to which this volume is addressed.

Specifically, we move from consideration of the relationship between bureaucratic organization and democratic government to an assessment of public bureaucracy's representative potential in terms of its personnel, structure, responsiveness to political authorities, and interaction with the public. We conclude that although there are inherent limitations on representative bureaucracy, there is also great potential that must be fulfilled if public bureaucracy and American democracy are to be integrated more successfully.

The authors have been concerned with representative bureaucracy for more than a decade. During that time we have benefited from the intellectual insight of many colleagues and friends, who are too numerous to list here, but whose work is often relied upon in the body of this book. We are grateful to them.

CONTENTS

Page

PREFACE vii

Chapter

1 Democracy and Bureaucracy: The Quest for Reconciliation 1

2 Representation by Personnel 31

3 Representation by Organization 75

4 Representation through Accountability and Direction 109

5 Representation through Interaction with the Public 157

6 Conclusions 185

Index 201

About the Authors 209

REPRESENTATIVE BUREAUCRACY AND THE AMERICAN POLITICAL SYSTEM

1

DEMOCRACY AND BUREAUCRACY: THE QUEST FOR RECONCILIATION

Political life in the twentieth century has been epitomized by "the bureaucratization of the world" (Jacoby 1973). Virtually everywhere one looks, whether in developed or developing nations, authoritarian or democratic regimes, public administration is organized bureaucratically. Moreover, despite its ubiquitous presence, bureaucratic power is almost universally decried. Nowhere is the rise of the bureaucratic state more perplexing than in democratic nations. These governments, based on nineteenth-century ideals and political developments, manifest systems of power, rule, authority, and legitimacy that are markedly opposed to bureaucratic domination. Although in earlier years the tendency was for democracy to suffer bureaucracy, seeking to contain and constrain it as much as possible, more recently this tendency has been substantially reversed: bureaucracy now pervades and engulfs democratic regimes. It transforms the nature of legislatures, chief executives, and the citizenry. Moreover, the relationship between democracy and bureaucracy is asymmetrical. Whereas modern democratic governments are unable to function without well-developed bureaucratic components, bureaucratic governments have little need for democratic political institutions. A central question for democratic regimes, then, is how public bureaucracies can be simultaneously efficient, effective, and responsive to elected political authorities.

BUREAUCRACY

"Bureaucracy" is a perplexing term. On the one hand it is often used to connote organizational inefficiency and governmental administration.

On the other, it is used in a technical sense to identify organizations having specific structural characteristics and behavioral attributes. Yet both of these approaches often miss a fundamental aspect of bureaucracy—it is a system of rule. In the words of Max Weber, "In a modern state the actual ruler is necessarily and unavoidably the bureaucracy" (quoted in Hummel 1977, p. 26). Indeed, as Ralph Hummel points out, although we are accustomed to thinking of public bureaucracies as service organizations, in reality they are "control instrument[s] of unparalleled power" (1977, p. 26). Only when this is fully understood can the conflict between democracy and bureaucracy be appreciated.

The most profound social scientific analysis of bureaucracy remains that presented by Max Weber. Although he sought to identify the major structural characteristics of bureaucracy and to explain their importance, his theory of bureaucracy goes well beyond a mere classification of organizational attributes. It starts from the premise that what differentiates government from other organizations in society is that it has a "monopoly of the legitimate use of physical force within a given territory" (Weber 1958, p. 78). Thus, the state becomes a relationship of dominance: the rulers dominate the ruled, and political power is ultimately based on the ability to legitimately compel compliance through the use of physical sanctions. But compliance can be induced by other means as well.

Weber identified three types of authority by which rulers dominate the ruled, who accept the legitimacy of their control. First, there is traditional authority: "the authority of the 'eternal yesterday,' i.e. of the mores sanctified through the unimaginably ancient recognition and habitual orientation to conform" (Weber 1958, pp. 78–79). For instance, depending on the natures of individual cultures, governmental leadership may be hereditary, precisely because that is the way it has been for ages past. Similarly, political life may be controlled by one group or class, such as males or an elite, and others may accept this domination on the basis of the belief that one should not tamper with tradition.

A second type of authority is "charismatic domination." It rests on "the extraordinary and personal *gift of grace* (charisma), the absolutely personal devotion and personal confidence in revelation, heroism, or other qualities of the individual leadership" (Weber, 1958, p. 79). Being based on personal qualities, charismatic authority is often revolutionary and unstable.

Third, authority can be based on "rational-legal" domination, or "domination by virtue of 'legality,' by virtue of the belief in the validity of legal statute and functional 'competence' based on rationally created rules. . . . This is domination as exercised by the modern 'servant of the state' and by all those bearers of power who in this respect resemble him" (Weber 1958, p. 79). This type of authority is most characteristic of contemporary political systems. Its essence consists of a legal code, abstract rules, impersonality, obedience based on belief in the rationality of the system, and obedience to the system, rather than to specific individuals. Structurally, rational-legal authority is organized in such a way as to include continuous official tasks, specialization, hierarchy, formalization, and separation of official and private resources. According to Weber, bureaucracy is the purest form or ideal type of rational-legal domination. Consequently, as political development erodes traditional authority, and modern technological and social complexity reduces the efficacy of charismatic authority, rule by bureaucracy emerges as the major form of political domination in the contemporary state.

Thus, bureaucracy, which translates literally as rule by bureaus or desks, is a means of exercising rational-legal authority. Its characteristics are such that it stands in marked contrast with democracy, or rule by the people. Weber identified the following characteristics in fully developed bureaucracies:

> 1. The staff members are personally free, observing only the impersonal duties of their offices.
>
> 2. There is a clear hierarchy of offices.
>
> 3. The functions of the offices are clearly specified.
>
> 4. Officials are appointed on the basis of a contract.
>
> 5. They are selected on the basis of a professional qualification, ideally substantiated by a diploma gained through examination.
>
> 6. They have a money salary, and usually pension rights. The salary is graded according to position in the hierarchy. The official can always leave the post, and under certain circumstances it also may be terminated.
>
> 7. The official's post is his or her sole or major occupation.
>
> 8. There is a career structure, and promotion is possible by either seniority or merit, and according to the judgment of superiors.
>
> 9. The official may appropriate neither the post nor the resources that go with it.
>
> 10. The official is subject to a unified control and disciplinary system. (Albrow 1970, p. 125)

Although this list is comprehensive, at least two additional characteristics of bureaucracy implicit in Weber's analysis should be made explicit. First, as Anthony Downs notes, "The major portion of [bureaucracy's] output is not directly or indirectly evaluated in any markets external to the organization by means of voluntary quid pro quo transactions" (Downs 1967, p. 25). In other words, bureaucracies typically do not produce a product that can be freely bought and sold in the marketplace. Price tags may be attached to bureaucratic operations, but these are established through budgetary routines or monopolistic transactions, rather than by conventional market pricing mechanisms. Bureaucracies may show surpluses or deficits, but these should not be confused with profits and losses. Consequently, it becomes difficult to evaluate the efficiency of bureaucratic operations.

Second, in order to be fully bureaucratized, an organization must be large. Indeed, Weber argued that "only by reversion in every field—political, religious, economic, etc.—to small-scale organization would it be possible to any considerable extent to escape" bureaucracy's influence (Weber 1947, p. 338). The large size of bureaucratic organizations complicates the problem of making them accountable and responsive to outside authorities.

Bureaucratic Growth

Much of the world's population is accustomed to deriding bureaucracy, but nevertheless its growth during the twentieth century has been phenomenal. Bureaucratic development in the United States illustrates this well. At the federal level there were about 240,000 civil servants at the turn of the century, compared with about 2.8 million in 1980. Although the latter number has remained relatively constant for more than a decade, there has been massive growth in the number of state and local government employees in recent years. Indeed, the mean increase in their number between 1954 and 1974 was 149 percent. A few states witnessed more than 300 percent growth in the number of public employees during those two decades. To what can the expansion of bureaucracy be attributed?

According to Weber, the major reasons for the spread of bureaucratic organization lie in some of its key features. In his oft-quoted words, "The decisive reason for the advance of bureaucratic organization has always been its purely technical superiority over any other form of organization. The fully developed bureaucratic mechanism compares with other organizations exactly as does the machine with the non-mechanical modes of production" (Weber 1958, p. 214). One reason for this is that bureaucracy's "special virtue" is "dehumanization" or the elimination "from official business [of] love, hatred, and all purely personal, irrational, and emotional elements which escape calculation" (Weber 1958, p. 216). Consequently, in the Weberian view, bureaucracies are efficient as a result of their precision, discretion, speed, unity, and expertise. Other forms of organization simply cannot perform as well in the face of the quantitative expansion of tasks, the need to process large numbers of cases with little deviation in routine, or the increasing complexity of social, economic, and political life.

There have been several attempts to modify and further develop Weber's theory of bureaucratic growth. Some of these take a highly generalized form, whereas others are substantially limited to specific governments and political conditions. Perhaps the most encompassing approach is "Wagner's Law."

At approximately the same time that Weber was expounding his theory of bureaucracy, Adolf Wagner, a German economist, was attempting to explain the tendency for public spending to increase at a rate faster than the rise in community economic output. He found this tendency in complex and developing industrial societies, regardless of the political characteristics of their regimes. Among his conclusions were the following:

1. "Government expands in order to control and coordinate the many antagonistic sectors of an increasingly complex society" (Wade and Curry 1970, p. 78). Hence, regulatory functions and instruments for control, such as police, expand.

2. As "the size of industrial units increases," as a result of the disappearance of less efficient firms from the economy, "the response of government is again one of intervention" (Wade and Curry 1970, p. 78). "The government's purpose in intervening is to maintain social stability, either by expanding controls over private industry or by taking over the property and management of industry itself" (Wade and Curry 1970, p. 78). In this fashion the government may prevent the amassing of great power in the hands of a nongovernmental elite.

3. Demands and needs for certain social services, such as education, arise and, given the costs and collective benefit of underwriting such services, government often seeks to provide them.

4. The scale of certain tasks is so great that only government can procure the resources required. A contemporary example would be the exploration of space.

Although "Wagner's Law" has been subject to considerable criticism and, strictly speaking, applies only to government expenditures (as opposed to public employment), discussions concerning the growth of the latter tend to identify similar factors. Donald Warwick (1975, pp. 7-8) delineates the following:

1. "Population growth increases the normal administrative demands made on governments—for police and fire protection and record-keeping, for example. Public employment expands to meet these demands."

2. In complex societies ". . . there is rising pressure for the government to act as agent of the public welfare and the arbiter of private conflicts."

3. As the concentration of corporate power increases, "governmental bureaucracies arise to: (a) provide the political and economic stability needed to protect the investments of the corporate giants; (b) protect the interests of society against the corporations; (c) prevent political chaos by mediating between large corporations and organized labor; or (d) act as agents to stimulate economic activity by corporations and channel it in constructive directions."

4. "The increasing specialization of knowledge favors the rise of a new 'managerial elite' in both the public and the private sectors. . . . Their presence in government swells the size of the public bureaucracy."

5. "Increased levels of abundance generate new demands for services typically provided by public organizations, including education, welfare, health, and recreation. In many cases no single arm of government is willing or able to take full responsibility for a given set of services. The action is divided among several agencies, with considerable duplication of effort and demands for interagency coordination."

The causes of bureaucratic growth are not entirely external to such organizations; bureaucracies possess internal pressures for growth as well. Anthony Downs (1967, pp. 16–18) has identified several of these:

1. "An organization that is rapidly expanding can attract more capable personnel, and more easily retain its most capable existing personnel."

2. "The expansion of any organization normally provides its leaders with increased power, income, and prestige; hence they encourage its growth."

3. "Growth tends to reduce internal conflicts in an organization by allowing some (or all) of its members to increase their personal status without lowering that of others. Therefore, organizational leaders encourage expansion to maximize morale and minimize internal conflicts."

4. "Increasing the size of an organization may also improve the quality of its performance (per unit of output) and its chances for survival."

5. "Because there is no inherent *quid pro quo* in bureau activity enabling officials to weigh the marginal return from further spending against its marginal cost, the incentive structure facing most officials provides much greater rewards for increasing expenditures than for reducing them."

Thus, bureaucracy develops out of the need of the state to dominate the ruled without sole reliance on the use of physical force. Once rational-legal authority becomes the dominant mode of exercising political power, bureaucracy becomes central to the political community. Its expansion is assured as a result of external and internal pressures. More aspects of life are penetrated by bureaucracy, more bureaucratic units are created, more personnel staff them. Consequently, during the twentieth century, at least, there has been an aura of inevitability about bureaucracy. And with its growth in size and scope, the issue of its political power has emerged.

Bureaucratic Power

Bureaucracy not only proliferates in terms of size, but also increases its power in society over time. As Weber expressed it:

> Under normal conditions, the power position of a fully developed bureaucracy is always overtowering. The "political master" finds himself in the position of the "dilettante" who stands opposite the "expert," facing the trained official who stands within the management of administration. This holds whether the "master" whom the bureaucracy serves is a "people," equipped with the weapons of "legislative initiative," the "referendum," and the right to remove officials, or a parliament, elected on a more aristocratic or more "democratic" basis and equipped with the right to vote a lack of confidence, or with the actual authority to vote it. (Weber 1958, p. 232)

The sources of bureaucratic power are numerous. As Weber indicates, expertise is of fundamental importance. Simply put, modern societies are dependent upon governmental bureaucrats for the formulation and implementation of public policy. Their independent power is both tolerated and granted because, essentially, "government would come to a standstill if our 'closet statesmen' in the civil service suddenly started doing only what they were told" (Storing 1964, p. 152). Indeed, "If the official stops working, or if his work is forcefully interrupted, chaos results, and it is difficult to improvise replacements from among the governed who are fit to master such chaos" (Weber 1958, p. 229). This is the essence of rational-legal domination. Despite constant complaints about bureaucrats, the rational and legal aspects of bureaucracy serve to legitimize their power and make the society dependent upon it.

Although expertise and rational-legal authority are the ultimate sources of bureaucratic power, there are additional elements in the formula. First, as an outgrowth of specialization and expertise, bureaucrats tend to develop a language of their own. As Ralph Hummel puts it, "the function of bureaucratese is fundamentally to make outsiders powerless" (Hummel 1977, p. 147). Thus, professional translators such as lawyers and accountants are sometimes employed when dealing with bureaucracy. The long tenure that bureaucrats often enjoy places them at a distinct advantage vis-à-vis temporary and even transient political authorities. Not only does the short tenure of the latter detract from their ability to develop the expertise with which to challenge career bureaucrats, but the bureaucrats are often secure in the belief that delay itself will mitigate efforts by external authorities to control them. For example, in the United States high-ranking career bureaucrats often have some 20 years of service in a particular agency, whereas the average tenure of political executives is two to three years (Heclo 1977, pp. 103–05). Restrictions on dismissing or demoting career bureaucrats are a common limitation on the ability of their nominal political superiors to control their behavior.

The specific sources of a given bureaucracy's power are likely to depend upon its functions and the cultural and political setting. Some generalizations in the context of the United States federal bureaucracy are illustrative. Among the elements of importance to an agency's power are the following:

1. Independence and autonomy. Theodore Lowi (1966) suggests that agencies having distributive or regulatory functions benefit from independence within the executive branch. This frees them from direct control by the president or the Executive Office of the President, thereby enabling them to develop support among relevant constituencies. For agencies having redistributive functions, which generally cannot be administered without the support of the president's constituency, Lowi suggests that independence is undesirable.

2. Relationship with Congress and congressional committees. It is generally essential for a bureaucratic agency to have strong support in at least one congressional committee. Lacking this, it can become overwhelmed by Congress's immense potential power over an agency's budget, mission, number of personnel, and mode of operation. Any bureaucratic agency that can count Congress among its constituents—as in the case of the Army Corps of Engineers—is bound to be very powerful within its policy domain.

3. Serving a large number of interests. This provides the potential of developing a powerful but diverse constituency. The agency can then play

interests off against one another, and thereby avoid being "captured." Agencies serving a single or a few powerful interests are especially prone to becoming spokesmen for these groups. In some instances public power is effectively captured by these private interests (McConnell 1966).

4. Interest-group support. Generally, agencies without strong, organized interest-group support, such as those dispensing foreign aid, are weaker than others. Consequently, strong interest-group support is an important element in bureaucratic power. However, it may also lead to the domination of an agency by an interest group.

5. Decentralization. Agencies with decentralized policy formulation are better able to cultivate "grass roots" support and adapt national policies to local conditions. Decentralization is an especially significant contributor to bureaucratic power in the policy area of distribution.

6. Leadership. The quality of agency leadership can contribute immensely to agency power or can detract from it. Thus, for many years the power of the FBI was augmented substantially by the leadership of J. Edgar Hoover. The power of other agencies has suffered as a result of poor leadership.

7. Ideology. In the view of Downs (1967, pp. 238–39), bureaucracies develop ideologies for the following reasons: "to influence outsiders to support the bureau, or at least refrain from attacking it"; "[to] develop stronger goal consensus among their own bureau members"; "to attract potential members who will contribute to stronger goal consensus, and to repel those with adverse goals"; and "to make decisions when other criteria of choice are impractical or ambiguous." Where ideologies are effective, they will enhance the bureaucracy's power accordingly.

There will be marked differences in the power of bureaucratic agencies, and their relationships with outside groups will vary. Yet it is a virtually universal consensus that public bureaucrats have great power. Wallace Sayre expresses this development well with regard to the United States in a passage that is worth quoting at length:

> The staffs of the executive branch agencies have come to exercise an important share of the initiative, the formulation, the bargaining, and the deciding in the process by which governmental decisions are taken. They are widely acknowledged to be leading "experts" as to the facts upon which issues are to be settled; they are often permitted to identify authoritatively the broad alternatives available as solutions; and they frequently are allowed to fix the vocabulary of the formal decision. These powers are shared and used by the career staffs in an environment of struggle and competition for influence, but the relatively new fact to be noted with emphasis is that the others who share the powers of

> decision . . . now rarely question the legitimacy of the career staff spokesmen as major participants in the competition.
>
> Great power also belongs naturally to those who carry out decisions of public policy. In this state, the career staffs have a paramount role. The choice of means, the pace and tone of governmental performance, reside largely in the hands of the federal government service. . . . [T]he civil servants have a position of distinct advantage in determining how public policies are executed. (Sayre 1965, p. 2)

DEMOCRACY

The rise of bureaucratic power places severe strains upon democratic government. Structurally, procedurally, and psychologically, bureaucracy and democracy are almost diametrically opposed. Their bases of legitimacy are also at marked variance. Whether the two kinds of rule can be successfully integrated remains an open question.

Although technically defined as rule by the people, democracy is typically thought to require government based upon consent of the governed and political equality. These underlying principles cannot be met unless every citizen has an unimpaired opportunity to do the following:

1. Formulate political, economic, and social preferences
2. Signify these preferences
3. Have these preferences weighed equally in the conduct of government.

In order for these opportunities to prevail, democratic government further requires several institutionalized guarantees (Dahl 1972, p. 39):

1. Alternative sources of information
2. Freedom of expression
3. The right to vote
4. Free and fair elections
5. Competition among political leaders for votes and support
6. The right to run for public office
7. Freedom to form and join organizations, including political parties

8. Institutions for making government policies depend on votes and other expressions of preference.

Any polity fulfilling these conditions to a substantial extent would be considered a democracy and would also be likely to have a thriving political system.

It is evident, however, that bureaucratic power militates against each of these requirements. First, bureaucratic government considers the consent of the governed, but may ignore it in favor of direction by expertise rather than by popular support. In any event, bureaucracy does not rest directly upon popular consent. Ultimately, of course, bureaucratic government without popular support might prove unstable.

Second, political equality is not a fundamental condition of bureaucratic government. On the contrary, bureaucracy assumes that because citizens do not possess equal knowledge, information, and expertise, they should not share equally in the right to participate in the formulation and implementation of public policies. Those whose participation is deemed desirable are chosen through bureaucratic criteria, such as merit, seniority, and technical expertise. Indeed, even within bureaucracies political equality is largely disregarded in favor of the principle of hierarchy.

Third, bureaucratic government militates against the citizen's opportunity to develop and express preferences and have these taken into account in policymaking. Thus, bureaucracies tend to favor secrecy, which makes it more difficult for the typical citizen to formulate meaningful preferences. Aside from secrecy, which may be reduced through the Freedom of Information Act, "sunshine" legislation, and the like, bureaucracies develop specialized languages that place the average citizen at a disadvantage when trying to interact with them or to assess their performance. Moreover, information flowing from bureaucracies may be distorted by bureaucratic ideologies, by attempts to generate support for their programs among various segments of the society, and sometimes by the need to disguise their objectives. A good example of the latter occurred in the United States in the summer of 1979, when the Department of Energy purposely allowed local gasoline shortages in California and on the East Coast to reach crisis proportions in order to convince the population that scarcity was a reality.

However, even if the citizen in the bureaucratized polity were able to formulate meaningful policy preferences, there would not necessarily be a meaningful way of presenting them. Although freedom of expression may prevail, it may be rendered ineffectual by the refusal of bureaucrats to take these preferences into account in the formulation and implementation of public policy. Formal channels by which bureaucrats can be made dependent upon citizens' preferences are not likely to exist. And even if they do, they may be ineffective.

Fourth, bureaucratic government militates against the institutionalized guarantees required by democracy. Although some public bureaucracies, including the federal executive branch in the United States, are fragmented and provide a wide variety of alternative sources of information, the overriding tendency of bureaucracy is to develop and project unity. Hency, "leaks" are frowned upon and efforts to coordinate bureaucratic activities and positions are stressed. Freedom of expression may also be compromised by public bureaucracies, especially with regard to their own employees, who may be restricted from engaging in political activities and political speech (Rosenbloom 1971). However, limitations on freedom of expression may also extend to clients and citizens who are dependent upon bureaucratic largess. Thus, citizens receiving welfare or work-relief may find their political rights restricted. Indeed, even those seeking the "privilege" of obtaining a driver's license may find that a Motor Vehicles Department withholds licenses from persons advocating overthrow of the government, as in New York State.

Although bureaucratic government does not necessarily restrict the right to vote or interfere with the fairness of elections, it does tend to reduce the relevance of elections in influencing the political direction of the polity. There are several reasons for this. Because bureaucrats are not elected, they are not directly dependent upon popular votes for candidates. Where the right of referendum exists, however, elections may be of greater importance to bureaucrats, as in the case of California and Proposition 13, for instance. In addition, the importance of the franchise is reduced to the extent that elected leaders are unable to control, direct, or influence the course of bureaucratic policymaking and implementation. Yet, there are several substantial barriers to the effective control of bureaucracy by elected officials. Certainly, those with limited expertise and tenure are unlikely to have a lasting impact upon public bureaucracies.

Moreover, it is one of the perversities of the modern bureaucratic state that elected officials come to rely heavily upon bureaucracy for their incumbency. Morris Fiorina observes:

> The nature of the Washington system is now quite clear. Congressmen (typically the majority Democrats) earn electoral credits by establishing various federal programs (the minority Republicans typically earn credits by fighting the good fight). The legislation is drafted in very general terms, so some agency, existing or newly established, must translate a vague policy mandate into a functioning program, a process that necessitates the promulgation of numerous rules and regulations and, incidentally, the trampling of numerous toes. At the next stage,

> aggrieved and/or hopeful constituents petition their congressman to intervene in the complex (or at least obscure) decision processes of the bureaucracy. The cycle closes when the congressman lends a sympathetic ear, piously denounces the evils of bureaucracy, intervenes in the latter's decisions, and rides a grateful electorate to ever more impressive electoral showings. Congressmen take credit coming and going. They are the alpha and the omega. (Fiorina 1977, p. 48)

The dependence of the elected upon bureaucracy goes beyond the advantages reaped by providing services for constituents. Bureaucratic decisions may affect the amount of governmental funds expended in the districts of elected officials. These funds, in turn, may affect the level of employment, general prosperity, and quality of life in the district. R. Douglas Arnold has closely studied the relationship between the United States federal bureaucracy and congressmen from this perspective. After analyzing various programs allocating funds to congressional districts, he concluded that

> . . . bureaucrats appear to allocate benefits strategically in an effort both to maintain and to expand their supporting coalitions. When it furthers their purposes, they broaden their program's geographic scope and increase the number of shares of benefits so that more congressmen can be brought into their supporting coalitions. When necessary, they allocate extra shares of benefits to leaders and to those who are crucial coalition members. . . . Each [allocational strategy] is specially tailored to fit a program's peculiar situation in Congress, to compensate where general-benefit strategies have proven weak, and to reward those congressmen who are especially important to a particular coalition's success. (Arnold 1979, p. 207)

And, as Fiorina observes, these allocations are a key factor in protecting congressmen's incumbency: ". . . a lesser proportion of congressional effort is now going into programmatic activities and a greater proportion into pork-barrel and casework activities. As a result, today's congressmen make relatively fewer enemies and relatively more friends among the people of their districts" (Fiorina 1977, p. 46). Hence, bureaucratic government may impair political competition.

An additional reason why bureaucratic government militates against meaningful elections is that in a fully developed bureaucratic state, governmental units composed of elected leaders, such as legislatures or chief executive positions, may themselves undergo bureaucratization. For example, the Executive Office of the President of the United States has expanded and undergone bureaucratization, partly as a result of the president's ongoing struggle to control the rest of the federal bureaucracy.

Similarly, the Congress created the Congressional Budget Office to assist it in responding to the budget proposals put forth by the executive branch. Anthony Downs has captured the nature of these developments in the form of a "Law of Control Duplication: Any attempt to control one large organization tends to generate another" (Downs 1967, p. 262 and ch. 12). In other words, it takes bureaucracy to control bureaucracy. But to the extent that elective institutions become bureaucratic, power and influence devolve into the hands of their staffs. As a result, elected leaders lose some control over their own branches of government (Nachmias and Rosenbloom 1980). Hence, elections are not likely to result in effective representation of the electorate.

The relationship between bureaucratic organization and freedom of association is complex. Bureaucracies may attempt to constrain the exercise of this freedom by their employees and client groups. Thus, membership in "subversive" or otherwise undesirable organizations may prompt bureaucratic agencies to take action against their employees. The same might prove true for clients. In some nations with highly politicized bureaucracies, services are provided primarily to the party faithful and withheld from others. For example, this was true not only in the United States in the age of machine-dominated politics, but also in nations such as Israel with comprehensive political parties (Fein 1967). In the United States another kind of coercion has also been present. As Theodore Lowi (1969) and Grant McConnell (1966) have pointed out, bureaucratic agencies sometimes seek to organize constituencies in order to enhance their own strength. In their zeal to do so, they may rely on coercive techniques, as was the case with the founding of the American Farm Bureau Federation under the auspices of the U.S. Department of Agriculture. Once organized, such groups may be dominated by the bureaucratic agency. Potential clients who seek to avoid membership may suffer discriminatory treatment.

Finally, as suggested above, bureaucratic government places a substantial barrier between elections and the formulation of public policy. To the extent that public policymaking occurs in bureaucratic agencies, elected figures are of diminished importance. Even when they are deeply involved in policymaking and monitoring bureaucracies, they are often dependent upon these agencies for information and knowledge. Consequently, links between popular votes and the content of public policies are generally weak in bureaucratized governments.

In sum, there is a substantial tension between the needs of democratic government and the dominant tendencies of bureaucratic government. The nature of the conflict can be put forward in the following shorthand fashion:

Democracy Requires	Bureaucracy Requires
Equality	Hierarchy
Rotation in office	Seniority
Freedom	Command
Pluralism	Unity
Citizen participation	Participation based on expertise
Openness	Secrecy
Community	Impersonality
Legitimacy based on elections	Legitimacy based on expertise

These differences between the two forms of rule raise the question of whether bureaucracies can be held accountable to political authorities in democratic polities.

THE QUEST FOR ACCOUNTABILITY

Throughout much of the political development of democratic nations, it appeared that bureaucracies could be held accountable to elected political authorities. The traditional approach was formulated as follows:

> Power emanates from the people and is to be exercised in trust for the people. Within the government each level of executive authority is accountable to the next, running on up to the President or the Cabinet. The executive authority as a whole is accountable to the Congress or Parliament, which is assisted in its surveillance of expenditures by an independent audit agency. Officials are required to submit themselves to periodic elections as a retrospective evaluation of their performances and to receive a new mandate from the people. (Smith and Hague 1971, pp. 26–27)

Today, however, it is frequently recognized that there are two fundamental shortcomings in such an approach. First, because of the nature of bureaucracy, the tenure and expertise of public bureaucrats, and the style of bureaucratic politics, "accountability gets lost in the shuffle somewhere in the middle ranges of the bureaucracy" (Smith and Hague 1971, p. 27). The processes by which this occurs are discussed in chapter 4, and need not be elaborated upon at this point.

Second, and relatedly, bureaucratization of the polity alters the traditional role of elections. Although we have already touched upon this point, some further elaboration is necessary. Elections can serve to assure the accountability of public bureaucrats to the public only if they enable the electorate to signify clear policy preferences that can subsequently be made operational by the elected. Bureaucracy interferes doubly with this process. It affects political competition through its allocation of resources and funds by rewarding supportive legislators with a greater chance of maintaining their incumbency. In addition, as previously noted, bureaucracy limits the extent to which elected officials can control the nature of public policy and increases the extent to which they are dependent upon information and policy alternatives flowing from the bureaucrats.

Elections remain "media events" and grist for political science journals. Yet their growing irrelevance in terms of the accountability of public bureaucrats and the formulating of public policy is widely recognized. Morris Janowitz is among those who are critical of the traditional approach:

> Modern political theory continues, nevertheless, to emphasize elections as the crucial device for the democratic control of political power. The election process has come to be seen as a device of popular sovereignty in that organized factions engage in competition. The public derives its power from the ability to chose periodically between political opponents who are claiming the right of temporary monopoly of political power. By contrast, a system of political theory which would outline the desired relations between government bureaucracy and the public in a democratic political system is relatively undeveloped. (Janowitz et al. 1977, p. 2)

Indeed, a majority of the United States population shares Janowitz's disdain for the traditional approach. In 1973 a Louis Harris study found that 65 percent of the public agreed that, "The trouble with government is that elected officials have lost control over the bureaucrats, who really run the country" (U.S. Congress 1973, pt. 2, p. 115, and pt. 3, p. 61). Only 17 percent disagreed with this statement, the rest being uncertain. Surprisingly, 57 percent of a sample of elected officials also agreed. At most, elected officials can be considered intermediaries between the public and the bureaucrats.

Under these conditions the character of elections is transformed. Rather than being devices for registering policy preferences, elections become predominantly means of legitimizing political power. Hence the concern with low voter turnouts.

But if accountability is thwarted by the bureaucratic polity and elections no longer serve to assure "popular sovereignty," how can democracy and bureaucracy be reconciled? As Frederick Mosher observes, this is a central question of our bureaucratic age:

> The accretion of specialization and of technological and social complexity seems to be an irreversible trend, one that leads to increasing dependence upon the protected, appointive public service, thrice removed from direct democracy. Herein lies the central and underlying problem. . . . [H]ow can a public service so constituted be made to operate in a manner compatible with democracy? How can we be assured that a highly differentiated body of public employees will act in the interests of all the people, will be an instrument of all the people? (Mosher 1968, pp. 3–4)

As Janowitz and associates suggest, political theory on this point is underdeveloped. Yet, one central point is clear: A direct relationship between the public and public bureaucracy is of critical importance; elected representatives of the public, even ombudsmen acting as third-party intermediaries, cannot sufficiently protect the essence of democracy in the face of bureaucratization. For the public to have a major political role in a bureaucratized polity, the bureaucracy must in some sense be an agent of the public. Two complementary theories concerning the possibility of establishing such a relationship have been advanced.

THE THEORY OF DEMOCRATIC BALANCE

The theory of democratic balance seeks to avoid the pitfalls of accountability theory by specifying the direct relationship between the citizenry and the bureaucracy that is desirable in democratic nations. Originally developed in the 1950s by Janowitz and associates, this theory has been a basis for a few more recent empirical investigations of the consequences of bureaucratization for democratic citizenship (Eldersveld et al. 1968; Nachmias and Rosenbloom 1978b). It starts from the premise that because the hallmark of democracy is continual competition between various factions, parties, and candidates, none of whom can dominate the political system in all issue areas, "balance" must be "the central concept for the analysis of the administrative process in a democratic political system" (Janowitz et al. 1977, p. 5).

Such "balance" is important in two ways. First, public bureaucracy must not emerge as the sole or overwhelmingly dominant political force in the polity. Rather, public bureaucracy must be so constituted that it is in competition with other political forces in the polity. Theoretically, such a condition might be achieved in various ways. In practice, however, the most successful method is likely to be the institution of the principle of competition within public bureaucracy. Thus, agencies, offices, and programs can be made to compete with one another over values, authority, and funds. That is, there can be forceful checks on bureaucratic power within the bureaucracy itself. The greater the extent to which bureaucratic policymaking can be made to resemble an adversary process, the more likely that the interests of democracy will be served.

Second, democratic balance is important in reducing the polarization of the polity. As Janowitz and associates point out, "Democratic government must provide for all classes a degree of social stability and economic security sufficient to keep these elements loyal to the community of purpose that makes the state possible. Democracy itself will collapse if it creates irreconcilable minorities" (Janowitz et al. 1977, p. 6).

The theory of democratic balance specifies two types of imbalance, each of which bears upon the relationship between public bureaucracy and democracy. First, a bureaucracy that dominates the political system and the public is out of balance because it is "despotic." Second, one that is subject to "capture" by interest groups or political factions, or is otherwise unable to play an independent role in the political system, is not balanced because it is "subservient." An administrative organization of the latter kind, however, is not likely to be "bureaucratic" in the technical sense of the term, and consequently is unlikely to possess the characteristics that make bureaucracy in the Weberian mold so powerful. In short, the desired role of public bureaucracies in democratic nations can be summarized as follows:

> The special kind of practical wisdom that characterizes the civil servant points to a more fundamental political function of the bureaucracy, namely to bring to bear on public policy its distinctive view of the common good or its way of looking at questions about the common good. . . . Like judges, civil servants have a special responsibility to preserve the rule of law. (Storing 1964, p. 154)

What, then, are the components of "democratic balance"? Janowitz and associates identified four (Janowitz et al. 1977, pp. 7-8):

1. Knowledge. The public must have an adequate level of knowledge about the operations of the public bureaucracy. Inadequate knowledge facilitates despotic administration, whereas too much knowledge theoretically could deprive an administrative agency of essential autonomy and produce subservient behavior.

2. Self-interest. The public must consider that its self-interest is being served by the public bureaucracy. . . . [T]he public must be aware . . . of the bureaucracy's capacity to act as a neutral and impartial agent in resolving social conflicts.

3. Principle Mindedness. The public must be of the general opinion

that the public bureaucracy is guided in its actions by a set of principles guaranteeing equal and impersonal treatment. Administrative routines, however, must be sufficiently flexible to cope with individual differences in order to insure adequate dealings with clients.

4. Prestige. Public perspectives toward the public bureaucracy must include adequate prestige value toward public employment as compared with other types of careers. . . . A very low prestige could tend to bring about subservient administration, while extremely high prestige could tend to result in despotic administration.

Studies of public bureaucracies in India, Israel, and the United States suggest that democratic balance is difficult to achieve. Thus, among other things, Eldersveld and associates found that in India about 60 percent of the population is convinced that more than half of all public bureaucrats are corrupt (Eldersveld et al. 1968, p. 93). Moreover, only a minority of Indian citizens felt efficacious concerning the bureaucracy (Eldersveld et al. 1968, p. 26). In Israel it was found that the general population could be categorized into three groups having distinct reactions to the bureaucratization of public life. The best-adjusted to this development—the smallest group—came closest to manifesting the conditions necessary for "democratic balance". They tended to be more aware of the impact of the Israeli bureaucracy on their daily lives and on national development. They also felt somewhat efficacious in their dealings with the national bureaucracy. Their evaluation of the national bureaucracy was more positive than that of the other groups. However, the conditions for democratic balance were clearly absent from a second and larger group. These citizens found the national bureaucracy to be complex and unfair. They viewed it as an unwelcome and threatening force in their lives, and felt inefficacious concerning it. Their image of the bureaucracy and public bureaucrats was quite negative. A third group fell between these two polar opposites in their reactions to the bureaucratization of Israeli life (Nachmias and Rosenbloom 1978b).

In the United States, reactions to the bureaucratization of public life have been complex. Overall, the citizenry recognizes the extent of bureaucratization. By 1973, 73 percent of the citizenry agreed that the federal government had become too bureaucratic (U.S. Congress 1973, pt. 2, p. 115). In fact, this seemed to be an almost universal contention—80 percent of the nation's elected officials agreed with this statement (U.S. Congress 1973, pt. 3, p. 60). In addition to there being too much bureaucracy, both the citizenry and its elected leaders agreed that the federal bureaucracy had become too powerful. This perception of the rise of bureaucratic power is coupled with a decline in the citizen's feeling of efficacy vis-à-vis the government (Nachmias and Rosenbloom 1980, ch. 9). Indeed, Daniel Katz and associates found that "despite the number of people who knew about the possibility of appealing [a bureaucratic decision], only a very low proportion actually tried that route" (Katz et al. 1975, p. 74).

Thus, a large proportion of citizens in the United States feel that the federal bureaucracy is too large and too powerful, and that there is too little that they can do about it. In this sense, the conditions for democratic balance are poorly met. In addition, despite the public's awareness of government's provision of services through bureaucratic agencies, these services are underutilized: "There is conspicuous underutilization of government services. On the average, about one-third of the people with problems for which government agencies provide help do not go to public offices" (Katz et al. 1975, p. 60). Lack of knowledge of the proper agency and the available programs was found to be the largest single reason for this.

The public's evaluation of bureaucracy is complicated. In general, Americans seem satisfied with their interaction with what might be called "service" agencies, such as employment services, job training, and welfare. Katz and associates found that, "In addition to rather high degrees of satisfaction elicited from those with service agency experiences, three out of five clients felt that their situations had been improved or their problems resolved by the agency that they visited" (Katz et al. 1975, p. 115). It is also important to note that, "Most respondents tended to view the service bureaucracies as operating on an equitable basis. Three out of four felt that they had been treated fairly, and only one in four felt that some groups of people received preferential treatment" (Katz et al. 1975, p. 115).

On the other hand, public interaction with constraint agencies (motor vehicle bureaus, police, tax agencies) were characterized by far more negative evaluations: "A majority of the constraint agency respondents felt negatively about the procedures used by those agencies. One-fifth of the constraint group stated that they had been subjected to threats and pressures, although there was wide variation across the . . . constraint areas" (Katz et al. 1975, p. 116). And "On the question of equitable treatment, a much lower proportion of constraint agency respondents than service agency respondents felt that they had been treated fairly (45 percent as opposed to 76 percent)" (Katz et al. 1975, p. 116). Overall, about 61 percent of the population felt that by and large most governmental agencies do a good job (Katz et al. 1975, p. 116).

Studies of the prestige value of public employment in the United States suggest that achieving a "democratic balance" is a complex endeavor. Analyses dating back to the 1920s indicate that government is an attractive employer mostly to the poor and disadvantaged segments of the society (White 1929; White 1932; Kilpatrick et al. 1964; Janowitz and Wright 1956). By the 1960s this had been perceived as a serious problem.

For instance, in 1960, Senator Henry Jackson complained that, "The fact is, we have encountered disturbing difficulties in securing first rate talent at the very time when the national security calls for the country's 'best brains' to man key posts at home and abroad" (Kilpatrick et al. 1964, p. 4). Similar difficulties have been pervasive in Israel, where in 1973, 65 percent of the citizenry indicated no desire to be employed in the national bureaucracy (Nachmias and Rosenbloom 1978b, p. 155).

The theory of democratic balance provides a useful guide for the integration of public bureaucracies and democratic political systems. Yet the evidence to date, drawn from polities as diverse as the United States, India, and Israel, strongly suggests that in practice, achieving such a balance is elusive. This fact seems to confound further the effort to develop a harmonious relationship between democracy and bureaucracy. However, another approach, which can be viewed as augmenting the theory of democratic balance or as wholly independent from it, has been advanced. This is the theory of representative bureaucracy.

REPRESENTATIVE BUREAUCRACY

Can a public bureaucracy be made into a representational institution despite such organizational features as hierarchy, specialization, and formalization? This question is at once immensely important and perplexing. At stake is the possibility of effectively integrating bureaucratic power into democratic government.

Although some democratic theorists stress the need for limited governmental involvement in the life of the society, the extent of governmental power is more generally treated as a secondary concern. From the perspective of predominant democratic theory, power is neither good nor bad in and of itself. Thus, the amassing of power in government does not preclude it from being democratic. The critical question is whether governmental power is legitimate from the point of view of democratic values. Such legitimation is generally conveyed through governmental representation of the public (that is, government of the people) and by public participation in government (government by the people).

Consequently, if public bureaucracies could be constituted so as to provide political representation of the general public, their power could be made to comport substantially with democratic values. If, in addition, meaningful mechanisms by which the public might participate in bureaucratic policymaking were present, then bureaucracies might be sucessfully combined with democratic political systems. In short, it is not the power of public bureaucracies per se, but their unrepresentative power, that constitutes the greatest threat to democratic government. If this power cannot be constrained by legislatures and political executives, it can nevertheless be made to operate democratically by making it representative of the public.

The notion of a public bureaucracy acting as a representative political institution is controversial. Part of the controversy results from the difficulty inherent in understanding the concept of representation itself. It has been said, for example, that "in spite of many centuries of theoretical effort, we cannot say what representation is" (Eulau 1967, p. 54). According to Hannah Pitkin (1967, pp. 8–9), this is partly because "representation, taken generally, means the making present in some sense of something which is nevertheless not present literally or in fact. Now, to say that something is simultaneously both present and not present is to utter a paradox, and thus a fundamental dualism is built into the meaning of representation." Much of the discussion of representation since the nineteenth century has centered on the issue of whether representatives should be considered the instructed delegates of those whom they ostensibly represent, or simply conceived of as general trustees of the public's interests who can ultimately be held accountable in some fashion.

Another aspect of the controversy surrounding the concept of representative bureaucracy is whether representation is feasible in the absence of elections. Despite the overwhelming concern of politicians, the media, and political scientists, it is both nearly self-evident and well-documented that elections do not guarantee representation (Miller and Stokes 1963; Campbell 1979). Moreover, it is certainly possible for nonelected leaders to represent their followers, as in traditional patrimonial societies or families.

In principle, therefore, the concept of representative bureaucracy is not self-contradictory. Representation can take place within bureaucratic structures. Three related aspects of representative bureaucracy have been advanced.

Representation by Personnel

The notion that administrative power and democratic government can be integrated through the composition of a civil service has a long tradition. For instance, in the United States, President Thomas Jefferson developed a concept of partisan representation in the nation's fledgling administrative system. He reasoned that the partisan composition of the federal service should broadly reflect the partisan balance found in the electorate at large. In 1829, President Andrew Jackson expanded upon this concept of representation by seeking to make the federal service reflect the social composition of the nation. He sought to ensure that the "road to office" was "accessible alike to the rich and the poor, the farmer and the printer" (Rosenbloom 1977, p. 35). Although much had occurred in the intervening years, in 1970 the Civil Service Commission voiced a related commitment: "We believe that to the extent practicable organizations of the Federal Government should in their employment mix, broadly reflect, racially and otherwise, the varied characteristics of our population" (Rosenbloom 1977, p. 109). Other nations, such as India, have established formal mechanisms to ensure the representation of various social groups in their public bureaucracies.

Contemporary intellectual interest in the concept of representative bureaucracy can be fairly dated from 1944, when J. Donald Kingsley's book by that title appeared. Although by present standards, Kingsley's *Representative Bureaucracy* bearly scratched the surface of the issues involved, he did advance the thesis that, at least in the context of British administration,

> There are obviously points beyond which a man cannot go in carrying out the will of another; and the fact that those limits have seldom been approached in the conduct of the Civil Service since 1870 bears witness to the unity of the middle class State. The convention of impartiality can be maintained only when the members of the directing grades of the Service are thoroughly committed to the larger purposes the State is attempting to serve; when, in other words, their views are identical with those of the dominant class as a whole. (Kingsley 1944, p. 278)

Thus, the propositions have been advanced that public bureaucracies can be transformed into representative political institutions through the partisan, social, and attitudinal composition of their work forces. These propositions raise at least three additional issues. First, can public bureaucracies be socially representative despite their need for expertise and middle-class skills? Will they not inherently overrepresent middle-class elements? To date, the evidence gathered suggests that such over-representation is likely, especially in societies with relatively small middle classes (Subramaniam 1967). (This matter will be addressed in some detail in chapter 2.) However, here it should be noted that the political importance of middle-class overrepresentation varies directly with the extent to which politics in a given society revolves around social class divisions.

Second, there is the issue of whether public bureaucrats will retain values and attitudes stemming from their social backgrounds. Certainly, bureaucratic recruitment patterns and socialization processes may go a long way toward destroying any connection between the bureaucrat's background and his or her current attitudes and values. As Frederick Mosher writes:

> The fact is that we know too little about the relationship between a man's background and pre-employment socialization on the one hand,

> and his orientation and behavior in office on the other. Undoubtedly, there are a good many other intervening variables: the length of time in the organization, or the time-distance from his background; the nature and strength of the socialization process within the organization; the nature of the position . . . ; the length and content of preparatory education; the strength of associations beyond the job and beyond the agency; etc. (Mosher 1968, p. 13)

Similarly, Kenneth Meier maintains that "the assumption . . . that socio-economic characteristics determine values for upwardly mobile, adult bureaucrats is in need of revision . . ." (Meier 1975, p. 529). How much in need of revision, is an issue addressed in chapter 2.

To the extent that bureaucratic representation through bureaucratic personnel takes place, however, several benefits for democratic government can be achieved. As Harry Kranz has argued, a representative bureaucracy would do the following:

> Lead not only to more democratic decision-making but to better decisions because it would expand the number and diversity of the views brought to bear on policy-making (1976, p. 110)
>
> Improve bureaucratic operations and outputs . . . by ensuring that the decisions and services were more responsive to the needs of agency clientele and potential consumers, particularly members of minority groups (1976, p. 110)
>
> Promote a more efficient use of the country's human resources (1976, p. 112)
>
> Increase, both symbolically and actually, the legitimacy of . . . [governmental] institutions . . . (1976, p. 115)
>
> Elevate social equity and justice to prime political values at least as important as the prevailing paradigm of "economy and efficiency" and its fellow traveler "stability" (1976, p. 116).

Thus, there is potentially much to be gained through representative bureaucracy by personnel, but, as discussed in chapter 2, obtaining such representation can be problematic.

Representation by Administrative Organization

Public bureaucracies can also represent various interests found in the political community through their organizational structures and missions. Indeed, this is reflected in the names of governmental departments, agencies, and bureaus. Thus, in any modern nation one is likely to find departments or ministries of agriculture, labor, education, health, and commerce. In addition, bureaucratic organizations may represent the interests of various social groups, such as minorities and women. A system of representation along these lines is well developed in the United States. A few of the groups given formal bureaucratic recognition are consumers, farmers (including the specific representation of those producing various crops), aliens, Indians, children, the aged, urban populations, rural populations, women, the handicapped, and refugees.

Inevitably, there will be gaps in bureaucratic representation by organizational structure and mission. Some interests will go unrepresented; some agencies will be poor spokesmen for the groups they are presumed to represent. Nevertheless, it may be possible to reach a level of pluralistic representation in public bureaucracies that cannot be matched elsewhere in government. For instance, with specific reference to the United States federal bureaucracy, Roger Davidson observes that "the conflict between Congress and the executive can best be understood as a test of the representational capacities of these two institutions," and that "in many respects, the civil service represents the American people more comprehensively than does Congress" (Davidson 1966, pp. 378–95). Norton Long is among those who would concur with Davidson: "The bureaucracy is recognized by all interested groups as a major channel of representation to such an extent that Congress rightly feels the competition of a rival" (Long 1965, pp. 17–18). He points out that, "The party system provides no enduring institutional representation for group interests at all comparable to that of the bureaus of the Department of Agriculture. Even the subject matter committees of Congress function in the shadow of agency permanency" (Long 1965, p. 17).

This form of representation is likely to be most pronounced for groups that are organized. In public bureaucracies such as the United States federal service, the group organization process is spurred by bureaucratic fragmentation. Long points out:

> It is clear that the American system of politics does not generate enough power at any focal point of leadership to provide the conditions for an even partially successful divorce of politics from administration. Subordinates cannot depend on the formal chain of command to deliver enough political power to permit them to do their jobs. Accordingly they must supplement the resources available through the hierarchy with those they can muster on their own, or accept the consequences in frustration—a course itself not without danger. Administrative rationality demands that objectives be determined and sights set in conformity with a realistic appraisal of power position and potential. (Long 1965, p. 16)

Consequently, bureaucratic agencies often turn to, or even create, organized interest groups to supplement their power in the legislature and elsewhere. In Long's words, "agencies and bureaus more or less perforce are in the business of building, maintaining, and increasing their political support. They lead and in large part are led by the diverse groups whose influence sustains them" (Long 1965, p. 18). Moreover, this form of representation "extends the principle of representation over into administration, since it is predicated on the assumption that law making bodies and conventional procedures cannot and ought not make law" (Lowi 1969, p. 96). In the most pronounced cases of this kind of representation, the government agency may organize the constituency, as in the case of the Department of Agriculture and the American Farm Bureau Federation, and/or the interest group may come so to dominate the agency that for all intents and purposes there is "the conquest of segments of formal state power by private groups and associations" (McConnell 1966, p. 162), as has commonly occurred with federal regulatory commissions. (This form of bureaucratic representation and the problems associated with it are discussed in chapter 3.)

Representation Through Citizen Participation

Closely related to bureaucratic representation of organized interest groups is such representation through citizen participation. One major distinction between the two kinds of representation is that in the former, interest groups may not adequately reflect the perspectives of the segments of society for which they claim to speak or of whom they are considered legitimate representatives. Another is that in the latter form, the citizen may participate as an individual or as an individual representative of the larger community.

As William Morrow points out, in the United States, "generally speaking, citizen participation in administration has assumed three forms: the citizen committee as an advisory group; the citizen committee as a governing group in a specific policy area; and the idea of neighborhood government, where citizens have direct responsibilities in a number of policy areas" (Morrow 1975, p. 191). Examples of each of these forms can be found in national and subnational bureaucracies in various political settings. To the extent that such representation is effective, it forges a link between the public and the government in the form of bureaucratic agencies. As such, citizen participation can contribute much to the integration of democracy and bureaucracy. (This topic is discussed in chapter 5.)

REFERENCES

Albrow, Martin. 1970. *Bureaucracy*. New York: Praeger.

Arnold, R. Douglas. 1979. *Congress and the Bureaucracy*. New Haven: Yale University Press.

Campbell, Bruce. 1979. *The American Electorate*. New York: Holt, Rinehart and Winston.

Dahl, Robert. 1972. *Democracy in the United States*. 2nd ed. Chicago: Rand McNally.

Davidson, Roger. 1966. "Congress and the Executive: The Race for Representation". In *Congress: The First Branch*, edited by A. DeGrazia, pp. 377-413. New York: Anchor.

Downs, Anthony. 1967. *Inside Bureaucracy*. Boston: Little, Brown.

Dresang, Dennis. 1974. "Ethnic Politics, Representative Bureaucracy and Development Administration: The Zambian Case." *American Political Science Review* 68 (December): 1605–17.

Eldersveld, Samuel, J. Jagannadham, and A. Barnabas. 1968. *The Citizen and the Administrator in a Developing Democracy*. Glenview, Ill.: Scott, Foresman.

Eulau, Heinz. 1967. "Changing Views of Representation." In *Contemporary Political Science*, edited by Ithiel de Sola Pool, pp. 53–85. New York: McGraw-Hill.

Fein, Leonard. 1967. *Politics in Israel*. Boston: Little, Brown.

Fiorina, Morris. 1977. *Congress: Keystone of the Washington Establishment*. New Haven: Yale University Press.

Heclo, Hugh. 1977. *A Government of Strangers*. Washington, D.C.: Brookings Institution.

Hummel, Ralph. 1977. *The Bureaucratic Experience*. New York: St. Martin's.

Jacoby, Henry. 1973. *The Bureaucratization of the World*. Berkeley: University of California Press.

Janowitz, Morris, and Deil Wright. 1956. "The Prestige Value of Public Employment: 1929 and 1954." *Public Administration Review* 16 (Winter): 15–21.

Janowitz, Morris, Deil Wright, and William Delany. 1977. *Public Administration and the Public—Perspectives Toward Government in a Metropolitan Community*. Westport, Conn.: Greenwood Press

Katz, Daniel, et al. 1975. *Bureaucratic Encounters*. Ann Arbor: Institute for Social Research, University of Michigan.

Kilpatrick, Franklin P., Milton C. Cummings, Jr., and M. Kent Jennings. 1964. *The Image of the Federal Service*. Washington, D.C.: Brookings Institution.

Kingsley, J. Donald. 1944. *Representative Bureaucracy*. Yellow Springs, Ohio: Antioch University Press.

Lipset, Seymour M. 1952. "Bureaucracy and Social Change." In *Reader in Bureaucracy*, edited by Robert K. Merton et al., pp. 221–32. New York: Free Press.

Long, Norton. 1965. "Power and Administration." In *Bureaucratic Power in National Politics*, edited by Francis Rourke, pp. 14–23. Boston: Little, Brown.

Lowi, Theodore. 1969. *The End of Liberalism*. New York: W. W. Norton.

———. 1966. "Distribution, Regulation, Redistribution: The Functions of Government." In *Public Policies and Their Politics*, edited by R. R. Pley, pp. 27-40. New York: W. W. Norton.

McConnell, Grant. 1966. *Private Power and American Democracy*. New York: Knopf.

Meier, Kenneth. 1975. "Representative Bureaucracy: An Empirical Analysis." *American Political Science Review* 69 (June): 526-42.

Miller, Warren, and Donald Stokes. 1963. "Constituency Influence in Congress." *American Political Science Review* 57 (March): 45-56.

Morrow, William. 1975. *Public Administration*. New York: Random House.

Mosher, Frederick. 1968. *Democracy and the Public Service*. New York: Oxford University Press.

Nachmias, David, and David H. Rosenbloom. 1980. *Bureaucratic Government, USA*. New York: St. Martin's.

———. 1978a. "Bureaucracy and Ethnicity." *American Journal of Sociology* 83 (January): 967-74.

———. 1978b. *Bureaucratic Culture: Citizens and Administrators in Israel*. New York: St. Martin's.

Pitkin, Hannah. 1967. *The Concept of Representation*. Berkeley: University of California Press.

Rosenbloom, David H. 1971. *Federal Service and the Constitution*. Ithaca: Cornell University Press.

Rosenbloom, David H. 1977. *Federal Equal Employment Opportunity*. New York: Praeger.

Rosenbloom, David H., and Jeannette Featherstonhaugh. 1977. "Passive and Active Representation in the Federal Service: A Comparison of Blacks and Whites." *Social Science Quarterly* 57 (March): 873-82.

Rosenbloom, David H., and Douglas Kinnard. 1977. "Bureaucratic Representation and Bureaucrats' Behavior: An Exploratory Analysis." *Midwest Review of Public Administration* 11 (March): 35-42.

Sayre, Wallace, ed. 1965. *The Federal Government Service*. Englewood Cliffs, N.J.: Prentice-Hall.

Smith, Bruce and D. Hague. 1971. *The Dilemma of Accountability in Modern Government*. New York: St. Martin's.

Storing, Herbert. 1964. "Political Parties and the Bureaucracy." In *Political Parties, USA*, edited by Robert Goldwin, pp. 137-58. Chicago: Rand McNally.

Subramaniam, V. 1967. "Representative Bureaucracy: A Reassessment." *American Political Science Review* 61 (December): 1010-19.

U.S. Congress, Senate Committee on Government Operations, Subcommittee on Intergovernmental Relations. 1973. "Confidence and Concern: Citizens View American Government." 93rd Congress, 1st Session.

Wade, L., and R. Curry. 1970. *A Logic of Public Policy*. Belmont, Calif.: Wadsworth.

Warwick, Donald. 1975. *A Theory of Public Bureaucracy*. Cambridge, Mass.: Harvard University Press.

Weber, Max. 1958. *From Max Weber: Essays in Sociology*, translated and edited by H. H. Gerth and C. W. Mills. New York: Oxford University Press.

——. 1947. *The Theory of Social and Economic Organization.* Translated by A. M. Henderson and Talcott Parsons, edited by Talcott Parsons. New York: Free Press.

White, Leonard. 1932. *Further Contributions to the Prestige Value of Public Employment.* Chicago: University of Chicago Press.

——. 1929. *The Prestige Value of Public Employment in Chicago.* Chicago: University of Chicago Press.

2

REPRESENTATION BY PERSONNEL

The selection of government officials has a central importance in any society. In Plato's discussion that importance centers upon competence; the public official was the helmsman of the boat. If he lacked skill, he could run the ship of state on the rocks. Greek society is inferentially criticized for its use of other criteria, notably popular choice. Aristotle recognizes the right of the nonexpert to evaluate performance even in specialized areas: "the guest may judge of the feast as well as the chef." Ultimately, though, both see the issue as one of competence, disagreeing with each other on acceptable measurement. They are united, too, in rejection of such egalitarian dreams as those that motivated choice of officials in the Athenian democracy. (We will comment on the hedges apparently involved in that later.)

Whatever theorists have thought, rulers have known better. Rivaling, and probably outstripping, sheer competence in their requirements has been loyalty. Family connections and long service indicating allegience have been sought eagerly, and signs of wavering have often been the basis for dismissal of the most competent. While the emphasis has been on personal loyalties, dynastic allegience is often sought by royal families and emphasized by generations of retainers. Regimes in our times have realized that allegience to a form of government is also feasible. The present German Constitution, remembering the halfhearted support the bureaucrats of the Weimar Republic gave democracy, requires officeholders actually to defend the regime—the "fighting democracy" concept. Other regimes have learned the need, to their sorrow. Lack of loyalty can be fatal. But loyalty is not everything. The Communists and the Nazis both have shown how incumbent bureaucracy lacking in loyalty can be forced to train its own replacements. And the demise of the Shah's regime in Iran was hastened, it is said, by overemphasis on loyalty over competence or even simple honesty. The result was widespread resentment of and contempt for his administration by the new middle class that should have been his natural supporters.

In short, "competence" is one of a system's several needs. Faithfulness, or lack of it, is not an irrelevancy; it contributes to effectiveness. Wisdom or expertise is not the same as honesty. And the face one presents to the public has consequences as great as any of the other factors. Who is in office, and what he or she represents to others, can have similar effects.

All of this has been obvious to rulers, who have never been blinded by expertise. Indeed, most societies at most times select their rulers from those who are above average, but well below the highest level of ability. Overly qualified leaders like Olaf Palme of Sweden, Helmut Schmidt of West Germany, and Pierre Trudeau of Canada are perceived as arrogant, and are most successful if they "humble themselves." People seek empathy, a feeling that they can understand each other. Rulers, in turn, have not sought those who "think too much; such men are dangerous," preferring those "that sleep o'nights" and accept matters as they are. But they have also understood the need to have servants who can communicate with the public, and therefore have introduced into their entourages representatives of different "constituencies" and geographic areas. Conscious "coalition formation" of a sort also has been attempted. Marriages, too, have been both symbolic and real efforts to secure representation. Insofar as wives (but not concubines) have been concerned, the harem has been as much a political as a sexual institution.

It is, then, this hidden set of functions that have come to the fore in the modern era, both in response to perceived failure of other mechanisms and as autonomous demands in their own right. Since democratic (or, even more sharply, nondemocratic) structures have been seen to have only intermittent control over bureaucracies, defense of or justification for the existence of the latter in political theory becomes more difficult. That they must exist is a fact of life, ultimately best verified by their inexorable acceptance and expansion by the very politicians who come to office swearing to cut them. But necessity is only the reason that we must accept them, not a justification.

The easy and traditional way of analyzing all this is to empahsize institutional neutrality of bureaucrats who rest their claims on expertise, and to maximize external controls. These points are not so much invalid as bounded. The traditionalist argument captures some of reality, to be sure, but it leaves out much more. The later chapters will be concerned with those issues and their limits; this discussion will center on the representational issue, but it is well to summarize and focus that discussion as a negative backdrop to the need for a case. Institutional neutrality has been vindicated in many instances, but also has been absent under crucial circumstances. Bureaucrats accept the formalism of legal limits and control by superiors, and this is certainly not a negligible constraint. The expectation of Thorstein Veblen, James Burnham, and others that "engineers" or technicians were taking over, misfired because technical questions and answers cover a relatively narrow domain. Technocrats are used to looking elsewhere for resolution of broader, framework problems. Department of Justice lawyers will resist an order not to prosecute a clear criminal case, but expect to share responsibility for setting aggressive or more moderate antitrust policy, and expect broad budgetary decisions to be made almost entirely elsewhere.

But the inertial power of bureaucracy is inevitably not neutral, and it is strong in its effects. Particularly where their own interests and programs are involved, bureaucrats can, in quite a different way than usually meant, "vote with their feet"—or some other part of their anatomy. Their staying power is not less in this era of complexity. Implementing change requires presidential (or equivalent) drive and determination. Though the president is likely to prevail if persistent, his success and the methods he uses are not remarkably different from his power to manipulate the major elements of the "private market" sector.

EXPERTISE

There are pockets of unadulterated expertise in the federal bureaucracy; these operate largely in autonomous fashion, subject to external controls. It is relatively easy to distinguish between technical problems in the Bureau of Weights and Measures, where true detached expertise may be expected to prevail over the details of the domain, and the question of American adoption of the metric system. Many—it is believed a growing number of—bureaucratic positions display that type of special skill. But the generalized important policy roles are not held by technicians or specialists, and a good number of specialists occupy roles in which their specialty is useful but neither necessary nor sufficient. Rather, key governmental positions are held by professional amateurs or generalized professionals whose skills are managerial, synoptic, and transferable, so that they can deal with important technical input but essentially make decisions much more broadly based than the "objective" data. For instance, defense systems require a blend of tax policies, an eye for future innovation, and an understanding of geopolitical patterns that far transcends even the technical capabilities and military considerations obviously involved. Thus, the "expertise" is long on alleged wisdom, experience, and "feel." It is largely undemonstrable and easily contestable—one man's hero in these areas is another man's goat. George

Kennan made a classic argument for foreign-policy professionals conducting foreign policy in the 1950s, but presidents continue to look to lawyers-turned-diplomats or detached academics and, increasingly, away from the State Department professionals.

In some ways the negative case against the traditional justification is stronger than the positive argument for representative bureaucracy. Put more succinctly, it is the great vacuum, the absence of any theory of administrative power in modern society, and its even more conspicuous absence in American constitutional theory, that focuses attention upon the bureaucracy and possible justification.

This chapter, then, examines the processes of bureaucracy itself for sources of restraints and constraints that might supplement, if not supplant, the older theories. At this point it is not so much "the argument" as it is the basis for an argument that is being developed. In tracing selection, training, and value inculcation, the argument suggested here has been a movement toward meeting some of that need.

The growth of emphasis upon representativeness fits in well with the relentless rationalization and the spirit of egalitarianism to which even the most rigid of societies show deference and exploit their symbols. Nondemocratic societies tend to emphasize their devotion to liberation of the downtrodden. Democracies are under constant pressure to bring into the political arena groups once denied an active role. This drive toward ending of what former Supreme Court Justice Abe Fortas called the "nonperson" in American law has its counterparts elsewhere in the world. It is "unthinkable," or at least intellectually indefensible, that a special group might have a monopoly on government service, or even that a narrow spectrum might dominate a particular policy through a stranglehold on key offices. Access to both jobs and policy is seen as a human right, limited by the complexities of job qualifications. And, like other human rights, it is suspended between the easy service of the lips and the more difficult achievement in the fact.

SELECTION

In *The Great Railway Bazaar,* Paul Theroux suggests that each nationality sets up its railway cars in a characteristic fashion. With a little imagination any social activity can be shoehorned into patterns that suggest national character. But administrative selection is so vital a process that it truly and almost inevitably reflects national character. Societies tend toward habitual patterns in the ways they handle situations. And at times societies have deliberately constructed selection processes for many different objectives.

To secure qualified individuals and maintain loyalty, most social systems wish to accord good financial returns, career lines, and high status to bureaucrats. But the accumulation of material benefits often is accompanied by loss of loyalty, perhaps even grandiosity and egoism. Machinery has ingeniously been constructed to try to channel, limit, and satisfy these conflicting motivations.

For example, the Chinese mandarin examination was an extended ordeal, so that those who rose to success were the intellectual cream with links and loyalty to the system. Furthermore, they had invested extremely long periods of time, so they identified with the "brass ring" and knew there were no alternatives as rewarding. The examination system took different forms, and passing grades changed with need; those who achieved certain minimum grades but failed the ultimate test received compensatory positions.

Even more effective was the Ottoman Empire's solution to this set of problems. It was quite usual in Moslem countries for those bureaucrats who had to deal with foreigners to be chosen from among Christians and Jews. The contact with non-Moslems was viewed as morally contaminating or degrading. Just as physically degrading labor was performed by nonbelievers, so was work that was considered morally degrading. The Ottomans went a step further. Mamelukes (Christians), preferably orphans, were trained from childhood in the service of the sultan. As unrooted servants, they were treated well in material terms but continuously reminded that their position depended on performance and loyalty, and that another regime would have no use for them.

This device was generally imitated in milder form by the British Empire, which favored Copts (Christians) in the Egyptian civil service and minority Chinese in parts of Asia. By utilizing Brahmins in India, they helped widen the gulf between that caste and the tens of millions of untouchables. In that instance the practice was perhaps accidental. The natural alliance of the British with the Bengali middle castes who first agreed to become their clerks and subordinates was later modified, perhaps to accord with Indian practice and patterns.

Such organizations were in effect the antitheses of representative bureaucracies. They eschewed the advantages of social representation in order to ensure subservience. Interestingly, they achieved great internal efficiency, but within the context of a weak regime lacking the ability to secure allegiance or much coherence. The Ottoman Empire disintegrated with World War I, but earlier was bound together only very tenuously. The Indian civil service was technically proficient but socially irrelevant (or nearly so). In the latter instance a foreign power disguised the weakness until independence exposed it.

In continental Europe the solution was to create a complex promotion system. With more important titles and small increments of pay, with perquisites and trappings of office given in small, piecemeal fashion, and a heavy stake in pensions, loyalty was engendered by utilizing the need for recognition and security.

Societies have quite different approaches to recruitment, reflecting to some degree their attitudes toward social divisions as well the need for political or administrative efficiency. The British had a long tradition of awarding posts as sinecures or to accommodate high-born families. Expansion of empire and a spurt in the need for capable talent both paralleled and changed attitudes toward the striving middle-class. First, India House as a training center, and then a conscious reconstruction of the "public school" to admit and support worthy middle-class talent willing to effect upper-class behavior, changed the structure of opportunities for the talented who were identified while young. The bureaucracy and army—indeed, the society—still sharply differentiated between those who were assimilated early and achievers in later years, with entry closed to the latter. The clerical and executive classes could rise to the top of a limited service, just as an enlisted man could only become a top sergeant; only the administrative class, drawn largely from "Oxbridge," could expect to rise to the permanent undersecretaryships and similar elite bureaucratic posts. (As Winston Churchill remarked, Erwin Rommel *might* have risen to be a sergeant in Her Majesty's service.) Escape from one stratum to another was a minor miracle. This rigid, almost castelike division is characteristically British; other examples are the barrister-solicitor dichotomy and the judge-master relationship.

It was in contrasting the highly stratified British system with the open American arrangement, permitting vertical promotion to elite status, as well as lateral entry at a high level, that led J. Donald Kingsley to coin the term "Representative Bureaucracy." The novelty of urging the British to imitate American practice was greater in the 1940s than it is today, and Kingsley's notions were readily absorbed only into the analysis of class politics at that time. Today his ideas—perhaps, more accurately, his side comments rather than his major thesis—seem prescient and informative. (We shall return to them in more theoretical form in chapter 4.

Other societies re-create their social divisions, not so much in strata or layers of prestige as in separate structures. The controversy between religious Catholics and rationalists (schoolteacher, free Mason) in continental Europe is in many countries resolved by assigning these forces different governmental departments as preserves—"colonizing," Brian Chapman calls it. Thus, the Ministry of Culture may be dominated by believers and the Ministry of Education by skeptics—or vice versa. Linguistic controversies may be represented in similar fashion, with separate divisions of the same ministry—say, Walloon and Flemish—

operating side by side. In essence the solution is to accept the division as permanent and unresolved, and to isolate the points of view as completely as possible.

Again, structures may be organized to maximize the regulated grouping's power and to minimize it. The development of a permanent cadre of officials in a subject-matter domain tends to co-opt these officials and to mute self-awareness. The American system establishes such clientele-oriented structures, together with a specialized legislative committee structure in which members of a profession (or others vitally affected) are actually preferred for positions. Typically, a teacher elected to the House of Representatives will serve on education committees if that is desired. In contrast, in Britain both legislative and administrative decision-making posts are normally rotated and assigned somewhat at random. This professional amateurism is maximized, and the interactions are characterized by different people in the same roles rather than continuous interaction of the same players. Clearly, the identification with a generalized bureaucratic role is the core of the identity of the administrator in Britain, while in the United States, identification with the area of regulation gets stronger, the longer the regulator serves.

Social class is also significant in the acceptance of bureaucrats, and more subtly affects selection. An Internal Revenue Service (IRS) official who goes to homes or offices is selected for social standing more often than not; a local boy rather than a CPA. While detached service workers are generally more carefully chosen than those in standard service—they are self-supervising, after all—the need for semi-voluntary cooperation impels use of more acceptable agents than those who call taxpayers to the office for a more limited discussion. Thus, in the early years of affirmative action, taxpayers in some southern cities were asked if they objected to a black IRS agent coming to their home. In contrast, a policeman with a search warrant need not be "socially acceptable." (However, it has been speculated that the main reason that lower-class use of the police for social welfare functions, including resolution of family disputes, is so great is not that middle- and upper-class families have alternative and nonstigmatizing resources, but that they perceive the policeman as essentially upper working class, and therefore not an appropriate mediator.)

In short, societies and bureaucracies have various structural solutions to the problem of adaptation to the social environment as well as pure efficiency of their internal processes. Since there generally is imperfect competition, at best, the tendency to prefer objective efficiency is small. They need only avoid being so grossly incompetent as to avoid certain dangers:

1. The effects of incompetence must not be so pervasive as to

encourage other societies to use forceful means (assuming the incompetence extends to inability to defend oneself), as was the case with China and India in the late nineteenth century or Austria-Hungary and Turkey in the early twentieth.

2. Internal incompetence should not promote rivals—either a revolution and replacement, or disintegration of the political system and a set of new governments as rivals.

3. Lapses should not encourage private institutions to take on their specific functions and compete.

The post office can be supplanted by private services, and where this is forbidden, telephone or computer communication might substitute. If they are bureaus of the same government, how these rivals are linked organizationally, and other organizational imperatives, will modify the disadvantages of inefficiency. If, on the other hand, the competitor is nongovernmental, the authority to limit the competition clearly involves some loss of service.

The crudity and immensity of these limits suggest that governmental agencies operate in rather safe environments, and some have doubted that they are often constrained by them at all. Political argument about their relative efficiency, however, may have great consequences, particularly for specific managers or regimes. But efficiency under such conditions is just one of many criteria by which the managers are judged—criteria such as social purpose, taste and manners, loyalty, and morality are other considerations that may crowd out the cost of waste. In any event, the reputation of good operation and its actuality are not identical. Unless many crucial units (or a whole sector of government) fail badly in efficiency, the very weak political and administrative checks are more usually operating than unit cost or other efficiency restraints. Furthermore, insofar as government is monopolistic in many areas, yardstick measures of efficiency are difficult to find or agree upon. Here again, the public sense of appropriate means or goals may well predominate over an undefined standard of getting the job done.

RECRUITMENT

Systems of recruitment of course constrain, if not determine, selection. In one of his less successful and less humorous formulations, C. Northcote Parkinson suggested that the ideal system would be one in which the definition of the position led to only one applicant—the right person for the post (Parkinson 1957, p. 53). In point of fact, the definition of a position, the development of candidates, and the selection from among them present remarkably complex problems that are seldom solved with the neatness Parkinson outlined.

Job description or definition of position is an advanced idea. Most loose structures recruit specific individuals and assign them a conglomeration of duties. The large-scale bureaucracies of older times seem to have recruited by cadres and assigned individuals to specific posts or allowed superiors to select from among them. The effort to standardize positions seems to have begun with the Prussian civil service.

By and large, recruitment as a systematic activity is a modern concept, and arises from notions of universality more than from a need for candidates. In most societies there is a surplus of applicants, so that what is sought by formal processes is a better pool and a finer sieve.

At the dawn of the modern nation-state, a dominant social factor was the lack of good career lines with which to properly place second and subsequent sons. For scions of good families, traditionally the church, and in some places and times the officer corps of the military, were the means to respectable livelihoods. Visible and usually honored public service was an appropriate analogue. Competition for such posts was great, and it was not uncommon for them to be sold—as, of course, was done with choice positions in the church or military commissions. (Alternatively, kings and lesser disposers of patronage were under strong pressure to make appointments in return for conspicuous service—military, political, or personal—by the candidate or a sponsor.)

All of this is the stuff of seventeenth-century novels. Not recruitment, but a process of fighting off job seekers, was required. And since the job and income represented a prize bought and paid for (in pecuniary or other coin), the expectancy of performance was low. Most positions were seen as sinecures with little more than moderate-to-negligible duties. Under the old regime it was said that "there was never such a thing known as a man . . . in a public office because he was supposed to be fit for the place" (Kingsley p. 35). Rather, places were allocated on an "eleemosynary basis," according to Kingsley. This was a welfare state in reverse that found places "for those members of the aristocracy who might otherwise fall into a state that would inevitably bring disgrace upon rank . . . frequently the feeble-minded, the incompetent or the illegitimate" (Kingsley 1944, pp. 28–30).

We have already noted that the British drive toward empire expanded the need for talent at the same time that business was becoming a respectable career for second and subsequent sons. England was being transformed by the growing social acceptance of the new entrepreneurs and the political rights accorded the middle class. As the "public schools" opened up to talented students, and as the East India Company and other far-flung enterprises gave middle-class youths (or even the trained lower-class scholarship boys) room to exercise daring or even competence, government service was also transformed. Indeed, India House's training was to become not just a model for the government services, but its essence. And, with success in business and administration as moral capital, and with their growing political power, the middle class was in a strong position to move for reform. The wave that passed first through the schools, and then through business affairs, inevitably dashed against the bulwark of a cozy, inefficient, privileged governmental service. And it washed away at least the complaisant justifications for upper-class welfare at the expense of the underprivileged average citizen.

Paralleling the triumph of the middle-class moralists in Great Britain, the continental bureaucracies grew more efficient partly in competition with each other. The French bureaucracy had always been awesome and surprisingly autonomous, and the Prussian civil service was emerging as the rival of the military. Its operations were part of the means by which their ruler was to become emperor of all Germany, one of the main props of unification. Whereas the weaker empires—Russian, Turkish, and Austro-Hungarian—were perceived to be weakened by bureaucratic ineptitude, the Prussian service was clearly an asset. (It should be noted that the Austro-Hungarian service had many more strengths than the other two).

The American reformers were closely allied with, and imitated, their British counterparts. Their efforts, tactics, and origins have been brilliantly chronicled by Ari Hoogenboom (1961), who finds the motive power in an emerging professional and technical group anxious to develop some basic positions. The middle-class moralism was in part following patterns pioneered by the British and in part responsive to the tenor of politics of the time. The tactics generally were successful in making a class issue a universal one. It was seen as part of the struggle against corrupt bosses and machines, and as a revolt against the excesses of the period that Vernon Parrington labeled "the great barbecue."

The assassination of President James Garfield by a disgruntled patronage seeker was the turning point in the crusade. The new president, Chester Arthur, a characteristic product of the very patronage system being inveighed against, sought respectability through reform. The Pendleton Act (1883) was the bedrock of reform and has, with modifications, remained the Magna Carta of the American civil service system. Reform was "merit," and merit was the institutionalization of testing. This strange and largely unexamined examination system remains the basis of operations today. Its pseudo precision has been challenged, but not really shaken, by experts and movements of the 1960s; its usefulness had been confronted much earlier, and its limitations were well-known. Yet it has survived.

That testing remains the normal mode for entry is due not to its own merits, but almost entirely to the problems with other methods. In institutional terms, as with politics, "you can't beat somebody with nobody." We shall develop in the next few pages the advantages and limitations of testing for job selection, the major alternatives to date, and some reasons for the survival, and even proliferation, of tests.

TESTS AS QUALIFICATIONS

The assumption of the classic Chinese written examination was that a Confucian education led to competent administration. The ancillary advantages of permitting long preparation time and adjustment of success to bureaucratic need was subordinate to this underlying premise, which also protected and hid the secondary goals.

The British used a form of examination in customs and excise as early as 1820. The Napoleonic Wars had strained the Exchequer, and debts required the protection of public revenue through more rigorous standards of selection. The conjunction in 1853 of T. H. Macauley's efforts to secure competition for the East India service and the Northcote-Trevelyan Report calling for open recruitment for the Home Service constituted a watershed. Macauley's effort resulted in an examination schedule in 1854, and the following year Willaim Gladstone carried the day in the Cabinet for competition to enter the Home Service. Parliament, however, remained hostile to open competition in the Home Service, even after sactioning it for the East India Company. Consequently, the Order in Council of 1855, the foundation of the civil service examination system, represents Cabinet action. It instituted only a compromise "pass examination" mode, however, and in 1870 a further Order in Council instituted competitive open examinations as the normal, through nonexclusive, mode of recruitment.

Macauley brilliantly expounded on the difference between the two types of exams in Parliament debates. Thus the reforms of the Indian service—Macauley's program of 1853-54—became the models for the entire British service.

> Under a system of competition every man struggles to do his best; and the consequence is that, without any effort on the part of the examiner, the standard keeps itself up. But the moment that you say to the examiner, not "Shall A or B go to India?" but "Here is A. Is he fit to go to India?" the question becomes altogether a different one. The examiner's compassion, his good nature, his unwillingness to blast the prospects of a young man, lead him to strain a point in order to let the candidate in if we suppose the dispensers of patronage left merely to the operation of their own minds; but you would have them subjected to

> solicitations of a sort it would be impossible to resist. The father comes with tears in his eyes; the mother writes the most pathetic and heart-breaking letters. Very firm minds have often been shaken by the appeals of that sort. But the system of competition allows nothing of the kind. The parent cannot come to the examiner and say: "I know very well that the other boy beat my son; but please be good enough to say that my son beat the other boy." (*Hansard* ser. 3, 198:754-55)

The original Macauley scheme represented a broad "liberal observation" concept, with selection in two stages. The test to distinguish fine minds was a broadened version of university tests of that time, and Macauley's weighting is of considerable interest:

> Nor do we think that we should render any service to India by inducing her future rulers to neglect, in their earlier years, European literature and science, for studies especially Indian. We believe that men who have been engaged, up to one or two and twenty, in studies which have no immediate connection with the business of any profession, and of which the effect is merely to open, to invigorate, and to enrich the mind, will generally be found, in the business of every profession, superior to men who have, at eighteen or nineteen, devoted themselves to the special studies of their calling. . . . We have, with an anxious desire to deal fairly by all parts of the United Kingdom, and by all places of liberal education, framed the following scale, which we venture to submit for your consideration:

English language and literature:	
Composition	500
History	500
General literature	500
Greek	750
Latin	750
French	375
German	375
Italian	375
Mathematics, pure and mixed	1,000
Natural sciences	500
Moral sciences	500
Sanskrit	375
Arabic	375
	6,875

> It seems to us probable, that of the 6,875 marks, which are the maximum, no candidate will ever obtain half. A candidate who is at once a distinguished classical scholar and a distinguished mathematician will be, as he ought to be, certain of success. A classical scholar who is no mathematician, or a mathematician who is no classical scholar,

> will be certain of success, if he is well read in the history and literature of his own country. A young man who has scarcely any knowledge of mathematics, little Latin, and no Greek may pass such an examination in English, French, Italian, German, geology, and chemistry that he may stand at the head of the list. (From Report [1853], reprinted as Document No. 1 in White 1930, p. 11).

After qualification in a general sense, the apprentice civil servant was to be trained for the Indian Service, through semi-applied courses in such subsets as Indian culture and political economy. After satisfactory completion of courses and examinations, the apprentice became an officer.

The tension between the notion of a civilized, well-educated man and one who could perform specific tasks was resolved in the American context much more in favor of specialization. Modifications involved a great emphasis on needs of the position—though usually the relationship was vague—and a drive toward objectivity in measuring achievement. The emergence of testing as a major preoccupation in American psychology had social ramifications for the art of civil service and the application of such tests. Oddly, the relationships between the testing industry and civil service have yet to be studied.

Above all, the aim of the reformers was to prevent abuses. Tests were labeled a good screening device, and the "rule of three," by which an administrator was not bound to a specific appointment, seemed not only to accommodate some compatibility notions but also to permit room for judgment on nonintellectual and nontechnical aspects of qualifications. "Character" is the way it can be most simply described.

The point can be carried to ludicrous extremes, but it seems fair to characterize nineteenth-century thinking as emphasizing a generalized "talent" or "intelligence." Though recognizing a few specific aptitudes such as art or music, the general view was that they were somewhat freakish. People's differential achievement was due to some accident of involvement or enthusiasm, or a product of "character" or commitment. Though the invention of intelligence testing and other devices directly reflected this point of view, it nonetheless also provoked other positions and provided some means of challenging it. And since intelligence testing continues to sustain (though in mitigated form) some semblance of claims for merit in the outside world, it has been a target for those less artistic social perspectives. Both the hereditary/learned distinction (of relatively minor import to our concerns) and the problem of whether there is an "intelligence" versus the possibility of multiple traits of intelligence are issues strongly linked to views of human nature and the reward structure of society.

Inquiry in those areas has not been unbiased; indeed, it has been demonstrated that the only internationally famous hereditarian, Cyril

Burt, whose work was the basis of the majority of precise efforts to measure nature/nurture influence, was a consummate faker who made up all of his data. Indeed, had he not been lazy enough to duplicate identical tables for different phenomena—requiring a statistical near miracle—and credited nonexistent collaborators as coauthors, we could only suspect invalidity. On the other hand, those who have come up with legitimate data and more solidly based conclusions that, though less starkly or surely, still support the existence of some strong innate capacities have rather readily been labeled as racists. And since aptitute tests of the sort used in civil service have had similar consequences, we shall necessarily return to this issue several times. They, too, have been under a cloud.

In the first half of the nineteenth century, the American school of psychological testing was inclined to mute the nature/nurture issue as largely unsolvable, and it was rather more interested in the question of single trait versus multiple aspects. Ernest Thorndike and his school pretty well demonstrated the multidimensionality of intelligence to everyone's satisfaction. This result confirmed the common sense of the matter; there are a number of traits, some highly correlated, that pass under the name of intelligence. So, for example, command of words (vocabulary) is a surprisingly good surrogate for several other dimensions. Some double-talk specialists, however, master words easily, but score poorly on concepts behind them, even as there are "idiot savants" who can perform intricate arithmetical operations with little or no concept of what they are doing.

The implications of these findings for testing were rather pronounced, more in a basic than in a day-to-day way. Certainly Greek and Latin mastery was finally disestablished as the key to intelligence. Traditional subjects survived as testable only on the assumption that they were reasonably job-related. Failure to learn Latin well would indicate probability of problems in Greek or Spanish, but might not be a reasonable predictor of aptitude for Chinese, let alone computer programming, physics, or microbiology. Subject matter did not emerge from those inquiries as a good framework for probing intelligence clusters. Functional categories seemed somewhat more promising. Whereas Macauley's committee would presume and prescribe a core of common training for all entrants, in the American environment, where it had never been present, it was difficult to demand it in the face of such strong evidence that it might not be useful. Yet even the Macauley report embraced the idea of diverse knowledge and intelligence in general. The already broad list of studies beyond the trivium would have to be expanded in the twentieth century. Even as designed, it went beyond the complacent attitude that Latin trains the mind and knowing Latin prepares one for all things.

In short, what the American testers largely demonstrated was the inappropriateness of any one test—and thus the need for many types of tests. It was a reassuring discovery, confirming both the psychologists' predilections and their purposes. IQs were seen as being reasonably good predictors of school success, but specific aptitudes were to be tapped by more specialized sets of inquiries.

For civil service purposes, too, a much greater variety of examinations was called for. From the beginning much more diversity had been sought, though the essence of different tests was perhaps more uniform than was acknowledged. A package thus emerged for civil service planners. A position about to be filled required analysis of its duties, skills, and difficulty. On the basis of this analysis, a place in the scheme of salaries was allocated and the proper testing procedure and instruments were specified. Candidates could be tested and then certified to the hiring agency. All of this was reasonably systematic and was justified as proceeding from concepts of merit and equality. Selection was based on the best estimate of achievement on standards deemed appropriate to the position. Access was seen as open and advertised. Individuals in like positions were, as closely as practicable, to be rewarded similarly.

All of these steps were acknowledged to be art forms, products of experience and guesswork, and subject to some error. Careful management effort and experience gradually improved the process. The main point was that errors in judgment on all those points would be made unintentionally by a disinterested expert concerned with the position and not the individual. The focus on objectivity was seen as a means of elevating the entire process above systemic political patronage, and even above personal patronage networks that co-workers develop on a day-to-day basis.

The system did work well in helping to establish the claims of civil service and removing the stigma of patronage. And the sleepy federal service adjusted with remarkable resiliency to the dramatic challenges of two world wars and a depression. Yet the feeling that reform had missed the mark was increasingly evident. In the zeal to prevent the worst, it was increasingly argued, obstacles had been interposed to achieving the best. Furthermore, even the preventive measures were not as effective as they had appeared to be.

The lesser of the two arguments was easily confirmed. The system remained monopolized by those who ran things. Indeed, this was one of the few mitigating factors, alleviating the more serious first objection: for example, it is perfectly possible to define a position to fit the proposed candidate rather than the opposite—and, having set requirements to define the result, to get the product desired. (It is the civil service equivalent of shooting the arrow and painting a bulls-eye around it.) In

1979 one of Washington's perpetual conference arrangers was quoted in the *Post*'s civil service column as estimating that fully 60 percent of all the middle- and upper-range positions are filled that way, officially or covertly. In general, personnel officers have cooperated with the supervisors in most nonflagrant evasions of merit—and more than a few crude ones. Racial discrimination, for example, was clearly practiced at a time when it was explicitly forbidden (Bradbury 1952).

But evasions undoubtedly are practiced at the fringes. The cumbersome process involved in most appointments discourages many quality people and makes matching of opportunity and skill difficult. Missed connections, long-term appointments on an acting basis, and forced appointments of individuals not really wanted are some of the costs. At a very minimum the sense of mission of supervisors is undercut by the way process dominates.

This paradox—the politicization of higher and more sensitive civil service positions and other corruptions of the system while effective leadership is undermined—receives its most elegant treatment in Hugh Heclo's work (1977). This sense of frustration to reform had reached public notice with such well-known critiques as John Fischer's article "Let's Go Back to the Spoils System" (1945).

With the effects of civil service called into question, its means became more vulnerable. As with many other parts of American society, the civil rights movement put both means and effect to the test. The merit system probably gave a moderate relative benefit to blacks; the American government was generally a less discriminatory employer than all but a tiny segment of private industry. But, judged by the pretense of merit employment, even in the early 1960s it was well behind equality, and demonstrably behind the milder standard of availability. Bluntly put, the federal service of the 1960s did not meet current standards, and most units could have been found guilty of discrimination by the standards used by courts and boards and commissions. Prior to the 1940s this represented an evasion of the generalized standards of civil service. After World War II it became a specifically prohibited mode of behavior. Thus, it represented a gross violation of the letter and spirit of merit employment. Because Washington has only gradually been Yankeefied and a good deal of the service located below the Mason-Dixon line, much of this was undertaken in reflex action. Where presidents were segregationists—as Woodrow Wilson was—and where Southern leadership dominated an agency (as with the Department of Agriculture, once known fondly as "the last remaining stronghold of the confederacy") official policies implemented discriminatory actions.

Armed with a strong, virtually irrebutable case, black leaders moved for a new approach and close examination of suspect mechanisms. With some support, first from Eisenhower and then vice-president Nixon, and later much firmer support from Kennedy and Johnson, affirmative action programs were mounted to eliminate covert as well as overt discrimination. On a more positive note, such changes as new recruiting mechanisms altered the institutional outcomes. Reflecting the big-city and Washington-centered, bureaucratic locations of its labor force, the U.S. civil service today has a distinct over-representation of blacks relative to total populations at least in part due to such efforts. On the other hand, although progress has been slowly and steadily made, there is still significant under-representation at higher levels. The commitment of the government to "goals" for each unit is in part a goal to achieve amelioration, if not eradication, of this nagging remaining disproportion at key positions, with its implications for both social and political progress. Such efforts can be seen as either a supplement to a merit system or an attack upon it. This issue is one we will return to in detail in later chapters, for it is one that has been joined in both the legal and political arenas.

The raising of problems with regard to testing was one application of the inquiry into past covert and overt discrimination. Many of the problems raised in the IQ controversy were raised in a civil service context. Additionally, aptitude tests in an academic setting have been validated at a medium level of confidence. Though this is not a tight relationship, accounting for only 10–20 percent of the variance, it is a better predictor than any of the other widely used measures: grades, interviews, and recommendations. A fair-minded discussion of claims, advantages, and weaknessess of such tests is found in Sindler (1978, pp. 110–61.) Furthermore, such tests have been shown to be slightly better predictors of black than of white academic performance. On the other hand, testing has not been carefully validated against "real life," at least in part because of the inherent vagueness of what constitutes success or failure in "real life." Thus, while scholastic tests are attackable but reasonably defensible, and have easily survived court attack—the best judgment possible is an impressive enough legal argument—the civil service examination system has been more vulnerable. The soul-searching has led to considerable advances in thinking about the essence of testing, and to refinement of what had been a largely nonrationalized mechanical operation.

What are the criteria for a test of performance? Obviously performance itself would be the ideal. But this requires keen analysis of what constitutes job performance for a particular position; securing an adequate sample of activities to provide stable and fair assessments; development of criteria and scoring that are reasonably objective and/or understandable. All present difficulties for positions of any reasonable complexity.

It is fairly easy to distinguish a task-based test for a typist or other worker with a relatively homogeneous job. That homogeneity tends also to make scoring easy and sampling not difficult. The test for a typist is to type. An executive-secretary position involving a combination of clerical functions, staff assistance to the supervisor, and relations with the public presents a challenge to assessment. The principal issues here—sorting out the components and assigning weights—present no insuperable obstacles to analysis, so long as the frequency of discretion, the more difficult it would be to establish reasonable testing methods. But it is the third problem—making the test manageable for the evaluators in terms of their time and their ability to arrive at reasonably similar evaluations—that prevents performance tests or simulations from becoming standard for positions of reasonable responsibility by large numbers, as in the middle and upper levels of the civil service. Constructing a durable sample of work tasks is itself an intricate notion, and the result is seldom a simple matter to score. Since convenience to evaluators, cost of preparation, and relative confidence in reliability in scoring are important aspects of performance tests for complex positions, surrogates are invariably sought for performance—surrogates that have those convenience factors.

For example, simple tests for mechanical portions of a position may be—and usually are—supplemented by personal interviews. In point of fact, the interview is not merely an unreliable instrument. A long succession of studies by psychologists seems to firmly establish the fact that negative information is introduced into calculation by the interview. Personal evaluation is wrong more often than it helps. Selectors, it would appear, invariably would be better off using tests, previous records, and others' evaluations. But since many executives pride themselves on their own skills as "judges of horseflesh," such studies have not really shaken the emphasis on interviews and intuitive judgment.

For simpler positions, performance tests have been devised. In general, blacks and other non-Caucasian, nonmiddle-class people do relatively less well on these. To a varying extent this reflects another of the few constant findings on aspects of testing: that blacks do much better on vocabulary and other verbal aspects of aptitude than on quantitative and visual aspects. Why that should be so has been freely speculated upon but poorly studied.

After reviewing this rather fragile state of knowledge, civil service officials returned to pen-and-pencil tests as not demonstrably inherently race-biased or class-biased, and more convenient and not more inherently less reliable than known alternatives. The "vindication" was more akin to the Scottish verdict of "not proven," as opposed to a clean bill of health, but it has been sufficient to restore vitality to the approach. The emphasis has moved to smaller, more precise indications, and more sensitive evaluation of specific tests, assuming, in the absence of new negative information, that the global question of their use at all can be answered affirmatively.

Testmakers now distinguish several ways of approaching the problem of validation. First, at its simplest level, items may have a clear relationship with a position (typing for a secretary, being able to read a timetable for a travel agent). This very crude level of analysis, known as "face validity," is a minimal test that can cull out more than it can confirm. Testing for knowledge of classical Greek in order to hire a traffic control expert is unreliable enough that strong evidence to justify its use can be demanded, or it can be summarily eliminated. But how esoteric a knowledge of computers is demanded for a position remains a judgment call.

Second, items may be studied for internal consistency. If item 141, for example, is answered correctly more often by low-scorers than high-scorers on the test as a whole, the item should be thrown out, the rest of the test should be thrown out, or some notion that it taps a different dimension should be developed and justified. The rule of consistency permits tests to measure more and more fully whatever it is they measure. But a test cannot validate the desirability of what is being measured. Should diverse facets, producing different cuts of the test takers scoring well, be sought, the question of relative weights becomes an important issue. In general, what is being done in this type of inquiry is increasing reliability, but this does not address the question of validity.

Third, tests may validated by using scores as the criterion for predicting success and failure in the task. To the degree to which scores are known to supervisors and become the basis of judgment, the testing process is contaminated. A double-blind system that has a relatively small criterion group taking the test, is on individual scorers, and has evaluators of performance who do not know the scores, is the best way of developing such instruments. Later modifications are developed with larger groups. Such modifications may still suffer from the problem of self-fulfilling prophecy—people do well because they have high scores, rather than the score independently measuring ability. Where performance can be evaluated in relatively brief periods of time, this method is desirable. At upper ranges of discretion, performance success is often much more ambiguous and subjective, and can be fairly judged only over long periods—months or even years. This method may then be rendered inconvenient or even unusable.

Fourth, closely related, but with greater conceptual difficulties, is performance evaluation with the test score as the dependent measure. Individuals held to be successes or failures are tested and their patterns on items are isolated. When the tests are administered to applicants, those who score like the successes are assumed to be "winners," and those who resemble "losers" are rejected. Cause and effect are difficult to disentangle in any such effort that is fundamentally correlational. So long as that correlation remains high in testing, the exact mechanism may not be too important, but it remains worrisome. Though extrapolating from high score to success because others have done it may be spurious, it is reasonably logical. Working backward has a built-in logical problem. Present-day high achievers may have high scores, but may not have had them when they were applicants. The method, in short, is simpler but even more questionable.

Most tests are compiled through methods that partake of these approaches in some ways. They are not fundamentally exclusive or contradictory, and creative methods of combining them are clearly possible.

Armed with this more precise underpinning of the instruments, civil service has delimited its claims rather than contracted its domain. Tests reflect greater concern for specific skills, and claims for more global tests are more modest. Reforms have been instituted to provide greater freedom for those who choose among applicants for positions involving judgment on intangible and not easily measured capabilities. Such modifications constitute a tacit admission that precise, determinable technical expertise is much less the basis for selection than was formerly claimed. If a demonstrable, graded score represented a presumably demonstrable advantage in filling a post, entry to the position was to be obtained by that demonstrated extra skill or knowledge. Whatever the problems, test-based competence claims appeared both demonstrable and objective. (This is, for example, the advantage of claims based on experience, which we all find hard to reject. Measurable claims, even those based on weak probabilistic grounds, are more likely to prevail than amorphous ones.)

If we now say that intuition is a better judge of that *je ne sais quoi* that marks a good top-echelon bureaucrat, then selection becomes, at the very least, an elusive and imprecise process, and one assumes that the true nature of the position falls into that category as well. One can argue that ultimately testing will be perfected to measure that *je ne sais quoi,* but until that time its objective, real nature is not visible. In short, the contemporary doubts about the nature of examinations, though not very successful in changing practice, have subtly and significantly undercut some of the rationale for their use. This, in turn, has had very serious consequences for claims to legitimacy of the bureaucracy in terms of its asserted competence. Except in an highly constricted domain, tests do not obviously certify competence; screening devices are defended as better than nothing, but are not functioning as a sufficient basis for bureaucratic authority. This represents a significant crisis in the legitimacy of civil service action, but one that is not being faced or examined.

The controversy over alleged discrimination through tests also has serious ramifications for claims of legitimacy. Obviously, many blacks and egalitarians view the basic process with greater suspicion than they did a few decades ago. Then they attributed unequal results to improper intent by individual officials. Now they see the basic mode of selection—the instruments themselves—as the enemy of racial progress. That these suspicions have not been confirmed in any way other than in differences in scores achieved by different groups is not viewed by them as exculpatory. They do not, as the courts do, regard the evidence as indicating that tests are better predictors than anything else. Even this weak endorsement seems to them to be approval of a forbidden result through sleight of hand. In short, on the issue of discrimination, the vindication of aptitude tests is only strong enough to permit continued use, not to dispel the cloud of doubt surrounding them. Controversy not only undermines some of the aura of expertise; it also raises doubts among a considerable segment of the population about the representativeness of the bureaucracy—or, even more starkly, about the fundamental fairness of its social composition.

RECRUITMENT, EDUCATION, AND SOCIALIZATION

We have already noted that emphasis on selection presupposes a surplus of applicants, and constitutes only a segment of the issue of social allocation of positions. How one describes a position constitutes a form of selection. So do the process of advertisement and procedures of choice.

The beginnings of the affirmative action program sensitized understandings on this point. The initial assumption of advocates of equal opportunity was that the elimination of discrimination was all that was necessary to effect major change. That proved reasonably true at the lower levels, where the discrepancy between supply of job applicants and federal jobs available was not great. At upper levels and in many specialized positions, little or no change occurred. A more sophisticated understanding of the process of recruitment was necessary.

The processes of recruitment for employment are as informal and personal as the job environment itself. People seek employment when they have some knowledge of an opening and an expectation of useful work. But the network of friends and word of mouth, which supplement advertisements and formal rolls, cannot be built in a day. Career lines require elaborate support systems—people reinforcing each other and informing each other of options. Ghetto youths have historically been made aware of rewards in sports and music rather more often than of opportunities in mechanical engineering, for instance. New expressions of interest in black recruitment by personnel officers were not even heard. Old relationships and patterns of recruitment did not indicate a deep desire to change hiring behavior. Convincing qualified blacks to venture into formerly hostile agencies was to prove more of a challenge than had been assumed. Calling attention to new opportunities required recruiting at black colleges or big city universities in addition to Ivy League and traditional southern schools. And streamlining the pipeline has demonstrated that the root problem of recruitment runs back to the very earliest motivational periods.

This ultimate problem of early preparation and involvement is, however, one seminal problem we need not deal with here. It is enough to note that social networks and early predisposition quite clearly count as much as restriction of opportunity for Greek restaurateurs, Irish policemen, Italian stone workers, and Jewish doctors. That is to say, generational kinship and friendship groups combine in subtle and not so subtle ways to ease and encourage the following of some standard paths in occupational commitment.

Even though careful studies, such as the work of Otis Dudley Duncan and Harold Wilensky, show most people have a much more complex work history than is implied by the term "career," the impact of social networks has emerged as basic even in "retracking" (what appear to be sharp changes in occupational involvement). Christopher Jencks, for example, suggests that a large portion of the vast, unaccounted-for variance in success may be due to friendship and—though this is speculative rather than data-based—may be more determinative than family origins or education (1973, pp. 226–29, 250–53).

The obverse is also demonstrable. The absence of such networks constitutes a severe handicap, and operates to further restrict entry by a group. Furthermore, the conspicuous absence of a social group from an occupation often leads to reinforcing attitudes, whether they be engendered by selective recruitment of those wishing to avoid that group, unconscious (or conscious) justification of the discrepancy, or the simple "we-they" aggressive tendencies that people seem to exhibit (and therefore may be innate). It is not merely lack of interest or aptitude that accounts for non-representation of Jews in insurance, blacks in the engineering professions, or women in high posts in the communications industries.

Federal agencies that sought to change whom they recruited invariably found it necessary to change how they recruited. This involved changes in the locales of the search. For positions requiring college training, black schools or universities with black enrollment had to be visited on a regular basis. For lower-level posts, the posting of vacancies in neighborhood headquarters was necessary to bring in a pool of talent not used to applying centrally. The symbolism of black recruiters and black supervisors in person and in advertisements really signaled that promotions and worthwhile stepping-stones were available. And as networks developed and gossip spread, agencies were judged and rated on delivery as well as on promise.

Closely related to this is the problem of education. In general, education is measured by years (or by "credits"), degrees attained, and specific courses completed, where the content of specialized work is relevant and useful. For example, the number and complexity of courses in accounting may be specified for tax agents, or organic chemistry courses for a food-and-drug researcher. While some attention is paid to the quality of the work (and in some posts this may be vital), in most instances successful completion at any level of quality is sufficient.

What is being measured, however, is ability to perform tasks. It must be, and is, recognized that achievement of degrees and the certification that one has sat through a course do not guarantee subsequent performance. They do not even fully validate a specific level of past performance in course work, since standards of grading vary from teacher to teacher and institution to institution. (It must be realized that evaluation of work is not merely an entry-level problem. It goes on through life, and looking at the grades earned at age 22 by a 50-year-old Nobel laureate, to stack the deck a bit, is simply grotesque.)

However, grades do emerge as a moderately strong surrogate for general ability and a fair predictor of types of achievement. That is so for many reasons. In general, ability and achievement tests are well correlated with grades. Grades, for one thing, are determined by end-of-term "achievement" tests, which by their nature involve some estimation of ability. Grades have the added predictive dimension that they represent work do e—not just potential or accretive knowledge. To some degree they indicate the motivation of the individual, the disposition to use what is potential, and the ability to marshal that potential, given the disposition.

Furthermore, grades represent a reasonably stable measure of what they evaluate, since a series of individuals have contributed their estimates. For most persons—we shall modify this—an average evaluation emerges from the educational record. Furthermore, the clump of work represented is a much larger sample of effort by an individual, and in most respects a less variable judgment than an examination.

Of course, that clump contains evaluations by many different people. In general, it "averages out," most of the time. But in any comparison A's courses in organic chemistry and higher mathematics are not strictly comparable with B's public speaking and modern film studies. Second, institutions vary importantly in regard to both content and difficulty.

Third, the long period of judgment involved in grading discounts today's potential. A high grade on an examination today may be a freakish occurrence, but it also might represent newly found physical or mental health, or new intellectual motivation. The trade-off in the stability of the grade measure is the ransom it pays to the past. Fourth, a test may be honed to exclude much of the excess baggage and test for what is useful to the job. While grades may reflect poor performance in mathematics and good performance in French, for instance, a few tests may ignore either factor or inflate its importance, depending on whether the job is that of calculation or diplomacy. Education has been retained as a criterion because it is in some respects a better surrogate for performance than state-of-the-art examinations prove to be. Like a qualifying examination, education is an index of probable behavior rather than of the behavior itself—and therefore not a precise measure. For that reason, it is a standard easily subject to sham and counterfeit.

The standard of education required for a position may be in error even when the attempt is made to prescribe the most reasonable "package." It is, however, possible to deliberately overstate or "goldplate" requirements. Many motivations go into such over-credentialing (Berg 1969). Examiners may resort to such devices merely to simplify their task; additional qualifications act as another sieve in a complex selection process. Just as we have noted that the examiners in imperial China altered the examination and requirements to accommodate needs and availability, so examiners may prefer to "objectify" criteria by changing requirements and minimizing decision strain, on the one hand, and recriminations, on the other. (Generally people respond with less hostility to rejection for lack of previously stated qualifications than to their invocation as the basis of a decision on worthiness. There are subtle differences in our attitudes toward criteria for eligibility and criteria for selection. Selection criteria arouse a more heated personal reaction, whereas unjust eligibility criteria are sweeping and generally absolute. Such criteria may establish solidarity within a category, and may breed widespread social, as opposed to isolated personal, discontent.) Educational requirements lend themselves very neatly to more systematic, social, purposive selection processes. In all societies we know, including socialist ones avowedly opposed to inherited or ascriptive positions, educational achievement correlates highly with parental social position. There are differing explanations advanced for this phenomenon, and the degree to which it is a fact varies from society to society.

First, a purely meritocratic system will, nonetheless, regularly produce a skewed class distribution in educational achievement, provided the selection process rewards more "intelligent" people. A society need not select its people optimally to meet this criterion; all that is necessary is that, by and large, some net selectivity occur in the right direction. Almost certainly every regime meets this weak criterion. Deliberate preference for the least able is not in itself a social goal. Since "intelligence" of parent and child is highly correlated, the combined probabilities will usually produce the results noted. Oddly, the very best correlations may have some built-in limits. The higher the selectivity of the system, leading to higher achievement/intelligence scores of parents, the lower the correlation (rather than the greater the convergence) between parent and child ("recession toward the mean"). Presumably this affects the educational level of offspring.

Second, in simple, real-world situations, an open meritocratic system is not pure. Information available to high-status persons on opportunities and how to use them, informal access to gatekeepers or persons who can influence gatekeepers, and the fiscal opportunities to take advantage of educational openings are usually class-bound factors.

It has been assumed that motivation also is generally correlated with class. In particular, it is asserted that the middle class, with its strong emphasis on morality, is achievement-oriented. In the 1960s, however, the "greening" phenomenon was a largely middle-class rebellion against striving. Impressionistic studies suggest that some of the rebels were left stranded, without a real possibility of recovering social position. (It is more likely, in our view, that the bulk of the "greeners" faded back into the community without great cost, and that those reported on are more conspicuous than typical.) But certainly the phenomenon of ennui and decadence is not unknown to history.

An interesting variant on this finding is the consistently high aspiration levels of blacks compared with their achievement/aptitude scores. Though the blacks as a group still have lower aspirations than the white majority, at any given level of test scores, blacks have higher aspirations than whites. This can be interpreted in many ways, and is not a subject of sufficient study to characterize definitely. A conservative view would be that blacks recognize the present advantages accruing to those among them with talent, and aspire to take advantage of that. Thus, overaspiration is real, and is a rational response to artificially inflated opportunity. A liberal interpretation is that the tests remain faulty, and achievement is in fact blocked by prejudice disguising that faultiness. The tests "predict" because they emerge from the same mentality. In this view, the problem is a racist society and a subculture that nurtures lack of confidence and aspiration.

In spite of some areas of doubt about specific types of inducements or advantages, it seems fairly well established that even "neutral" systems encourage and abet achievement by children of successful parents. Societies differ mainly in the extent to which they articulate that stand and to which they institutionalize such advantage.

Third, there is an invisible seam between societal neutrality and active promotion of advantage. In most societies the handing on of social position has some degree of approval. We may note, for example, the differentials in alimony and child support awarded to different people on the theory of maintaining individuals "in the style to which they have become accustomed." Achieved status is an entitlement for royalty, heirs to great fortunes, or offspring of great political families. The desire to care for one's children is evidenced in biblical stories and Greek legend as well as ancient and modern history. And the childless, too, tend to favor "their own kind," and to respond consciously or unconsciously to people like themselves. (Nicky Hilton explained that his success was based on the fact that one day he ran into his father at one of his hotels "and he took a liking to me.")

Once it was quite literally true that new appointees were personally known by the department head to be of good character. In the formative period of the nation-state, personal loyalties prevailed over national ones, and personal knowledge was an inadequate, but perhaps the only, means of judging character. Subsequently, such personal knowledge remained useful as an evaluatory device. "Old boy" networks survive precisely because they are based upon personal knowledge of the one to be enlisted by an individual whose evaluative skills are known to the hirer. Allowances can be made for harshness or generosity. A certain sloppy coziness is the price paid for such information. In the drive for equality and universalism, that coziness is increasingly seen not as minor favoritism, but as an affront to the basic values of fair opportunity. Such subterfuges as educational criteria represent a last gasp of class favoritism, particularly an emphasis on specific schools—"Oxbridge" in England, the Ivy League in the United States. The picture is quite complicated because these institutions have been undergoing changes, and have maintained quality (and often superiority) in fact as well as in the memories of alumni.

The extent to which this can be carried is shown by the former British practice of sharp distinction between type of government position so that entry into a low-grade past carried with it a ceiling on life-time aspirations, this lack of mobility between position types remarkably preserved the British class system. But, under pressure from the Labor Party, the class system has been altered in educational terms—admission to Oxford, establishment of new universities, and expansion of existing rivals—leading to modification of the virtually complete separation between the administrative and supervisory classes.

There is evidence that the East European Socialist leadership gives its children educational and career preference. Carried to the utmost, as in Romania and North Korea, this involves formal installation of sons as direct heirs to political power. Less obvious is the situation in which all life decisions are bound together in a package whose shape is largely determined by a single integrated power structure.

Explicit restriction or enhancement of opportunity to occupy bureaucratic positions may exist; almost invariably much the same exceptions or rulings exist for access to education. Thus, Malays are accorded advantages to overcome the Chinese propensity to succeed; the untouchables in India are assigned a quota (which need not be filled but is available to all minimally qualified); and Israelis of Sephardic descent are given bonus points on tests. The rare restrictions that are administered across the board are interesting and revealing. It was thought that a member of the House of Lords could no longer be a member of the British Cabinet; some Laborite peers therefore gave up their birthright. But Lord Home qualified and ended this "ineligibility." An index of a decrease in class emphasis generally is the lack of concern generated by the whole matter. Again, quotas based on language generally do not involve preference for admission to education, since that is almost meaningless; rather they take the form of a push for parallel institutions.

In short, bureaucracies are at times deliberately unrepresentative by social class and other characteristics, and also by social chance. These modes often overlap, so that it is difficult to disentangle them. Raymond Boudon (1973) has even shown that, given equal abilities distributed throughout a population, stratification that comes from different perspectives and aspirations may easily and adequately account for differential social achievement even in the absence of other constraints.

SOCIAL CLASS AND SOCIAL COMPETITION

We have already indicated that there are limits to the potential representativeness of bureaucratic service. These are dictated by inherent needs for functions and skills, so that the inconstant domain of what a society regards as "public enterprise" alters even that aspect. New social enterprises change the composition of the bureaucracy. In general, those groupings outside the work force because of age and minimum ability are also not present in bureaucracies. Those who are underrepresented by choice in the market are often overrepresented. Those whom a society regards as able to perform, but are handicapped, are utilized to differing degrees by different societies, in government service.

Children and the elderly are not generally employed in bureaucracies even to the degree that they can be found in the work force. Bureaucracies employ surprisingly large cadres of blue-collar, manual, and routine workers, and secretarial, filing, messenger, and other personal-service posts abound in many regimes. Thus youngsters and oldsters are not necessarily completely excluded even if they are unable to perform at the level of their rivals aged 18–65. When governments enter various forms of business activity—post offices, shipyards, railroads—they add labor forces that more closely resemble standard units. As computers and other modern organizational and information devices develop, there will be a shift from blue-collar to white-collar employees and from low-level (clerical) skills to modern and higher-level skills (keypunch operator, programmer, systems analyst). This tendency—government moving to take on more standard tasks, while internal changes sharply increase its middle-skill levels—is simultaneously making it difficult to spot a clear trend. That is, offsetting tendencies are complicating who is and who is not employed or employable by government. (In a paper at the 1979 American Political Science Association convention, James Guyot made an interesting attempt to argue for convergence of the public-sector and private-sector bureaucracies. The data are work, so the argument is ingenious and rewarding rather than convincing. It does, however, show real promise of new directions.)

We have already noted that in the golden age of Islam, rulers preferred to utilize the services of Christians and Jews for diplomacy, collection of imports, and port authorities. This was done both on religious grounds—fewer Moslems need contaminate themselves by contact with nonbelievers—and for strategy reasons—such groups were more dependent on the ruler, and therefore could be presumed to be more loyal. Governments have been, and are, complex in treatment of women. When male copyists began to be replaced by women secretaries as a result, in part, of the use of the typewriter, government was quite open to the development. (Why this should have occurred—women can use pens as well as press keys—is not quite clear. It is probable that the required social discontinuity in careers for the male copyists was the pretext for a change dictated by economics. This also occurred with a fortuitous social change in urban home life.) While business may well have been more willing at first, government quickly became a favorite and more flexible employer of women, at least in the United States.

Similarly, blacks have had complex relationships with bureaucratic employment. In the past they usually saw federal employment as a less prejudiced job environment than private industry. It is probable that in the urban South after World War II it was more discriminatory than industry, but figures tend to support the prevailing impression that the government has been a consistent pioneer.

If we consider physical handicaps—not disabling in terms of the specific job, but perhaps affecting "presentability"—government, particularly under merit systems, is often a benign employer. At other times it simply is not. Currently, efforts are being made to develop a serious program.

On the other hand, those gentlemanly groupings that in various societies have seen themselves as above trade or manual posts—literal or figurative Brahmins—find posts in government generally inviting, even when the actual duties may be the same as in despised private-sector jobs. (After all, middle-class, educated women who eschew being waitresses find it glamorous to be airline flight attendants.)

In essence, it is the prevalence of upper-class individuals, and of children of middle-class parents, in the upper reaches of the bureaucracy that has drawn the attention of most scholars and critics. J. Donald Kingsley's work, done under the influence of Harold Laski, the noted Marxist theorist and charismatic teacher at the London School of Economics, saw the problem of representative bureaucracy as a class issue. Subsequent work has, however, challenged a good deal of that emphasis. Bureaucracies, after all, have certain functional needs. In every system analyzed, these needs result in a high-level, above-normal use of posts requiring middle-class skills. V. Subramaniam (1967) has shown that this intuitive understanding is empirically borne out by the data. Bureaucrats, then, are skewed toward having middle-class skills and occupying middle-class positions. This is a fact of life, at least as all societies currently operate.

Being drawn from middle-class families is not a fact of life with the same tautological import, but it is hardly unexpected. Middle-class people often have middle-class parents, and this symmetry is achieved without repression or special inducements or constraints. The normal predisposition of offspring to imitate their parents produces disproportionate carry-over of the same or similar status from one generation to another. In many ways what is remarkable is the weakness of the effect over several generations, rather than the continuity. Thus, a study of bureaucrats reporting middle-class origins is one of the dogs-have-teeth variety. Even a tilting toward bureaucratic parents is hardly surprising.

Kingsley did note that the British civil service also had a pronounced sex bias, and that representation on regional or linguistic lines was not adequate either. His arguments along these lines coalesced with observations by Laski and his colleague William Robeson about the relationship of "locals" and "colons" in the administration of parts of the empire, and helped to formulate a more comprehensive approach to the phenomenon. While the thrust of Kingsley's seminal *Representative Bureaucracy* is that Britain's administrative apparatus should become a structure open to talent, its influence emanates from the heavy emphasis on elimination of class differentials, some of which seem endemic.

Theoretically, any social characteristic can become the basis of differentiation for eligibility or success within bureaucracies, and there is considerable variety in what has been the basis of selection or discrimination. Most enduring are nationality or subethnic cleavages, particularly in balkanized societies—such as Yugoslavia and Canada—where they fall along mutually reinforcing regional, cultural, linguistic, and social status lines. Purely regional effects and geographic affinities always have some influence, but where virtual subsocieties exist, bureaucracies cannot escape the consequences. They must self-consciously move to alleviate the situation—as in Canada—or accept the division and reinforce it—as in most Belgian bureaucratic structures.

Class (or caste) lines become most significant in societies with enormous gulfs between groupings. Even vigorous "reverse discrimination" in India over a period of three decades has just begun to have significant payoffs for the untouchables.

Religion and language generally emerge as issues joined to other divisions. Religion is often intertwined with ethnicity, and sometimes social class. In societies that are homogeneous in religion, minor sectarian differences or degrees of belief or observance may be divisive. "High Church" and "Low Church" have been key dividers in British society, in tandem with class position and political preference. (The Episcopal Church has been described as "the Tory Party at prayer"; it is also averred that "the Labor Party owes more to Methodism than to Marx.") In Syria, at the time of this writing, the minority Alawites are the dominant group. An Islamic sect looked down upon by the others as heretical, the Alawites have often entered military service. The clash of big powers in the Middle East has poured weaponry, and even more power than usual into the military. So a group with low status and poor connections, but with its own cooperative network, has become at least temporarily dominant. Similarly, in Belgium, France, and Italy, Free-masons, schoolteachers, and other traditional "freethinkers" have come to dominate specific departments and agencies, while orthodox groups dominate others. Indeed, Brian Chapman (1956) identifies such structures and describes the process of taking over a department and maintaining it as an enclave as "colonisation."

Because language is the skin of a culture, its clearest manifestation, vital language differences in a society signal deep-seated division—lifestyles, achievement levels, and lack of social trust. The advantages of a single language are so great and obvious, in social terms, that societies strive mightily to achieve it. The costs for nonpolyglot individuals is so great that they will resist. Genuine multilingual societies develop unsuspected flexibilities in people. The Swiss will switch languages as different subject matters arise or in response to subtle clues leading them to surmise the nationality of the person addressed. When a dominant, previously unchallenged language group has its power challenged—as in Canada and Belgium—the dynamics resemble similar situations in other areas (like religious dominance in Lebanon).

In short, what divides a society affects its allocation of scarce, often prestigious positions. Whether these positions are viewed as social prizes—attractive incomes, life tenure, and considerable security of income and perquisites—or policymaking posts, they are targets of opportunity for the same social groups that vie for other scarce goods. Only occasionally, as we have noted, are governmental posts regarded as déclassé and allocated to disprized groups. Thus women invariably have been drastically underrepresented or even totally excluded from such posts, as have most isolated and abject groupings—lower castes in India and exotic natives such as the Ainu in Japan or the Bushmen or the Eskimos.

Most typically a complex allocation system develops that generally provides a good glimpse into the realities and social workings of a society. Even the degree to which balancing is explicit or covert provides important clues. The clearest case of such a calculus is found in Lebanon, and is illustrated by the apocryphal anecdote told by Leonard Binder (1966, p. 213) about an incident during Lebanon's token participation in the 1948 war against Israel:

> On the Lebanese front in the Palestine war of 1948 a Maronite Lieutenant found a Greek Catholic platoon in a state of complete inactivity despite the unabating and still vigorous exchange of fire. "Sergeant," bellowed the company commander, "don't your men know that this is war? Why aren't they fighting? If they do not take up their arms at once, I shall have you and them executed as deserters." "But one of our men was just killed, sir. We are therefore waiting for three Maronites, two Sunnis, two Shi'is, two Greek Orthodox, and one Druze also to be killed before we resume fighting."

To deal with its division into Christians and Moslems of various sects—some regarded as heretic—a complex bargain was struck involving some fictions. Thus no census was taken after 1943, in order to maintain the notion that Christians were still the majority group. The president—with foreign policy predominance—was always a Maronite Christian, reflecting that community's involvement with trade and supra-Islamic connections. The prime minister—clearly number two in the system—was a Sunni Moslem, as were several other ministers in every Cabinet. At least a few major portfolios went to the Shi'ites and Greek Orthodox. The exact distribution was not as precise as suggested by the army anecdote; some rough equivalences of, say, deputies to Cabinet officials (depending on their importance) or bureau chiefs were partly preordained and partly bargained for. This, in turn, permitted some flexibility in terms of individual capabilities and nonethnic political contingencies. This rough formula was not limited to the government, but permeated all communal

TABLE 2.1: Distribution of Higher Administrative Positions Among Religious Communities in 1946 and 1955

	Maronite	*Sunni*	*Shi'ite*	*Greek Orthodox*	*Greek Catholic*	*Druze*	*Total Number of Cases*
Percent of posts, 1946	38.7	29	3.2	19.3	3.2	6.4	31
Percent of posts, 1955	40.0	27	3.6	11.7	9.0	7.2	111
Percent of population, 1956	30.0	20	18.0	10.0	6.0	6.0	1,430.908

Source: Binder 1966, p. 172, taken from Halim Fayyad, "The Effects of Sectarianism in Lebanese Administration" (M.A. thesis, American University of Beirut, 1956).

activities in Lebanon. The intransigence of the Maronite community to any alteration of the formula—in spite of a much larger birth rate among the Moslem groups, also ignoring their social and economic development—together with the catalyst of the Palestine Liberation Organization, produced a civil war in the late 1970s. Fearing that any reopening of the formula was a slide down a slippery slope, the Maronites clung to a false security too long.

Other societies generally have less clearly articulated formulas and much more flexible limits. It is rare to see anything like the Lebanese or Indian formula. (In the latter case the "temporary" divisions to benefit the "backwards and unscheduled castes" are sanctioned by constitutional amendment and essentially defined by statute.)

Subservient populations are usually identifiable because the government functionaries of that group are individuals who serve as liaison to their community, usually in nonpolicy-making posts. Such phenomena must be carefully observed. Paradoxically, the greatest show of strength of a group is its power over its regulators. (Thus, the medical and legal professions' dominance of legislative and executive posts dealing with their operations is an impressive demonstration of power, not of weakness.) But restriction of members of a group to such executive posts, and the limited authority in policy, particularly when nongroup members are affected, are hallmarks of weakness. (Consider, for example, the tribal authorities in South Africa.)

Ratios of power can be discerned particularly when the patterns persist over time. Thus, Great Russian dominance is demonstrable in the USSR from any studies taken of elite groups. Similarly, the absorption of some groups into power positions in American society, and continued discrimination against blacks, are both readily shown by such data.

But the concepts of representative bureaucracy that have proved alluring and powerful have not primarily been seen as measures of social reflexiveness, in the sense of simply seeing "who gets what and when and why." That, to be sure, is being done within other traditions. Rather, it is urged in the sense that policies will be better-informed if the bureaucracy reflects the general population in a broad sense; that, as we have noted, the "representative branches" need such supplementation in the modern world; and that groups have a right to such representation in policy formulation.

There are, of course, many ways to secure pluralistic accommodation, including consultative devices of varying degrees of formalism and effectiveness. Europeans, particularly the Scandinavians, have elaborate structures for consultation with both groups and outside experts. New measures, whether they are legislative or administrative, go forward after a very broad effort at consultation, negotiation, and a high degree of consensus. This, plus the high degree of governmental and political intervention in the society, has convinced a school of analysts—notably Phillipe Schmitter—that these societies are "corporatist" in nature—Benito Mussolini's old theory of fascism in essence, but without dictatorship or bullies or force or exploitation of labor. This concept will be analyzed later, in terms of our argument. At this point we can note that such a consultative society requires great civility, patience, and time to make the wheels roll effectively. The system also may work because of its implementation in relatively homogeneous societies that have cooperative traditions. Some severe strains have developed in recent years, too, suggesting the possibility that consultation may have worked because of its appropriateness to a particular epoch.

Where the total system is less structured, it is more difficult to get at the realities of consultation. In general, most "advisory" bodies attached to administrative units have proved to be of little use. They tend to be regarded by the bureaucrats as window dressing, or public relations devices, or—a leg up—as a political shield. They may be sounded out for advice, and wise boards probably have more influence than foolish ones. Usually, however, even the advice-seeking is for the purpose of co-optation to a policy that is largely predetermined. Isolated groups with no power and meeting sporadically, they tend to be controlled by the bureaucrats with their greater day-to-day involvement, concentration on the matter at hand, and clearer authority.

Still, special groups may come to dominate an agency, and that agency in turn may become the bargaining agency within the total bureaucracy for that group. In American public administration that is quite a usual pattern, and we refer to such structures as clientele agencies. The Departments of Agriculture and Labor are clear instances. The selection of experts in the field as administrators reinforces that control, but something close to an absolute veto inheres in the AFL-CIO and the larger agricultural organizations. The tradition of American legislative committees being composed almost exclusively of representatives having roots in such fields also contributes to the pattern. President Jimmy Carter gave some indication of the extent of such control when he made clear one of his criteria for selection of a new secretary of education was noninvolvement in and lack of beholdenness to the educational establishment. In fact, it is virtually certain that the new department, if it survives, will be quickly captured, in spite of Carter's heroics, given the high degree of structured representation and organization in the educational community and its political prowess. (To be sure, that sector's importance will be declining, with a smaller segment of the population involved in its programs, as we approach zero population growth. This in turn strengthens President Ronald Reagan's campaign to scrap the department.)

Such clientele structures are presumed to give emphatic clout to the groups involved, and it is likely, but not proved, that having a government mail drop is highly advantageous in ways other than prestige. For governance, the disadvantage of such a system is, of course, its inflexibility. Departments are not easily "uncreated" when their clients' importance declines, nor can every group achieve that bureaucratic status.

Finally, structures can be created with formal representatives from appropriate groups. Such structures have tended even more clearly to be excessively rigid, the representatives seeing themselves as instructed agents rather than creative architects of policy.

For the same reasons, the bureaucrats cannot be clearly entrusted or encumbered with the duty of speaking for the outside group. Even clientele agencies like the Department of Labor or, as was believed, the former Atomic Energy Commission, often must be at odds with their clients, if only for the sake of appearance. And they pay heavy prices in terms of bureaucratic, political, and public relations, according to the degree to which they are boxed in by parochial concerns. In short, what Frederick Mosher (1968) calls "active representation" by the bureaucracy is not only inefficient, but probably unworkable in a modern political system. Though some, like an early treatment by the distinguished Polish political scientist, Stanislaw Ehrlich, have thought it significant, most have not. Ehrlich dubbed it "advisory representation." Most commentators have found it illusory representation, and Mosher himself suggests that it is at most a useful adjunct of policymaking.

In sum, the "fair shares" notion of bureaucracy has little to do with policymaking. The "active representation" idea has little to do with reality. And the "corporate politics" concept implies an intermediary role for the bureaucracy; it describes the political structure of the society, but is not a description of the representational role of the bureaucracy.

When we talk about fair shares and representation, we are using what Hannah Pitkin (1967) suggests is almost a pun. That is, we are saying that the bureaucracy should "represent" society in the sense of "standing for" or "looking like" society. When we talk about the functional question, or what Mosher calls "passive representation," we are saying that the bureaucracy itself should incorporate some of the attitudes, positions, and understandings that prevail in society. Representational bureaucracy as a functional operation expands membership to stress diversity in policymaking as well as the desirability of the bureaucracy being able to sell its program to diverse groups in society. By increasing the range of those who function within the bureaucracy, we increase both the infusion of ideas into the bureaucracy and the dissemination of decisions to the outside world.

It is interesting, in that respect, to note that the concept of "penetration", of the need of a system not only to make decisions but also to disseminate and to persuade, was developed after viewing the functions of the Indian civil service—a very "efficient" bureaucracy in technical terms, but one that had very little impact on the outside. The Brahmin nature of the operation meant that its British-trained outlook was only "procedurally rational" rather than "substantively rational," to use Karl Mannheim's terms. That is, it did everything correctly, but what it did had very little to do with what was going on in the country. Whether the present Indian structure, which is not even procedurally very rational or effective, has greater penetration is of course doubtful. To say that a structure that is efficient will be enhanced by representativeness does not mean that a representative structure may not be ineffectual or inefficient.

The notions of representative bureaucracy have been analyzed at some length by critics. Most thorough and most vehement has been Kenneth Meier. In a vigorous attack, for example, Meier and Lloyd Nigro conclude that

> The "theory of representative bureaucracy" is inadequate as a normative theory of political control and as an empirical description of reality. Its theoretical linkages are critically weakened by unsupported empirical assertions, untenable assumptions, vague definitions, and poorly defined units of analysis. (1976, p. 467)

While the notions are vague, and the linkages weak, it is hard to see that the indictment is fully warranted. Indeed, no one has been pretentious enough to advance these propositions as a "theory." It is, as they suggest, a loosely articulated notion. But Meier's own reiteration of traditional notions of political control can be attacked in the same terms.

Meier's method is to reduce all assertions to sweeping either/or propositions, reasoning on his own as to what the implications should be. Thus, he argues, representative theorists suggest that each individual bureau should be representative, inasmuch as decisions are made at that level. He would not be able to produce a single supporter of that position if his life depended on it.

Again, he repeatedly identifies the position as asserting the primacy of social-origin notions and repeatedly "confutes" the position with evidence of life-cycle socialization processes. This unexceptional and nonnovel observation would hardly trouble Mosher. The naive notion that bureaucrats do not adapt to self-interest is an odd view to attribute to that perpetual cynic, Norton Long. Nor is the theory of social origins as influences uniquely Marxist, as Meier suggests. Indeed, many of the asserted relationships are clearly "epiphenomenal" and anti-Marxist—the emphasis on sex, for example. Meier often constructs a straw man, sets him on fire, douses the flames, and in the cloud of smoke announces that he has clarified what has never been in doubt.

But theorists have been doing that for a long time. They are particularly able to go through such manipulations with respect to any theory of representation. For, as Pitkin suggests, the very theory of political representation is an effort to get from the simple notion of agency (as lawyers currently use the term) to a notion that because the representative has some asserted identity with the populace, his or her action is in some sense theirs. It is always, she suggests, an exercise in semantic legerdemain. As in all other representative theories, weak and overlapping notions abound in the idea of representative bureaucracy. We have suggested that there are at least four intertwined and nonoperationally defined concepts, and I have no doubt that others would have no difficulty in finding a fifth or a sixth. But we would suggest it is the nature of the beast.

If Meier is more vitriolic than might be called for—though accurate enough in the thrust of his criticism—his empirical tests seem unworthy of some of the conclusions that he wishes to draw from them. Utilizing a mailing to 500 executives of a National Opinion Research Center questionnaire, Meier and Nigro found very little difference between the views of executives and those of the general public in a number of issue areas. From this Meier concluded that the representative bureaucracy has little or no effect in any passive sense. The questions utilized were not formulated for the specific purpose he intended. In spite of his identification of them as "issue areas," they reflect very broad attitudes that do not actually tap important social divisions within society.

Another major test of representative bureaucracy approaches the challenge by measuring degrees of difference between bureaucracies. Meier's use of this material resembles his test of opinions. That is, using Gini indexes, he sets off to compare the civil service, the noncivil service, the diplomatic service, and the army; and while he finds that the civil service is more broadly representative of the general public than the other three, the differences are not as pronounced as might be imagined and none of them falls along the perfect Gini correlation line. (A Gini index is a way of measuring cumulative differences in two populations. A perfect identity is 1.00. It is a simple variation of the Lorenz curve.)

At least in the first instance, what we are dealing with is a serious attempt to test the proposition that the theorists assert even if the particular items of analysis do not appear to be fully convincing. It is fairly clear that when he is measuring the representativeness of these four organizations, Meier is not testing what theorists are talking about at all. In Long's terms, at least the rest of the executive, and certainly the diplomatic, service is part of what Long would call the bureaucracy. We do not know how he would feel about the armed forces, but it is quite possible that he might incorporate them into that structure as well.

At any rate, what is being asserted is that the bureaucracy is decidedly more representative—has a lower Gini coefficient—than Congress or the presidency, and that is the proposition to be tested—not whether the diplomatic service is or is not more representative. Thus, a comparison of Congress and the bureaucracy, or of Congress and its staffs, or of occupants of the presidential office, or of the president and his staff and the judiciary, against the bureaucracy, would have been a valid test. To be sure, by its very numbers and nature the bureaucracy has an advantage, but that is essentially the argument of the advocates of representative bureaucracy. A more reasonable argument, if one were interested in "truth" as opposed to scoring points, might be that these differences between the branches are decidedly less than had been imagined.

In his work with Nigro and in an earlier article (1975), Meier introduces evidence that supports the notions, and also contributes to their refinement: The American bureaucracy closely approximates the general population (Gini coefficient of .12) and is more representative than others, though it underrepresents lower classes more than others. However, at the truly high levels, it is less representative, though pronouncedly more representative than other countries.

In their article Meier and Nigro assert the following:

1. The theory rests on assumptions that origin equals attitudes equals behavior.

2. The higher civil service, unlike the total service, is decidedly unrepresentative.

3. Demographic variables account for only about 5 percent of the variance in attitudes among higher civil servants in their responses to the NORC questionnaire.

4. In 34 of 132 possible correlations between demographics and attitudes, the correlations are statistically significant, though the highest correlation is .16. Using path coefficients, the number of statistically significant relationships is reduced to 29, but (as they do not choose to mention) the highest correlation jumps to .29.

5. Race is significantly related to attitudes (.80), accounting for about two-thirds of the variance.

David Nachmias and David Rosenbloom (1978) have proceeded on similar premises. Using fractionization procedures, as well as Gini correlations, they have measured progress toward fair shares and, like Meier, have compared different structures in their representativeness. Like Meier, like the Civil Service Commission, like those who run as they read, or who pore over the data meticulously, they conclude that departments and agencies vary considerably in the degree to which they are representative, and in particular the degree to which upper echelons have been integrated.

Rosenbloom and Jeannette Featherstonhaugh (1977) have sought to test the effectiveness of representativeness through attitude measurement. They assayed a secondary analysis of Brooking's data (1967) on political attitudes, and found a number of significant differences between black and white bureaucrats. They argue that inasmuch as the 1960s were a period of dispute between the communities, these political activities are especially revealing. However, by virtue of the items considered, their study is far from definitive.

That there is a relationship between demographic characteristics and attitudes is one of the stocks in trade of the most mundane social scientist, not just of the Marxist. Meier shows three score relationships while pooh-poohing the concept, whereas Rosenbloom and Featherstonhaugh claim victory on one somewhat fragile finding. A two-hour search in the library produced several other studies, in spite of the paucity of work on bureaucratic attitudes and the absence of any good search categories in the standard indexes. These include the following:

1. Lebanese bureaucrats sharply split on various lines—for example, Moslems advocated a "basic reform" in administration (significant at the .001 level); women bureaucrats indicated loyalty to family over sect or state, in sharp contrast with males (significant at the .0001 level.)

2. Responses of U.S. Defense Department officials to questions on equality are sharply different from those of officials in "social" agencies. Other agency officials' responses are in between, but closer to those of the "social" bureaucrats than those of defense officials.

3. Geographic mobility rates are vastly different between lower-ranking and higher-ranking bureaucrats, even controlling for government service moves.

4. Robert Putnam (1973) found Italian, German, and British government officials to have strikingly different attitudes toward politics and accommodation, as well as tolerance generally to minority positions. Striking generational differences emerged on these issues, especially in Germany. Technicians and specialists had less tolerance than generalists, even controlling for education.

5. Nachmias and Rosenbloom found ethnic differences in self-perception in the Israeli bureaucracy, with differences in career progress and propensity to exit ethnically correlated.

6. Dennis Dresang (1974) found that Zambian bureaucrats were perceived as particularistic in their treatment of clients, but were not

discriminatory on broad allocative policies, such as educational expenditure. He also found ethnic differences, especially the Bemba willingness to take the initiative, compared with other tribes, and to favor their own group.

In short, it is not hard to find instances of differential attitudes or behavior among bureaucrats when they are lumped into categories. It is thus easy to refute the extreme form of Meier's "demographic characteristics don't cut much ice" by finding a crisis or very sharp cleavage issue; refining the tests and standards involved; defining the target groups more closely; or taking another time slice. In a sense all of the above studies do one or more of these things.

Meier developed his excessive argument in response to those he alleges believe external restraint is nonexistent; thus he stressed representativeness as the only check on discretion.

The conclusions of Meier's article are, in contrast, useful and thoughtful. Since demographic characteristics are not the whole story, external restraints should remain part of the analysis if there are to be restraints. In the light of Stalinism and Hitlerism, to say nothing of Nixonism, few would dare quarrel with that. So we return to what should have been the starting point.

> Administrative responsibility, or political responsibility of any kind, is not an either/or matter of only internal or only external controls. If external political controls exist and internal control do not, violations of the "code of responsibility" will occur. Formal controls and sanctions have one serious fault; the costs of universal application far outweigh the gains from such an application. More simply expressed, those in the political branches of government (and in other control agencies) do not have the time, manpower, and perseverance to prevent all possible administrative abuse; their time is better spent on more important things. On the other side of the question if only internal, ethical controls exist, then violations of the "code of responsibility" will also occur. Internal controls may be thought of as society's way of instilling internal, positive reinforcement. But if no formal sanctions exist, the bureaucrat will eventually reach a situation when the utility from unresponsible behavior exceeds that from responsible behavior. If he does not have to consider the probability of external sanctions, he will commit the act. The conclusion is simple: In order to be effective any type of control must rely both on internal, ethical checks and on external sanctions; both must be present for the system of controls to function. (Meier 1975, p. 542)

The test before us is to develop a means of estimating the real influence of representativeness and its potential for improved operations. Nominal data, such as opinion preface, are inadequate. Here, as in the study of administration generally, the problem of numbers and sampling, and the difficulty of knowing what happened and what is significant, loom as challenges of frightening proportion.

To date, though, the study of representative bureaucracy has demanded a serious reexamination of the nature of bureaucracy, its symbolism, and its degree of autonomy. It has engendered serious examination and reexamination of data conventionally used in studies of large-scale agencies, and has found them wanting. All in all, it has demonstrated that a concept treated seriously has a life and purpose independent of its original matrix. It is, of course, the impetus from the doctrine of external controls that has caused a growing emphasis on representativeness as a legitimating device for the bureaucracy. The curious absence of any underpinning for bureaucratic authority in the American Constitution or the Anglo-American tradition accentuates this drive, for it is necessity, not love, that turns us to heavier and heavier use of administration.

While "representativeness" serves as a bureaucratic entitlement to authority, it also gives an authority to groups who demand that the bureaucracy live up to that concept. This in turn means some diminution of the normal political powers to select, fire, and reward bureaucrats, and further weakening of external controls. It leads to a populist-universalist system that Max Weber largely foreshadowed.

But representativeness as an exclusive theory of place cannot prevail, being hemmed in by many constraints, most notably by the functional needs of the service. It is inadequate by itself to guarantee quality of decision, and totally inadequate without external controls to responsiveness. An autonomous bureaucracy, however recruited, will ultimately represent itself best, at the expense of its social inheritance. The notion of representative bureaucracy is in no sense a paraphrase of Plato's espousal of unguarded Guardians.

But as a fact of life in modern societies and as an aspiration toward social justice, the notion of representative bureaucracy has powerful appeal. In the first instance, it serves as an analytic tool, and in the second as a legitimating device in an area where legitimation has always been uneasy and diminishing. The degree to which representativeness in fact does the things we believe it should, and trust it does, remains to be documented. In this area it is a challenge to future scholarship. The problem seems both susceptible to investigation and vital to our understanding of and faith in modern democracy.

REFERENCES

Berg, Ivar. "Rich Man's Qualifications for Poor Man's Jobs." *Transaction* 6, no. 5 (1969): 49–50.

Binder, Leonard, ed. 1966. *Politics in Lebanon.* New York: John Wiley.

Bradbury, William. 1952. *Racial Discrimination in the Federal Service.* New York: Columbia University Press.

Boudon, Raymond. 1973. *Education, Opportunity and Social Inequality.* New York: John Wiley.

Burnham, James. 1960. *The Managerial Revolution.* Bloomington: Indiana University Press.

Chapman, Brian. 1956. *The Profession of Government.* London: George Allen and Unwin.

Dresang, Dennis. 1974. "Ethnic Politics, Representative Bureaucracy and Development Administration: The Zambian Case." *American Political Science Review* 68 (December): 1605–17.

Erlich, Stanislaw. 1963. "Functional Representation." Unpublished International Political Science Association paper.

Fisher, John. 1945. "Let's Go Back to the Spoils System." *Harper's,* October, pp. 362–68.

Heclo, Hugh. 1977. *A Government of Strangers.* Washington, D.C.: Brookings Institution.

Hoogenboom, Ari. 1961. *Outlawing the Spoils.* Urbana: University of Illinois Press.

Jencks, Christopher. 1973. *Inequality.* New York: Harper and Row.

Kingsley, J. Donald. 1944. *Representative Bureaucracy.* Yellow Springs, Ohio: Antioch University Press.

Lipset, Seymour Martin. 1952. "Bureaucracy and Social Change." In Robert K. Merton et al., *Reader in Bureaucracy.* Glencoe, Ill.: Free Press.

Long, Norton. 1949. "Power and Administration." *Public Administration Review* 9 (Autumn): 257–64.

Meier, Kenneth. 1975. "Representative Bureaucracy: An Empirical Analysis." *American Political Science Review* 69 (June): 526–42.

Meier, Kenneth, and Lloyd Nigro. 1976. "Representative Bureaucracy and Political Preferences." *Public Administration Review* 36 (July/August): 458–69.

Michels, Roberto. 1956. *Political Parties.* New York: Dover.

Mosher, Frederick. 1968. *Democracy and the Public Service.* New York: Oxford University Press.

Nachmias, David, and David H. Rosenbloom. 1978. *Bureaucratic Culture: Citizens and Administrators in Israel.* New York: St. Martin's.

Parkinson, C. Northcote. 1957. *Parkinson's Law.* Boston: Houghton, Mifflin.

Pitkin, Hannah. 1967. *The Concept of Representation.* Berkeley: University of California Press.

Putnam, Robert. 1973. "The Political Attitudes of Senior Civil Servants." *British Journal of Political Science* 3 (July): 257–90.

Rosenbloom, David H., and J. Featherstonhaugh. 1977. "Passive and Active Representation in the Federal Service." *Social Science Quarterly* 57 (March): 873–82.

Sindler, Allan. 1978. *Defunis and Minority Admissions,* pp. 110–61. New York: Longman.

Subramaniam, V. 1967. "Representative Bureaucracy: A Reassessment." *American Political Science Review* 61 (December): 1010–19.
Theroux, Paul. 1975. *The Great Railway Bazaar*. Boston: Houghton, Mifflin.
Veblen, Thorstein. 1921. *The Engineers and the Price System*. New York: Viking.
White, Leonard D. 1939. *The Civil Service in the Modern State*. New York: McGraw Hill.

3

REPRESENTATION BY ORGANIZATION

Although the theory of representative bureaucracy maintains that public bureaucracies can be representative in terms of the social characteristics and the values of their personnel, it is equally true that they may also be representative in terms of their organizational structures and missions. Indeed, as noted in chapter 1, public bureaucracies are sometimes considered to be more representative of myriad economic, social, and political interests than are legislatures. Representation of this nature is explored in depth in this chapter.

NATIONAL BUREAUCRACIES: FRAGMENTATION AND UNITY

National bureaucracies can take many organizational forms. They can be relatively coherently and rationally organized; likewise, they can be highly fragmented and diversified. Whatever their form, however, it is of fundamental importance to recognize that the organization of national bureaucracies is overwhelmingly a function of politics and only secondarily an attribute of prevailing organization theory. This fact has been well demonstrated with reference to different types of political settings.

Traditional organizational theory in democratic nations tends to be concerned with accountability, responsibility, and efficiency. Its overriding focus is to develop a neat, rational organizational scheme that assures a clear chain of command reaching upward through political executives to presidents, prime ministers, and legislatures. In this fashion, it is assumed, political control can be exercised downward by the voters through elected officials. In addition, traditional theory emphasizes "efficiency" as a leading value because this reduces the cost that taxpayers and private businesses must bear to support government.

In sum:

> Orthodox theory is preoccupied with the anatomy of Government organization and concerned primarily with arrangements to assure that (1) each function is assigned to its appropriate niche within the Government structure; (2) component parts of the executive branch are properly related and articulated; and (3) authorities and responsibilities are clearly assigned. (Seidman 1970, p. 5)

Theories along these lines have become "deeply ingrained in our culture," (Waldo 1961, p. 220). However, they explain more about the rhetoric of proposals for reorganization of national bureaucracies than about the operation and actual organization of these structures. This is because the orthodox theory is largely apolitical. It is based on the premise that politics and administration are two separate endeavors that can be combined only at the price of inefficiency. Yet, in reality, the organization of any national bureaucracy will reflect political concerns.

Public bureaucracies are instruments of political power. Consequently, it is unrealistic to assume that politics will not play the dominant role in determining how they will be organized. For instance, in organizing the government of the United States in 1787, the participants at the Philadelphia Convention were cognizant of rational administrative organization, but they were far more concerned with rational political organization. Consequently, they created a governmental organization scheme that is an orthodox organization theorist's nightmare: Three equal branches of government coexist with no final arbiter of the authority among them. The legislature is divided into two branches with largely redundant powers. The national government and the state governments have several overlapping spheres of activity. The major purpose of these arrangements was to create a system of checks and balances that would serve to ensure that political power was used responsibly in the public interest. Why should the political power of public bureaucracies be treated differently?

A fundamental condition of the rise of the modern bureaucratic state is that political power accrues in the hands of bureaucrats and bureaucratic organizations. To a considerable extent, depending upon where one is in the contemporary world, bureaucracy is government and government is bureaucracy. Hence, the concerns of traditional organization theory are seriously misplaced. Politicians everywhere, and in democracies the public as well, are given to organizing public bureaucracies to achieve political rather than administrative ends. As Harold Seidman observes:

> Established organization doctrine, with its emphasis on structural mechanics, manifests incomplete understanding of our constitutional system, institutional behavior, and the tactical and strategic uses of organization structure as an instrument of politics, position, and power. Orthodox theories are not so much wrong when applied to the central issues of executive branch organization as largely irrelevant.
>
> Executive branch structure is in fact a microcosm of our society. Inevitably it reflects the values, conflicts, and competing forces to be found in a pluralistic society. The ideal of a neatly symmetrical, frictionless organization structure is a dangerous illusion. (Seidman 1970, p. 13)

Thus, it is to be expected that national bureaucracies will be organized so as to reflect different political concerns. The literature of comparative administration has pointed to two dimensions that are useful in categorizing the nature of national bureaucracies. One is the degree of economic and political development. John Forward has categorized bureaucracies according to the degree of development in the following fashion:

> Modern: generally effective and responsible civil service, performing in a functionally specific, non-ascriptive social context;
>
> Semi-modern: largely rationalized bureaucratic structure of limited efficiency because of shortage of skilled personnel, inadequate recruitment criteria, excessive intrusion of non-administrative organs, or partially non-congruent social institutions;
>
> Transitional: largely rationalized ex-colonial bureaucratic structure in the process of personnel nationalization and adaptation to the servicing or restructuring of autochthonous ["indigenous"] social institutions;
>
> Traditional: largely non-rationalized bureaucratic structure performing in the context of ascriptive or deferential stratification system. (Forward 1967, pp. 454–55)

Bureaucracies in less-developed nations, then, are likely to be imitative of bureaucracies in more developed nations, and less effective and efficient. They are also likely to be less autonomous and more characterized by a discrepancy between form and reality (Heady 1966, pp. 69–72).

A second dimension used to categorize the organization and operation of national bureaucracies is the extent to which political systems are autocratic or polyarchic. According to Ferrel Heady (1966), the following conclusions may be drawn.

Traditional-autocratic political systems are characterized by dominant political elites whose power position is the outgrowth of a long-established social system emphasizing aristocratic social status. Public bureaucracies have the dual role of fostering desired reform and inhibiting unwanted change. "The administrative machinery is the principal vehicle for action, but its ability to operate effectively is hampered by its own traditional characteristics and by the difficulties it faces in penetrating the community" (Heady 1966, p. 75).

Bureaucratic elite systems are often found in developing political systems in which the traditional elites have been displaced by career civilian or military governmental officials professing the goal of modernization. In Heady's view, they may have bureaucracies that are themselves elite and aloof from the society, yet effective in enabling government to operate and adapt to changing political conditions, as in Pakistan; or, by contrast, they may follow the model of Thailand, where "The total pattern of behavior is more concerned with the maintenance of proper personal relationships in the social system than with productive output" (Heady 1966, pp. 81–82). In the latter case the bureaucracy may be "well adapted to its environment."

Communist systems, although there is great variation among them, all have important elements in common, including the centrality of ideology in government and the justification of coercion and terror in the name of the promised social transformation sought by that ideology. In addition, these systems organize political power in the hands of one political party and do not allow competition between the party and other organizations in society. They seek to mobilize the masses and to administer virtually all aspects of the economy and culture. "The administrative apparatus required by such a regime is enormously complex, and it must be subjected to reliable party supervision, which in turn calls for a control network responsive to the narrow circle of elitist leadership in the party. . . . Even with overlapping personnel, this is an arduous obligation in a society plagued by a shortage of skilled manpower, but it cannot be avoided without risking the security of the regime" (Heady 1966, p. 96).

Semicompetitive dominant party systems have been described thus: "In a dominant-party semicompetitive system, one party holds a monopoly of actual political power, and has held it for a substantial period of time, but other parties are legal and do in fact exist" (Heady 1966, p. 88). India and Mexico present historical examples of this phenomenon. Although such political systems are exceedingly diverse, they share the common challenge of establishing functional working relationships between the dominant party and the civil service. In Mexico this has been accomplished by a highly fragmented, decentralized bureaucracy that is in constant consultation with the Mexican chief executive. In India a pronounced separation has existed between politicians, who make policy, and administrators, who carry it out. However, as Heady suggested, such a separation inevitably faces severe strains when a government embarks upon a course of deep penetration of a nation's economic and social systems.

Dominant party mobilization systems have been characterized by Heady:

> Important differences separate countries in this group from those just discussed. Permissiveness in politics is less; actual or potential coercion is greater. The dominant party is usually the only legal party. If other parties are permitted to operate openly at all, they are surrounded by restrictive controls designed to keep them weak and only symbolic of opposition. Ideology is more doctrinaire and more insistently proclaimed, although it may be adjusted for purposes of expediency. Greater stress is placed on mass demonstrations of loyalty to the regime. The elite group is young, urbanized, secularized, and relatively well educated, with a strong commitment to developmental nationalism. (Heady 1966, pp. 91-92)

At various times Algeria, Bolivia, Egypt, and Ghana have presented clear examples of this type of system. Bureaucracies in these systems are largely subservient to political leaders, and tend to play a very limited role in the formulation of public policy.

Polyarchical competitive systems exist in the United States and much of Western Europe. They are characterized by political competition and the elements required by democratic regimes discussed in chapter 1. Consequently, these political systems have less well defined elites and more fluid relationships among political actors. In these systems

> The hand of government will be weak when it attempts to collect taxes, impose regulations, or otherwise exert pressures that affect private interests. Public administration must be carried on without consistent political support even from the political instrumentalities that have previously made the formal policy decisions being administered. The bureaucracy itself may become one of the focuses for competition among contending political groups. (Heady 1966, p. 83)

Despite these pronounced differences among public bureaucracies in different types of political systems and in nations with different levels of development, there are also some unifying factors. Foremost among these are the general structure and behavioral attributes of bureaucracies. Although the shape of national bureaucracies may be different and their cultures may vary markedly, in general they all rely on hierarchy, specialization, formalization, and some measure of achievement orientation in their personnel systems. Moreover, in all types of regimes, bureaucrats, whatever their prestige and technical expertise, are likely to be looked upon, by political authorities at least, as constituting a potentially threatening power center. Hence, efforts will often be undertaken to constrain the power of public bureaucracies. National bureaucracies also share some common organizational characteristics in terms of the functions they provide. As Heady observes:

> A necessary consequence of hierarchy and specialization in large-scale organization is an orderly arrangement of units into successively larger and more inclusive groupings. This process of departmentalization has occurred in a remarkably uniform way in countries that vary greatly in their political orientation and in other aspects of their administrative systems. The basic unit is the department or ministry, with each one representing a major organizational subdivision of administration. Chapman identifies five "primordial fields of government"—foreign affairs, justice, finance, defense and war, and internal affairs—represented in Europe's past by primary ministries with origins dating back to the Roman system of administration. With the growth of governmental responsibilities and services, new ministries emerged from what had been the residual category of internal affairs, adding new ministries in such fields as education, agriculture, transport, trade, and more recently, social security and health. The contours of the sphere of governmental activities in each country will certainly affect the number and missions of the central ministries, but the impression one gets from reviewing rosters of ministries in many countries is one of uniformity or close similarity rather than of wide variation. (Heady 1966, p. 23)

In general, nations will have somewhere in the range of 12 to 30 ministries, depending on the degree of governmental penetration of the society, party and coalition politics, and factors peculiar to the experience of the particular political community. Thus, religious and quasi-secular nations may have ministries of religious affairs, those with a thriving tourist industry may have a ministry of tourism, and a nation perceiving massive challenges to its security may have a ministry of police, as in Israel. Of course, the extent of governmental bureaucratization does not end with ministries. There are also any number of other organizational forms, including agencies, commissions, and governmental corporations, and these will also vary somewhat with the political, social, and economic conditions prevailing in various nations. In addition, organizational missions may be stated with varying degrees of specificity.

ORGANIZATIONAL MISSIONS

Organizational missions are a key factor in determining whether a given interest group will have effective representation by a national bureaucracy. Where there is no public bureaucratic organization having a mission that is relevant to an interest group, that group is less likely to gain an effective influence on the development of public policy. Conversely, where agencies' missions comport well with the concerns of interest groups, representation will potentially be far greater. In some nations, public bureaucracies reflect almost all the articulated interests of political importance in the society. As noted in chapter 1, the United States presents an excellent example of this phenomenon. Indeed, despite the prevailing ideology favoring limited government, it is difficult to find a major interest in the society that is not in some way dealt with by some federal bureau, whether it be disadvantaged segments of the population, advantaged segments, those producing specific crops or products, consumers, urbanites and rural populations, or even illegal immigrants.

Thus, knowing the scope of organizational missions is an important prerequisite for effective representation by organization. The degree of specificity of those missions is also of great importance. Where missions are highly specific, bureaucratic discretion will be limited as will the ability of agencies to represent constituencies and clientele groups. Where missions are broadly stated and no explicit set of priorities among them is extant, representation by organization is likely to thrive. Again the United States presents a leading example.

The missions of the U.S. federal bureaucracy are best analogized to the planks in the platforms of U.S. political parties. Something is promised to virtually everyone. Explicit contradictions among these promises are avoided by the absence of clear priorities. The general assumption is that people will be attracted to the parties by virtue of the planks they find most salient, and will tend to subjectively reduce the importance or relevance of the others. In this fashion, coalitions and even consensus may be forged.

In a similar way, given the extreme fragmentation of the federal bureaucracy, federal agencies may find it necessary to generate support for their programs. Being unable to rely on any formal chain of command reaching from the president downward, they are impelled to develop the political resources necessary to carry out their missions. Support from clientele and constituency groups is important in this regard because these groups can bring pressure to bear on the legislature to insure adequate funding and favorable legislation. In fact, the fragmented quality of the legislature itself often leads to a situation in which a strong alliance is formed among the agency, legislative subcommittee, and interest group. Where such alliances envelop a major area of public policy concerns, they may evolve into "complexes," such as the "military-industrial complex," and may include some degree of interchange of personnel between the governmental and nongovernmental participants. As in the case of political parties, support can often be generated by the use of vague organizational missions calling for a host of benefits for divergent groups without creating an explicit set of priorities.

The food stamp program in the Department of Agriculture is a good example. The program carries benefits for economically disadvantaged segments of the society, farmers, food processors, and supermarkets. The artificial money (the stamps) created by the program can be used to purchase food, thereby creating a form of subsidization of each of these groups. However, any attempt to use the program to provide greater benefits for farmers, such as restricting the purchasing power of food stamps to surplus items, or to limit the subsidy to supermarkets by allowing purchases only on low-profit items, would almost surely lead to the dissolution of the coalition that brought these elements together in the first place. Indeed, even the liberal objective of eliminating the requirement that those using food stamps buy them was resisted for years by the more conservative backers of the program, who remain uncomfortable with its welfare, as opposed to agricultural, aspects.

The mission statement of the Department of the Interior presents an excellent example of the vague mandate approach:

> In formulating and administering programs for the management, conservation, and development of natural resources, the Department pursues the following objectives: the encouragement of efficient use; the improvement of the quality of the environment; the assurance of adequate resource development in order to meet the requirements of national security and an expanding national economy; the maintenance of productive capacity for future generations; the promotion of an equitable distribution of benefits from nationally owned resources; the discouragement of wasteful exploitation; the maximum use of recreational areas; and the orderly incorporation of Indian and Alaskan Native people into our national life by creating conditions which will advance their social and economic adjustment. (*United States Government Organization Manual* 1972/1973, p. 251)

Potentially, therefore, the Interior Department can gain the support of those who want to use natural resources and those desiring to conserve them, those favoring recreation and those favoring environmental preservation, Indians and those who would exploit their land. While a given decision may alienate some of these interests, other decisions may gain their favor.

The necessity of building support is an important impetus to the growth of bureaucratic programs offering some degree of representation to different interests within the society. Hence, pluralism of this nature has a self-reinforcing quality. Moreover, where deemed necessary, the bureaucratic agency may actually organize a constituency in order to assure an adequate level of support for its activities. In such a system, overlaps and redundancies are inevitable. Agencies often compete with one another to represent various interests, and such competition can lead to shared authority. Thus, it is not unusual to find a dozen or more agencies involved in related aspects of an overall policy area such as education, health, energy, or urban life.

The organization of national bureaucracies along these lines clearly violates the major tenets of orthodox organization theory, and has important costs. Overlaps and redundancies cause red tape, add to the personnel and operating costs of government, and beget other inefficiencies. They also obscure responsibility, authority, and the chain of command, thereby making control by elected officials and political executives difficult. Policymaking is largely transferred from the elected branches of government to bureaucratic agencies. And, in an ironic twist, the legislative veto becomes a common way of trying to establish such control. At the same time, however, it is undeniable that such vague and overlapping missions enhance the potential of the bureaucracy to represent various interests in society, even if not in a rational and orderly manner. Indeed, interests frequently demand the creation of programs and bureaus to provide such representation. Under the circumstances, the nature of organizational structures becomes important, for some structures are likely to be more representative than others.

ORGANIZATIONAL STRUCTURES

Where the provision of representation by bureaucratic organization is a fundamental characteristic of a political system, the question of how such representation is itself organized can be of critical importance. As pointed out earlier, while there are theoretical propositions covering the administrative aspects of this matter, political factors are likely to be largely dominant. Moreover, the latter are likely to follow idiographic or even ad hoc patterns.

While most nations have a core of ministries or Cabinet departments in common, exactly what is included in the missions of these units will vary, as will their relation to one another and to the chief executive. Nevertheless, the following generalizations are appropriate.

First, while there is not likely to be a very clear dividing line between ministries or Cabinet departments and other units in terms of mission, and perhaps of authority, some criteria are pertinent. Ministries and Cabinet departments will generally be differentiated from other bureaucratic units by the scope and national importance of their missions. They are likely to administer a wide range of programs and to be concerned with policies for which constant political supervision is deemed desirable. They are also apt to be created to symbolize national concerns. In terms of traditional organization theory, they are organized around purposes such as health, defense, and education. Yet, these generalizations notwithstanding, it must be pointed out that partisan and interest-group politics can play an important role in the specific nature of these ministries and departments. For example, such an organizational unit may be created to gain or maintain the support of a political coalition partner. Where this is a standard practice, the number of ministries or departments is likely to rise in relation to the necessities of forming governments. In addition, these units are likely to be more functionally specific. For example, in Israel the use of ministries as payoffs to coalition partners has created both these conditions (Nachmias and Rosenbloom 1978).

In such political systems, departments or ministries with amalgamated functions, such as Health, Education, and Welfare or Housing and Urban Development, are uncommon. Rather, separate units exist for each of these functions. Even where the need to form governing coalitions is less explicit, as in presidential systems such as the United States, political considerations will affect the creation of departmental structures. At times, efforts to combine missions within one department will fail because of political opposition waged by various interest groups, as when President Lyndon Johnson sought to merge the Departments of Commerce and Labor. At other times a broad mission may be a prerequisite for gaining the political support necessary to create a department, as in the cases of the Departments of Health, Education, and Welfare and Housing and Urban Development. Subsequently, though, as political forces and public policy undergo change, these may be divided. Thus, in 1979 the creation of a separate Department of Education was authorized.

It is evident that organizational and political logic may be quite divergent. While the former may dictate consolidation to reduce the number of bureaucratic entities that the chief executive must oversee, and to limit the extent of overlaps and redundancies, the latter may dictate fragmentation. Perhaps, in terms of subject matter, all that any nation needs is departments or ministries of national security, economic development, domestic policy, and justice. But politics inevitably dictate more.

Whatever the number and subject matter of ministries and departments, their political situations may vary considerably. Some, such as units for foreign affairs, defense, justice, and monetary matters (treasuries), may be under greater scrutiny and control by chief executives and legislatures. In the context of the United States, this distinction is often propounded in terms of the "inner" and "outer" Cabinets (Cronin 1975, pp. 191–202). Whereas the former is closer to the president, the latter, consisting of departments such as Agriculture, Interior, Transportation, Labor, and Commerce, is more constituency- and clientele-oriented. Even among "outer" Cabinet departments, it should be noted that

> Clientele interests rarely focus, however, at the departmental level. The department is valued mainly as a symbol. Departmental constituencies, even for acknowledged partisans such as Agriculture, Commerce, and Labor, represent a diversity of interests and may speak with conflicting voices. . . . Pressures are most intense when constituencies are narrowly based and united by a common interest in preserving tangible economic privileges. . . . It is the independent agency or the bureau which is most likely to be seized upon as the vehicle for safeguarding and advancing these interests. (Seidman 1970, pp. 126–27).

Moreover, some officials within the "inner" Cabinet may be officially considered to be representatives of certain interests. Thus, the comptroller of the currency in the U.S. Treasury Department has been, as noted by the *Comptroller's Annual Report* of 1923, ". . . the representative and partisan of the national banks" (Seidman 1970, p. 126).

A precise distinction between the missions of ministries and departments, and those of independent agencies of national bureaucracies, cannot be drawn. However, B. Guy Peters has identified a general tendency:

> The purposes served are clearly the most frequent basis of organization, as departments or ministries of defense, education, and health would indicate. Organization by process is more commonly found at subministerial levels, with divisions or bureaus of accounting, legal services, engineering, and the like. Types of persons or things dealt with would include organizations such as the Veterans Administration in the United States, similar organizations in other countries, the Bureau of Indian Affairs, and various boards and commissions for (or against) foreign workers in European countries. Finally, the area served is frequently used as an organizational principle at the subdepartmental level, as in the use of regional offices, but may also be institutionalized at the departmental level, as in the Scottish and Welsh Offices in the United Kingdom. (Peters 1978, p. 110)

Consequently, independent agencies commonly involve various overhead functions, such as budgetary, personnel, and supply matters, or the representation or regulation of various segments of the population, such as women, minorities, or veterans.

Again, however, the precise organizational forms often depend upon political configurations. As Seidman points out:

> Independent agencies come in all shapes, sizes, and forms. Both the Small Business Administration and the Federal Aviation Agency, prior to its incorporation in the Department of Transportation, were spun off from the Department of Commerce. . . . None of the independent

> agencies at present is an embryo executive department comparable to the Housing and Home Finance Agency, although NASA has some aspirations. As we have indicated, the General Services Administration and the Veterans Administration do exceed in size, measured in personnel and budget, smaller executive departments. Some, such as the Veterans Administration, General Services Administration, and Civil Service Commission, are expressly subject to Presidential direction or regulations, while others, such as the Farm Credit Administration, are almost outside the Government altogether. (Seidman 1970, p. 216)

In any event, such agencies are likely to be more specific in their missions and, where clientele-oriented, potentially highly representative of specific groups. For example, in the United States the Small Business Administration is an independent agency that is designed to represent the interests of small businesses. The U.S. Commission on Civil Rights and the Equal Employment Opportunity Commission are intended to represent the interests of members of minority groups and women. Because the constituencies of such units are generally narrower than those of the departments, the independent agencies often become forceful spokesmen for them, and may even become clearly subservient to them.

In the United States, independent regulatory commissions constitute a separate and especially representative form of bureaucratic organization. Generally these units are created to defuse a political issue by establishing an apparently nonpartisan, quasi-judicial and quasi-legislative administrative agency to deal with problem areas where governmental regulation is desired. By one set of legal definitions, these units "occupy no place in the executive branch" (*Humphrey's Executor* v *United States* 1935). By almost all calculations, they go through similar "life cycles" that lead them inevitably to be highly representative of—indeed, even subservient to—the very interests they are designed to regulate.

The life cycle of regulatory agencies was predicted almost from the moment they were created. Some five years after the Interstate Commerce Commission (ICC), the first of these, was established in 1887, the attorney general of the United States wrote a letter predicting that, first, the ICC would stop the public clamor for governmental regulation of the railroads; then, once the public lost interest, regulation would be nominal; finally, the ICC would emerge as a spokesman for the railroads (McConnell 1966, p. 284). This cycle came to pass, and a similar one has been observed in other regulatory commissions. Indeed, some observers believe that the regulatory commissions have become "a form of legal cartel for regulated firms" (Seidman 1975, p. 251, quoting Roger Noll), and others see them as a major channel by which private interests have been able to capture public power (McConnell 1966).

A great deal of attention has been paid to U.S. regulatory commissions, perhaps because they are illustrative of more general aspects of representation through organizational structure. Why do regulatory commissions and other bureaucratic organizations often represent the interests they were originally designed to regulate? Part of the answer lies in the need of independent agencies to develop political support. Any agency that is isolated from the rest of the executive branch and from the chief executive or legislature—that is, independent—will be unable to rely upon the support of those branches for continued or expanded funding, operating authority, and personnel. Consequently, it must develop a strong constituency to press for its objectives and survival among relevant governmental authorities.

Although the general public may be such a constiuency at the creation of a new bureaucratic unit, as the agency eliminates the abuses about which the public has complained, it will inevitably become less salient to the citizenry. Once it can no longer count upon massive public support for its mission, the interests it regulates become the relevant constituency. The opposition of these interests to the agency can be damaging in the legislature and elsewhere; their support can become the foundation of the agency's continued existence and authority. Moreover, as regulatory processes become heavily lawbound, the issues become more obscure to outsiders, whose interest may be declining in any event. In this fashion the agency and the interest group develop a dialogue that is largely uninterrupted by outsiders. Each has much to lose by provoking the other—and much to gain by acting in concert.

The process of representation through independent agencies is facilitated by the vague mandates that often accompany the creation of such bureaucratic units. One reason the regulatory commission exists is that the legislature does not want to be burdened with ongoing supervision of a policy area. Another is that the issue may be so controversial and politicized that elected officials would prefer not to have to deal with it substantively and thereby risk the public's wrath. Rather, it is addressed in procedural fashion through the creation of an administrative agency. But, for the same reasons, enabling legislation is likely to avoid clear standards for the use of the authority being delegated to the agency. For instance, the Federal Communications Commission (FCC) is charged with awarding licenses to broadcasters on the basis of the "public convenience, interest, or necessity" (McConnell 1966, p. 285). The mandate of the Civil Aeronautics Board (CAB) has been so vague that one of its chairmen admitted that "the philosophy of the CAB changes from day to day" (McConnell 1966, p. 286).

Despite the absence of clear mandates, however, a common thread runs through the representational behavior of these agencies: they overwhelmingly tend to represent established interests over those of would-be competitors. For instance, until recently the CAB had prevented additional carriers from entering the airlines industry, and the FCC prevented the development of competition between AM and FM radio stations by overwhelmingly awarding licenses for the operation of the latter to the owners of the former (Lowi 1969, pp. 90–91).

Independent agencies' quest for support and the broad discretion delegated to them by legislative bodies contribute to a dynamic by which the agencies become representatives of the groups they were established to regulate. A final factor in the representational equation is an interchange of personnel between the agency and the industry and, more generally, fraternization between the two. The interchange of personnel, whereby representatives of the industry are appointed to the agency and employees of the agency leave to take jobs in the industry, has a strong rationale in the need of each kind of employer for expertise in the regulatory process. Agency officials engaged in regulation must have thorough knowledge of the industry. Likewise, the industry can benefit from thorough knowledge of the agency. These needs become all the more acute when regulatory administration becomes highly legalistic. Consequently, it is not unusual for a "regulated" industry to gain a de facto veto over the appointment of top agency officials. Nor is it surprising when the head of an agency such as the CAB leaves the government to become the president of a major airline. Naturally, the process of interchange facilitates the development of a harmony of understanding between the agency and the industry. As Carol Greenwald points out:

> A study of nine regulatory commissions showed that between 1960 and 1975, 30 percent of the appointees came from the regulated industry; from 1970 to 1975, the figure increased to 50 percent. Personnel-industry ties are further reinforced by the practice of circular employment, whereby regulatory employees learn the byways of government and then leave for lucrative jobs with the industry they once regulated. . . . Between 1960 and 1975, 37 percent of the eighty-five persons who left nine regulatory commissions went to work in the industries they had regulated. . . .
>
> Inevitably human relationships turn regulation in the public interest into protection of private interests. (Greenwald 1977, p. 230)

Fraternization of agency and industry officials has similar roots. Both are deeply interested in the same kinds of issues and questions. They attend the same industry conventions and, of necessity, may be in frequent contact with one another. Again, this interaction facilitates the transformation of adversarial regulation into harmonious representation. Where it is most pronounced, the agency and the industry merge into one common actor.

An additional structural form worthy of mention is the government corporation. This may be used where the government is providing a service or a product, or developing natural resources. The extent to which political systems rely upon this form of bureaucratic structure is strongly related to political ideology. Communist and socialist systems make heavy use of it, as do developing nations, which are attracted by their potential for efficient and apolitical operation. Whatever the economic benefits to be gained from such organizations, their representational qualities tend to focus on three groups. First, such corporations may largely represent their own employees, and thereby become somewhat syndicalist. According to Brian Chapman (1959), this is not uncommon in Western Europe, where civil service unions are exceedingly strong. In the United States, collective bargaining arrangements in the Postal Service may eventually lead in this direction. Second, the corporations may represent the geographic area they serve. This is true, for example, of the Tennessee Valley Authority in the United States. Finally, corporations may represent their clients, who may also be geographically dispersed. Examples here would include the Federal Deposit Insurance Corporation and various governmental corporations dealing with farmers.

Finally, executive offices attached to chief executives may provide substantial representation to various interests. This has been pronounced in the United States, where the White House and the Executive Office of the President have expanded rapidly since the 1940s. Thomas Cronin observes:

> An important reason for the swelling of the presidency is the addition of interest-group brokerage to the more traditional staff activities of counseling and administration. During the late 1960s and early 1970s a large number of special assistantships or semi-institutionalized offices were set up explicitly to serve as brokerages or clearing-houses to provide greater access to presidential attention for professional, demographic, or specialized organizations. The interests thus provided for comprise a veritable index of middle- and upper-middle-class American society. . . .
>
> Interest groups and professions no longer seemed to settle for lobbying Congress; for influencing congressional aides engaged in casework or managing constituency relations to advance the interests of businessmen, veterans, labor officials, minorities, and so on; or for having one of their number appointed to departmental advisory boards or subcabinet positions. Although it now appears essential to interest groups to have their own man (or woman) right there in the White

> House, the White House itself seems to have seen the reciprocal political potentialities of the arrangement. (Cronin 1975, p. 123)

In sum, then, representation of nongovernmental interests by administrative organizations is a reality that can take several forms. Departments, agencies, and corporations may be officially viewed as representatives of various groups, or such representation may evolve over time. When most pronounced, the governmental unit comes to speak for the private interest; public authority and private power may merge in this fashion. Before examining these processes in greater detail, it is desirable to address the nature of organized bureaucratic constituencies.

ORGANIZED INTEREST GROUPS

An organized political interest group has been defined as "one whose shared activities include attempts to influence decisions made within the public policy-making system" (Greenwald 1977, p. 15). The number, scope, and activities of such groups depend heavily upon elements of political culture and ideology. In totalitarian regimes, only those groups officially sanctioned will be considered legitimate. Others may be eliminated through coercion and terror. In polyarchic systems, by contrast, the formation of interest groups and their interaction with government may be encouraged as a functional requirement of democracy. Because the term "interest group" can have a negative connotation and may be associated with practices, such as "lobbying" and the financing of political campaigns, that are sometimes considered unsavory, it is useful to pause momentarily to stress the extent to which interest groups may be officially viewed as beneficial to a polyarchic political system. For instance, it has been argued that in the United States the prevailing "public philosophy" is "interest group liberalism." Theodore Lowi describes the content of this philosophy thus:

> It is "interest group liberalism" because it sees as both necessary and good that the policy agenda and the public interest be defined in terms of the organized interests in society. In brief sketch, the working model of the interest group liberal is a vulgarized version of the pluralist model of modern political science. It assumes: (1) Organized interests are homogeneous and easy to define, sometimes monolithic. Any "duly elected" spokesman for any interest is taken as speaking in close approximation for each and every member. (2) Organized interests pretty much fill up and adequately represent most of the sectors of our lives, so that one organized group can be found effectively answering and checking some other organized group as it seeks to prosecute its

> claims against society. And (3) the role of government is one of ensuring access particularly to the most effectively organized, and of ratifying the agreements and adjustments worked out among the competing leaders and their claims. (Lowi 1969, p. 71)

Moreover, as Lowi and others point out, government support for interest-group liberalism may drive public agencies to organize such groups among their clientele. This may even occur where, as in the case of the War on Poverty and Model Cities programs, the governmentally organized groups subsequently demand radical changes in public policy and the political status quo. It is to be expected that where interest groups are so valued by prevailing political thought, their interaction with public bureaucracies will be a major feature of the political system. As will be discussed shortly, such groups may even have a clear statutory right to be consulted by bureaucratic agencies in the course of their implementation of public policy.

The political culture of a political system is another important determinant of the general importance of interest groups in the policy-making process. Some cultures are more group-oriented than others. For instance, it has been noted since the 1830s that, "The Americans of all ages, all conditions, and all dispositions constantly form associations. They have not only commercial and manufacturing companies . . . but associations of a thousand other kinds, religious, moral, serious, futile, restricted, enormous, or diminutive. . . . Wherever at the head of some new undertaking you see the government of France or a man of rank in England, in the United States you will be sure to find an association" (Alexis de Tocqueville, quoted in Greenwald 1977, p. 15).

Whether or not a population is generally inclined to join legitimate interest groups, it has been pointed out that there may be substantial benefits for individuals who become members. These can be categorized as follows:

Psychological benefits. According to Carol Greenwald:

> There are two basic psychological functions of individuals that can be affected by joining a group: an "orienting function" that mediates between the individual and the larger society (or the state) and a "personal identification" function that helps the individual to express personal feelings. (Greenwald 1977, p. 32)

Material benefits. Greenwald has this to say about material benefits:

> First, the group provides desirable "selective benefits," that is, benefits available only to members, such as the [U.S.] Farm Bureau's educational programs and low-cost insurance, the American Medical Association's or the National Society of Legislative Lobbyists' discount gift

> buying, travel, and insurance benefits. Second, individuals join groups when the value of the benefit [policy sought] or the need to be seen as a participant is important. Consequently the size of the group itself becomes a relevant factor. In a small group one member may contribute more than his share because he needs the benefits for himself; in a medium-sized group participation or nonparticipation of an individual may be noticeable, thus pushing the individual to contribute to a collective good. (Greenwald 1977, p. 36).

Although many have noted the tendency for interest groups to be oligarchic in their internal governance—an issue to which we shall return later—their formal organizational structures vary substantially. Some are unitary organizations in which there are no geographical, functional, or other subdivisions. Other are federated—that is, composed of suborganizations based upon characteristics of the members. Labor unions such as the AFL-CIO are examples of the latter; trade associations, such as the National Association of Manufacturers, often follow the former pattern. Membership size and the number of suborganizations in federated groups will vary substantially from organization to organization. Moreover, these attributes of interest groups have an important bearing on their ability to wield influence. The following are among the most important elements contributing to the influence potential of a political interest group in the United States. To a greater or lesser extent, depending upon political and electoral arrangements, they are also important in other polyarchic political systems.

Membership attributes have been described thus: "the size of the organization in terms of its percentage of possible members and in terms of its voting potential; the prestige of the occupation represented; the amount of internal cohesion; and the political reservoir of talents among members as derived from their educational backgrounds, available time for political activities, interest in such activities, and so on" (Greenwald 1977, p. 330).

Geographical distribution can be translated "into lobbying power when federated organizations . . . can ask their local units to use constituent pressures such as letter writing and votes to influence elected officials" (Greenwald 1977, p. 330).

Organizational linkages and leadership skills also are important. The stronger the leadership and the links between a federated national organization and its subunits, the better able the organization is to project unity and organize constituent pressures on local and locally elected officials. Leadership that fails to compel the support of the membership for specific political objectives may lose its credibility with the government, as has happened to some labor leaders.

Economic resources are important in two ways. "One is money . . . to assist in electoral campaigns, to offer soft services to candidates, to finance research, pay lobbyists, entertain decision makers. . . . Second, economic resources translate into political clout when [a corporation] is so important to the national economy that it receives attention in proportion to that fact rather than the democratically acceptable alternatives of vote power and citizen demand" (Greenwald 1977, p. 331). Automobile companies and defense industries are examples that come readily to mind.

Standing in the general social environment, according to Greenwald, ". . . is composed of two separate sets of assets—one tangible, one intangible. [Groups may have] a solid combination of economic/social or cultural status attributes plus money, educated . . . participants, and a well developed arsenal of lobbying tools. . . . [I]ntangible assets depend upon the relationship between the group as a complex of resources and the current climate of opinion which sets the boundaries for acceptable policy. This aspect of social standing reflects the legitimacy which officials accord the group to act as spokesman for its issues" (Greenwald 1977, p. 332).

In considering group assets, however, it must be borne in mind that there is no simple equation by which one group will become influential while another remains weak. The types of resources mentioned above can be used effectively or ineffectively. Groups may find a sympathetic or deaf ear in government. Their objectives may be easily won or largely unattainable. Moreover, in addition to these resources, the extent to which public policy encourages the formation of formal links between organized interests and government is an important element. In the context of public bureaucracies, this link is most pronounced in the form of advisory bodies.

ADVISORY BODIES

Interest-group contacts with public bureaucracies are a common feature of public policymaking in polyarchic political systems. As Henry W. Ehrmann observed:

> The diminished role of parliament has been parallelled usually, if somewhat unexpectedly, by a decrease in the weight of the political executive. Where Ministers used to tell the civil servants what the public would not stand for, the bureaus are now in direct contact with an organized public, viz., the interest groups. If a high degree of governmental controls has increased the power of Ministers and of their departments, such power is counterbalanced by their dependence on

> outside organizations. From the perspective of the bureaucracy interest groups are audience, advisors, and clients, foremost participants in the process of bargaining over governmental policy. From the perspective of pressure politics the administrative bureaus are a decisive center of power although this does not mean that for the interest groups their contacts with the bureaucracy have everywhere replaced other forms of influence. (Ehrmann 1971, p. 334)

In most of these political systems such links have become institutionalized in an important formal fashion through governmental recognition of interest groups as "advisory committees." For example, in the early 1970s there were close to 500 of these at the level of the central government in Great Britain and some 1,400 attached to the U.S. federal government (Ehrmann 1971, p. 330; Seidman 1975, p. 269). Their purpose is to provide representation: "The very proliferation of such committees forces many governmental departments to constantly 'keep in touch'; at almost every step it is necessary to take into account a large number of reasons and arguments" (Ehrmann 1971, p. 339).

The notion that advisory bodies should play a representational role is clearly spelled out in the U.S. Federal Advisory Committee Act of 1971 (PL 92-463, 86 Stat. 770, Oct. 6, 1971). It starts from the premise that "Congress finds that there are numerous committees, boards, commissions, councils and similar groups which have been established to advise officers and agencies in the executive branch . . . and that they are frequently a useful and beneficial means of furnishing expert advice, ideas, and diverse opinions to the Federal Government." The purpose of the act is to improve the extent of such representation within the bureaucracy by systematizing the use of advisory bodies, increasing the breadth of interests they represent, and opening up their proceedings to members of the general public. Thus, section 5B specifies that legislation mandating the creation of new advisory committees should "require the membership of the advisory committee to be fairly balanced in terms of the points of view represented and the functions to be performed by the advisory committee." Moreover, such statutes should "contain appropriate provisions to assure that . . . the advisory committee will not be inappropriately influenced by the appointing authority or by any special interest. . . ." Advisory committee meetings are generally to be open to the public, as are their transcripts, minutes, reports, and related documents. With some exceptions, such committees are to be established for a two-year term, after which time they may be renewed.

The evidence gathered to date indicates that advisory committees are often highly representative of the better-established and more elite elements within given constituencies:

> Of the 22,256 positions on federal advisory committees and commissions, 19,000 are public citizens appointed by the President or by one of the heads of the forty-five departments and agencies that operate these committees. Not only do these committees tend to overrepresent insider organizations and big corporations, they are also unrepresentative of women and black categoric groups: only 11 percent of the positions in 1975 were held by women, 4 percent by blacks; 50 percent of the committees were all white, 36 percent were all male. (Greenwald 1977, p. 222)

A study undertaken in the office of U.S. Senator Patrick Leahy in 1976 indicated that advisory committees were overrepresentative of the nation's largest and wealthiest corporations and replete with overlapping individual memberships. Although the study was confined to the Departments of Agriculture and Defense, it uncovered the multiple corporate representation presented in Table 3.1. Indeed, it found that elitism was sometimes formally built into the selection of members of advisory committees:

> Charters for the Flue-cured Tobacco and National Tobacco Advisory Committees require membership composed exclusively of representatives of tobacco companies affected by the advice and recommendations of these committees. The charter of the Distributors' Advisory Committee (for Georgia peaches) grants peach shippers a monopoly in giving government advice: "The three shippers who shipped the largest proportion of peach shipments during the preceding year are entitled to one member each. The remaining four members are selected from the remaining handlers. . . ." (Leahy 1976, p. 77)

In addition to these elements of elitism, the Leahy report found that 24 individuals had membership on more than one committee in the Department of Agriculture, and 97 had such multiple memberships in the Department of Defense (Leahy 1976, pp. 11–12). Moreover, "Several individuals have been on the same advisory committee for more than ten years despite a USDA regulation requiring rotation of committee membership every two years. Several advisory committee members at DOD have maintained their positions for more than a generation. Membership on DOD advisory committees for more than a decade is common" (Leahy 1976, p. 12).

Thus, in terms of their membership, the advisory committees are not necessarily representative of a broad segment of the constituencies for which they are formally empowered to speak. However, the evidence suggests that they do wield great influence in representing the firms and interests from which their members are drawn. For example, the following are among the findings of separate studies:

TABLE 3.1: Multiple Representation on Advisory Committees, Departments of Agriculture and Defense, 1976

Business-Industry	*Number of Memberships*
AT&T	95
RCA	95
ITT	86
General Electric	80
Communications Satellite Corp.	64
Exxon	48
IBM	40
Mitre	37
Boeing	36
Western Union	35
General Motors	33
Westinghouse	33
Raytheon	31
Lockheed	30
Rockwell International	29
Ford Motor Co.	28
RAND	28
Hughes	27
Honeywell	26
Mobil Oil	26
Aeonautical Radio	25
Motorola	25
United Airlines	25
Dupont	24
Gulf Oil	22
GTE	22
Bendix	21
R&D Assoc.	21
TRW	21

Source: Leahy 1976, appendix C-18.

1. The effect of business advisory committees on administrative decisions extends to both staff agencies as well as to executive departments. Senator Lee Metcalf (D-Montana), a long-time consumer advocate, has analyzed how such committees control decisions within the Office of Management and Budget. . . . In one case, involving research into the industrial water-pollution practices, OMB and its antipollution advisory council filibustered to delay such enterprise for seven years. The council consisted of representatives from some industries most guilty of water pollution. (Morrow 1975, p. 172)

2. . . . Edward Berlin, former assistant general counsel of the

> Federal Power Commission . . . said that in his experience they were not just advisory committees. "These committees do not advise the Budget Bureau; rather they determine what the Budget Bureau will accept or reject as far as FPC and other agencies are concerned. . . . I certainly felt that I would be shirking my responsibilities to the FPC were I not able to negotiate with the industry representatives and come up with something they agree to let us have. That was the nature of the ball game." (Greenwald 1977, p. 225)
>
> 3. Secretary of Commerce Sinclair Weeks was criticized severely by the Anti-Trust Subcommittee of the House Judiciary Committee in 1956 for creating advisory arrangements which "effected a virtual abdication of administrative responsibility on the part of Government officials in that their actions in many instances are but the automatic approval of decisions already made outside the Government in business and industry. . . . [H]e has allowed an agency of the Government to become an instrument for inside influence and advancement of special interests." (Seidman 1975, p. 269)

To some extent, limitations on the representativeness of advisory committees are not inherent in their institutionalization, but an outgrowth of their composition. The Leahy Report observes that the Agriculture Department's Advisory Committee on Hog Cholera Eradication

> . . . is composed of representatives of the swine or related industries, state and local government agencies, professional and scientific groups, the consuming public, and one representative of USDA. Many of the significant program actions taken as a result of its recommendations would not have been taken if they had been recommended solely from within the agency. Recommendations such as stopping hog cholera vaccination and strengthening market regulations received strong opposition from certain segments of industry. However, when recommended by the highly regarded members of industry on the Committee, the recommendations were accepted. (Leahy 1976, p. 88)

This example points to the potentially invaluable functions of advisory committees. First, they can be suppliers of vital technical information about the operation of various industries. As Ehrmann (1971) points out, bureaucracies in several nations, including Italy and France, are notoriously unable to obtain such information in another fashion. Yet, public policy based upon ignorance is virtually certain to fail.

Second, the use of advisory committees can legitimize bureaucratic policymaking and ease compliance with it by various sectors of the economy and society. This is the other side of representation: it allows outsiders to influence government while it enables government to function with less reliance on coercion. Again, however, legitimacy is likely to be related to the composition of advisory committees, and the perplexing question of how these groups can be "fairly balanced" becomes paramount. To some extent this is an issue of "constituency," a matter to which we will return after discussing the broad patterns that describe interest-group relationships with public bureaucracies generally.

INTEREST GROUPS AND PUBLIC AGENCIES: SOME PATTERNS

Interest groups can adopt various relationships with bureaucratic agencies. The nature of these relationships is influenced by the type of interest group, the type of bureaucratic agency, the nature of the policy area, political culture, and related factors. Nevertheless, it has been possible to discern four broad patterns of interest-group interaction with bureaucratic agencies. These have been synthesized and expounded upon by B. Guy Peters (1978). He finds the following patterns extant:

1. Legitimate interactions. As we have been seen from our discussion of advisory bodies, ". . . in some political systems, not only are pressure groups an accepted fact of political life, but they are also legally and officially involved in the process of making and administering public policy. The major examples of this type are found in West Germany, the Low Countries and Scandinavia, but a number of other countries have adopted legitimate roles for pressure groups in more limited forms" (Peters 1978, p. 143). Peters subdivides legitimate interactions between bureaucratic agencies and interest groups into two categories. One is required consultation, which characterizes many political systems in which bureaucratic agencies must confer with or seek the advice of interest groups before adopting new policies and regulations. He points out that, "One method of assuring such input is through the use of *remiss* petitions in Sweden and Norway. In both these countries, when policy modifications are being considered, the administrative agencies are required to ask for *remiss* from interest groups. These documents state the views of the group as well as some of the information that the group considers relevant to the case" (Peters 1978, p. 144). Norway also makes widespread use of advisory committees in this regard (Peters 1978, p. 144).

In the United States the nature of required consultation with interest groups is often less explicit. Generally, administrative regulations require public notice of proposed agency rulemaking and an opportunity for interested parties to respond. Although interest groups tend to monopolize these responses, the process is nevertheless open to the political community at large. Thus, a "public-interest group" or self-appointed champion of public or private interests is free to respond. To a considerable extent, however, the advice of advisory committees is sought more avidly and weighted more heavily. And, as we have seen, these committees tend to be dominated by interest groups.

Peters refers to a second form of legitimate interest-group interaction with administrative agencies as "implementation." Here, "interest groups serve as quasi-official arms of the political system in implementing some programs about which they are assumed to have expert knowledge and skills "(Peters 1978, p. 145). This approach is heavily relied upon in Scandinavia and the Low Countries, especially in the realm of agriculture, "where either commodity groups or local farmers' organizations administer regulations or acreage allotments or contractual relationships with the government" (Peters 1978, p. 145). Labor and economic regulations also are frequently implemented in this fashion. In the United States, publicly sanctioned occupational licensing and accrediting functions are sometimes implemented by private professional or occupational associations. From a policy perspective, Peters finds that legitimate interest-group relationships with bureaucratic agencies are most common in the realms of redistribution and self-regulation.

2. *Clientela* relationships. This type of interest-group relationship with bureaucratic agencies was observed by Joseph LaPalombara (1963) in the context of Italian politics. He defined a *clientela* relationship as a situation in which "an interest group, for whatever reasons, succeeds in becoming in the eyes of a given administrative agency, the natural expression and representative of a given social sector which, in turn, constitutes the natural target or reference point for the activity of the administrative agency" (LaPalombara 1963, p. 262; Peters 1978, p. 148). The major distinction between *clientela* and legitimate relationships is that in the former, "Each agency tends to select a single pressure group as *the* legitimate representative of its particular social sector and to avoid most other groups seeking to present information and advice" (Peters 1978, p. 148).

Clientela relationships also tend to center on self-regulatory and distributional policy. As LaPalombara points out, they provide substantial advantages to both the interest group and the bureaucratic agency: "In this relationship the interest group gains access; in exchange it provides the administrators with certain kinds of assistance, above all with certain guarantees that it can help the agency survive and get its job done" (LaPalombara, 1974, p. 333). Such relationships are pronounced in the United States, especially in connection with regulatory commissions, and in other industrialized nations. At the heart of this pattern is the stark fact that, "Administrators may lack the resources and the central political support to enforce programs of regulation in the face of opposition of powerful and well-organized groups, so that in essence they must gain support from these groups" (Peters 1978, p. 150).

3. *Parantela* relationships. Elaborating upon LaPalombara's discussion of this type of relationship, Peters observes: "A *parantela* relationship describes a situation of 'kinship' or close fraternal ties between a pressure group and the government or dominant political party. . . . *Parantela* relationships between pressure groups and bureaucracies involve an indirect linkage between those actors rather than the direct linkage discussed in the *clientela* relationship" (Peters 1978, pp. 151-52).

Typically, the *parantela* relationship is found in preindustrial societies with strong one-party political systems. Although it occurs elsewhere, it is most common in single-party African and Latin American states. Depending upon the strength of the dominant political party, pressure groups may be little more than pawns that are used by the party to exert leverage over bureaucratic policymaking. This appears to have been the case of the Indian National Trade Union Congress under the dominant rule of the Congress Party in India (Peters 1978, p. 153). However, in other instances, such as authoritarian Spain, the interest groups were observed to exert an independent influence (Peters 1978, pp. 153-54). Perhaps the closest approximation to a *parantela* relationship of importance in U.S. national politics is that involving the AFL-CIO and the Democratic Party. While the union may act outside in seeking to influence bureaucratic policymaking, it often beseeches the party to intervene on its behalf. *Parantela* relationships are most common in the policy areas of regulation and distribution.

4. Illegitimate relationships. "This denotes a variety of situations in which the interaction of pressure groups with bureaucracy may be defined as outside the pale of normal political actions, but they occur anyway" (Peters 1978, pp. 155-56). These relationships are of two types. First, they may involve corruption or illegality—as, for example, when an interest group makes illicit payoffs to politicians in return for some governmental or policy benefit. For instance, in one well-documented case in the United States, interest groups representing dairy producers were able to use contributions to the Republican Party to win "substantial policy victories such as continuation of the school milk program, setting of new dairy product import quotas, and the largest single increase in milk price supports made by any administration at the beginning of a marketing year—all this in contradiction to the stated Nixon administration proposal to move away from policies 'which mean massive subsidies to agriculture'" (Greenwald 1977, p. 5).

Another kind of corruption may emerge in political systems relying heavily upon planning, such as the Soviet Union. There, the disparity between planned operations and real production may lead to the development of "gray markets" through which various enterprises may manipulate bureaucratic agencies and policies in order to obtain the supplies or concessions they desire. Such arrangements can involve elaborate trade-offs. As David Granick observed:

> The Russian manager works within a fine mesh of rules, procedures, and detailed targets for all aspects of his operations. If he breaks these rules, he is not simply violating company policy. He is committing a criminal offense under Soviet law; for it is a sacred Soviet dogma that "The Plan is Law." Yet, if the manager is to operate at all, he must cut red tape. It seems a fair generalization that all Soviet managers are, ipso facto, criminals according to Soviet law. (Granick 1967, p. 229)

A second type of illegitimate pressure-group relationship involves organized and illegal disruption, such as strikes, violent protests, or terrorist activities. Complex modern societies are highly vulnerable to such activities. In some societies, such as Italy and several Latin American nations, the exercise of pressure in this fashion is a fundamental aspect of the political system. Elsewhere, as in the United States, such relationships are more sporadic. In either event, protests can involve "anomic" interest groups—that is, groups that "arise spontaneously, usually when a particular issue of policy becomes overheated or when people demanding or opposing a policy experience severe frustration. Such movements do not generate permanent organization" (LaPalombara 1974, p. 330). They also may articulate contradictory or hopelessly unachievable demands. Nevertheless, as experience in the United States in the 1960s indicated, riots and violent protests may have a profound impact on governmental policy.

It is evident that each of these patterns of interest-group relationships with bureaucratic agencies can afford a substantial degree of representation of the interests involved. Legitimate relationships create a right by which organized interests can express their points of view to bureaucratic agencies. While these can sometimes be ignored by the agency, more often there are incentives for the agency to take interest groups' views into account. This is especially true where interest-group access is through advisory boards. Seidman points out: "Advisory Boards may be utilized to lend respectability to new or controversial programs such as poverty and foreign assistance. It is hoped that board members will act as program missionaries and assist in mobilizing support for the program both in their home communities and in the Congress" (Seidman 1975, p. 267). In fact, it could be maintained that such legitimate access to public bureaucracy is a fundamental prerequisite for democratic policymaking in a bureaucratic age, as implied by the theory of democratic balance discussed in chapter 1.

Interest-group participation in the implementation of public policy also affords such groups a great deal of representation. Indeed, such implementation may turn out to be largely self-regulation, a process that maximizes the extent to which the values of a particular sector of the society can be taken into account by governmental regulatory administration. For example, as Grant McConnell has shown, in the United States a system of locally elected advisers was created under the Taylor Grazing Act of 1934, and "Their advice was followed in decisions on 98.3 percent of the more than 14,000 licenses issued during the first fourteen months of the Act's operation" (McConnell 1966, pp. 204–05). Ultimately, the advisers were elected by those receiving grazing permits. Therefore, self-regulation was nearly complete.

Clientela relationships also afford a great deal of representation for interest groups. Again, regulation has a tendency to turn into self-regulation. The values of the regulated industry or interest are given great emphasis in the process. For instance, although regulatory commissions in the United States have been widely criticized, it has rarely, if ever, been maintained that late in their "life cycle" they fail to take the perspectives of the regulatees into account. Indeed, clientela relationships are a major representational device for affected interests.

The case of parantela relationships is somewhat more complex. It is evident that an interest group may be no more than a puppet of the dominant political party or, perhaps, administrative agency. As such, the interests of the group may go largely unrepresented. Co-optation of the interest group and of would-be dissidents within it also may occur. In such cases little genuine representation is afforded, despite the ready access of the interest group to the ruling powers. In other cases, however, the interest group, despite its "kinship" relation to a political party or agency, will have an independent voice and exert independent influence, though it may be relatively weak.

Finally, illegitimate relationships also afford a degree of representation of various interests. Although such representation is by definition corrupt, illegal, illicit, or beyond the bounds of normal political activity, it should be remembered that such relationships may have "latent" aspects that are functional from the point of view of the political community. Access to government can be an important democratizing element, and one that can contribute valuably to the formulation of public policy. The fact that access can be bought may skew policy in one direction or another. However, it must be borne in mind that it is not the access, but the skewing, that is undersirable from democratic perspectives. Again, it would be difficult to argue that the problem with illegitimate relationships is that they do not afford representation to the groups involved. If anything, they afford too much representation.

CONCLUSION: REPRESENTATION AND MISREPRESENTATION

The discussion in this chapter points to the conclusion that national bureaucracies can be highly representative of interest groups. Bureaucratic organizational structures and missions may be highly reflective of the major interests to be found in the society at large. Each major sector of the economy and society may have some bureaucratic agency charged with looking out for its interests and welfare. Moreover, agencies may take the perspectives of representatives of various segments of the political community into account in the process of formulating public policy. Indeed, advisory bodies may proliferate for this very purpose. Other types of interest-group interaction with bureaucratic agencies may reinforce the extent of representation. In fact, representation may be so pronounced that government agencies come to speak for private interests. In short, whatever political rhetoric may hold, the standard concern in democratic polities has not been that bureaucracies are unrepresentative of organized interests but, rather, that they overrepresent these interests to the exclusion of the more general public interest. Thus, once again, the issue is one of balance.

Forceful critiques of bureaucratic representation of organized interests in the United States have been developed by a number of scholars. Grant McConnell has argued that

> [an important] characteristic of American government is the conquest of segments of formal state power by private groups and associations. Although it would be impossible to state with any precision what portion of the power of American government has been taken possession of in this way, it is certain that the portion is substantial and that the control involved is considerable. . . .
>
> The pattern by which this condition has developed varies, but several steps in the process are common. Local elites have become organized nationally, usually on a federal basis, and have then been able to assume the exercise of public authority within significant areas of policy. The public agency with a particular clientele is a familiar phenomenon. However, it is but one of various types of administrative body that serve the purposes of narrow groups. . . . In return for special consideration of its interests, the private group supports and defends the agency from attack and from demands that general executive policy be followed. . . . The function of policy-making is often turned over to the private group in what amounts to delegation. (McConnell 1966, pp. 162–63)

In McConnell's view, the capture of public power by private interests is not in the public interest, largely because it constitutes a case of misrepresentation. This is true for two major reasons.

First, the nature of the constituencies represented by interest-group interaction with bureaucratic agencies is inappropriate. These constituencies tend to be relatively small and to be narrow in their interests. They represent only one dimension of their members, and other dimensions may go unrepresented as a result of their broad, general nature. For instance, a dairy producers' association may represent its members by using campaign contributions to obtain favorable public policy, but at the same time the other interests of dairy farmers as citizens—in honest government, for example—will go unrepresented. They will go unrepresented because they are unorganized—or, if organized through some "public interest group," only weakly supported. However, pluralistic, fragmented public bureaucracies are unable to afford effective representation to interests lacking strong organization and highly focused demands. In McConnell's words:

> In general, the interests discriminated against in this manner are of two kinds. The first is the interest of a weak minority, which, if distributed evenly among many small constituencies, will lack the liminal numbers necessary to achieve any influence at all within these constituencies. Such a minority may be an ethnic group or any category of heterodox opinion. . . .
>
> The other type of interest discriminated against in a system of many small constituencies is that for which support must inevitably be diffuse and which is not central or preoccupying for any group—the kind of interest most commonly called "the public interest." . . . [such support] may have no effect in small constituencies and, if [it is] to succeed, must have the larger numbers of a big constituency from which to draw enough people with the time, money, and drive to work for a cause the benefits of which will be shared by all. (McConnell 1966, p. 109)

Second, even the narrow interests of small constituencies may be misrepresented by the leadership of these groups. It has long been argued, for instance, that there is an "iron law of oligarchy" (Michels, 1962) prevailing in private organizations, whatever their avowed principles. According to this view, the leadership of interest groups is largely self-sustaining, and often misrepresentative of the membership. The leadership typically controls the organization's budget and channels of communication, has greater expertise than the general membership, and can prevent political competition from developing within the organization. In McConnell's view there is a widespread illusion about private government that "in any group homogeneity is ever complete or that unanimity is ever possible" (McConnell 1966, p. 154). Hence, these governments are less involved in reconciling differences among the members than in obtaining a projection of unanimity through the use of tyranny of the majority and injustice to the minority. As a result, minorities within groups go unrepresented by the very organizations that public bureaucracies may recognize as speaking for them.

Theodore J. Lowi is another critic of interest-group representation by bureaucratic agencies. Although wide-ranging, his critique can be reduced to the following three points:

1. The prevailing nature of interest-group representation by bureaucratic agencies shuts the public out of policymaking. "They shut out the public, first, at the most creative phase of policy-making—the phase where the problem is first defined. . . . The public is shut out, secondly, at the phase of accountability. In programs in which group self-administration is legitimate, the administrators are accountable primarily to the groups, only secondarily to the President or Congress as institutions" (Lowi 1969, p. 86).

2. "Programs following the principles of interest-group liberalism create privilege, and it is a type of privilege particularly hard to bear or combat because it is touched with the symbolism of the state" (Lowi 1969, pp. 87–88). Thus, the governmentally recognized private organizations that become spokesmen for whole policy areas are able to forestall political competition.

3. "Government by and through interest groups is in its impact conservative in almost every sense of that term" (Lowi 1969, p. 89). The public is shut out, privileged interests become dominant in their various policy spheres, and the result is government that is stagnant and oriented toward the status quo. Before a new interest can be taken into account, it must be organized; and once it is organized, its leadership may be prone to enter into a mutually supportive relationship with an appropriate government agency. The whole process is stacked against change.

These criticisms are well taken. Bureaucratic representation by organizational structure, mission, and interaction with interest groups contains all these pitfalls to some degree. A few possibilities for correcting these deficiencies have been suggested. First, Lowi and others would prefer to push the interest-group representation process back to the legislature and away from administration. However, to do so effectively, the legislature would have to reclaim its place in the center of public policymaking. Without speculating upon whether this is even possible in a bureaucratic age, it must be recognized that the loss of public policymaking functions by legislatures to public bureaucracies is virtually a worldwide phenomenon that is a direct outgrowth of the nature and expertise of bureaucratic organization. Consequently, even if a legislature were inclined—and, as discussed in chapter 1, this is unlikely—to reassert itself, the process might be tortuous. Even if it succeeded, interest-group representation by legislative committees and subcommittees would present many of the same problems as representation by bureaucratic organizations.

A second possibility is to further organize the society so that virtually every important interest has some representation vis-à-vis the bureaucracy. While this could alleviate the problem of minority interests of which McConnell speaks, it would not eradicate it. Broad, general interests would still be unequally represented. The nonrepresentation of some groups or interests is only part of the problem; misrepresentation is the other part. Short of requiring full-fledged democracy within private groups, this feature of interest-group interaction with bureaucratic agencies cannot be overcome. Yet such a requirement would be virtually impossible to enforce and, in the United States, might even be unconstitutional.

Third, it can be recognized that interest-group representation by bureaucratic agencies has some very functional aspects, but needs to be augmented by other forms of bureaucratic representation. Such an approach has the advantage of realism. As long as bureaucratic agencies are engaged in the business of policymaking and policy implementation, their interaction with interest groups can have valuable consequences for democracy. Interest-group influence is harmful only to the extent that it drives out concern for the public interest. Communication between those creating or administering policies and the objects of those policies is hardly harmful in itself—and, in fact, may generally be beneficial. If the problem is that the public is shut out by this process, then the solution may be dealing the public back in. That is the subject of the next two chapters.

REFERENCES

Chapman, Brian. 1959. *The Profession of Government.* London: Unwin University Books.

Cronin, Thomas. 1975. *The State of the Presidency.* Boston: Little, Brown.

Ehrmann, Henry. 1971. "Interest Groups and the Bureaucracy." In *European Politics,* edited by Mattei Dogan and Richard Rose, pp. 333–52. Boston: Little, Brown.

Forward, John. 1967. "Toward an Empirical Framework for Ecological Studies in Comparative Public Administration." In *Readings in Comparative Public Administration,* edited by Nimrod Raphaeli, pp. 450–72. Boston: Allyn and Bacon.

Granick, David. 1967. "The Red Executive." In *Organizations and Human Behavior,* edited by Gerald D. Bell, pp. 218–30. Englewood Cliffs, N.J.: Prentice-Hall.

Greenwald, Carol. 1977. *Group Power*. New York: Praeger.

Heady, Ferrel. 1966. *Public Administration: A Comparative Perspective*. Englewood Cliffs, N.J.: Prentice-Hall.

Humphrey's Executor v. United States. 1935. 295 U.S. 602.

LaPalombara, Joseph. 1974. *Politics Within Nations*. Englewood Cliffs, N.J.: Prentice-Hall.

———. 1963. *Interest Groups in Italian Politics*. Princeton: Princeton University Press.

Leahy, Patrick. 1976. "A Report on Advisory Committees in the Department of Agriculture and the Department of Defense." Washington, D.C.: U.S. Senate. Unpublished.

Lowi, Theodore. 1969. *The End of Liberalism*. New York: W. W. Norton.

McConnell, Grant. 1966. *Private Power and American Democracy*. New York: Knopf.

Michels, Roberto. 1962. *Political Parties*. New York: Collier Books. First published in 1911.

Morrow, William. 1975. *Public Administration*. New York: Random House.

Nachmias, David, and David H. Rosenbloom. 1978. *Bureaucratic Culture*. New York: St. Martin's.

Peters, B. Guy. 1978. *The Politics of Bureaucracy*. New York: Longman.

Seidman, Harold. 1975. *Politics, Position, and Power*. Second edition. New York: Oxford University Press.

———. 1970. *Politics, Position, and Power*. New York: Oxford University Press.

United States Government Organization Manual. 1972/1973. Washington, D.C.: U.S. Government Printing Office.

Waldo, Dwight. 1961. "Organization Theory: An Elephantine Problem." *Public Administration Review* 21 (Autumn): 210–25.

4

REPRESENTATION THROUGH ACCOUNTABILITY AND DIRECTION

Institutionally, bureaucracies and the state have evolved in tandem. Bureaucracy has been the cement utilized by political regimes to hold societies together, the instrumentality that has made possible the set of sustained political operations we call the state. As those operations have grown in complexity, so have organizations needed to carry them out. Impressive social ingenuity and unappreciated creativity have been harnessed to create the apparatus that we now see all around us. Comparatively little thought has gone into the question of controlling that machine; the symbiotic growth has been so gradual that most of the time it has been assumed that formal legal controls continued to assure the predominance of political power. Today that premise seems inadequate, but there is little left to replace such a notion. It is the formal theory, its limited truth, its partial falsehood, and the role—a perhaps irreplaceable role—that it plays that concern us in this chapter. The gap that exists in constitutional—indeed, in all political—theory, whether democratic or other in form, is another way of characterizing the problem that faces us.

The two dominant trends that formed the historic identity of the bureaucracy were centralization and growth in complexity. The early state was in essence relatively simple, with minimal functions to perform. Government was a "minimal protective state" designed to repel invaders and to adjudicate relatively few matters between the units—normally families or congeries of families—upon which the society rested. Where there were distant, usually conquered, territories, government resembled a franchise. Not uncommonly, governors were sent out with general instructions, and had little or no continued communication with the center. For most decisions they were on their own. To carry the franchise analogy further, officeholders often paid for their positions, were assigned quotas to raise as tax collectors, and were expected to live on an anticipated surplus. Such arrangements did not make for gentle or popular tax collections, but were effective money raisers for rulers. Feudal arrangements can be regarded as a special form of these arrangements, though more centralized, with a schedule of duties and obligations transcending money remittance. The fuzzy line between the "franchise" and feudal systems conceals important differences, and it is arguable whether feudalism was a more primitive or more advanced structure.

The emergence of the nation-state was an involved process by which local officials were brought under central authority, given generalized directives, and put directly on the public payroll. The effect was to elevate central policy, for the official no longer lived off the land, but was dependent on the public coffers. By this action more efficient, more objective, and less self-involved decisions were sought and control was achieved. For much the same reasons as the contemporary polity seeks to eliminate the justice of the peace, the growing nation insisted upon ending the inefficiencies and injustices of the old systems. As Max Weber describes it:

> Everywhere the development of the modern state is initiated through the action of the prince. He paves the way for the expropriation of the autonomous and "private" bearers of executive power who stand beside him, of those who in their own right possess the means of administration, warfare, and financial organization, as well as politically usable goods of all sorts. The whole process is a complete parallel to the development of the capitalist enterprise through gradual expropriation of the independent producers. In the end, the modern state controls the total means of political organization, which actually come together under a single head. (Gerth and Mills 1958, p. 82)

Standardization of function by locality was supplanted by greater flexibility and accommodation to central politics.

Hand in hand with the new locus of control was the addition of state purpose. Cause and effect are difficult to isolate here. Certainly a growing concept of warfare played a major role, but internal changes were also significant. In Western society the state took formal authority over authorization and registration rites of passage away from the Church, buying that institution off by permitting a religious option for the actual ceremonies. It was not an anticlerical move, but rather an effort to control and register that the post-Napoleonic state needed for military, police, and tax reasons. Gradually, too, it took responsibility for education from the family, which had found the burden too great and sometimes had succumbed to the temptation to exploit rather than train the young. This abuse engendered welfare and health problems for the future. State control helped build a society better fitted for increasingly mechanized warfare and for technocratic competition in peace. Control of education was a means of developing loyalty to burgeoning governments. It was—perhaps less consciously—a device for mitigating surges and drops in unemployment, as well as—more clearly—a means for channeling individuals into employment.

Old-age and health benefits have generally come later, while public housing has varied in its emergence as a governmental program. Certainly many of the older capitals and metropolitan centers were quickly inundated by hordes of job seekers and, like Vienna and Moscow, were plagued by perpetual overcrowding and lack of housing.

The multiplication of functions carried with it the geometric growth of the bureaucracy. More than that, its structure became still more elaborate and refined. Where fiscal needs and physical power were the old areas of expertise, the new, elaborate structures had specialists on, for instance, wildlife in the same service as weights and measures people. Experts on the insurance business and authorities on mass murder were assembled together with experts on public health, sanitation, and education. In the bureaucracy, as in the outside world, they often had problems communicating across professional lines—even if they were reinforced by organizational parameters, special problems were created. Structure to overcome structure was needed, and interpretive "interface" types were needed.

All of this culminates in another factor similar to that found in productive societies in general: to deliver bureaucratic output, secondary and tertiary structures are needed in larger numbers. "Parkinson's Law" utilized evidence on this point to draw a perhaps misleading conclusion: that the Admiralty grew while the number of ships and sailors declined. (In our terms, secondary and tertiary structures were developed even as the primary arrangements waned.) Similarly, administrators of education proliferate while staff-line teachers and students become fewer, or the Department of Agriculture expands while the number of farms and farmers decreases. In some instances this is, as C. Northcote Parkinson argued, mere mitosis, the division and expansion of staff to fit promotion needs and psychic satisfactions; but a good deal of it is a product of relentless processes that enable fewer ships to deliver more deadly firepower, fewer farms to produce more wheat, and fewer accountants to deliver more Social Security checks while "headquarters" is expanding to plan, purchase, and coordinate this larger output and its infrastructure.

Government, however, seemingly has more than its share of service functions that do not easily yield long-term increases in productivity. Schools and hospitals seem to require close personal ties to accomplish their goals—affect leads to effect. The Postal Service is "mechanized," but there is little per capita increase in productivity. Other functions devolve upon government precisely because of the failure of their operators to find efficient means; mass transit in the United States and the coal mines in Great Britain are examples. Overall, though, it is clear that government generally participates in, and sometimes leads in growth of, productivity. Expansion, then, is at least in part a product of increased social demands and the complexity of those demands, together with diseconomies of scale that normally (but by no means always) offset the economies.

Our purpose is to explore the consequences in terms of people, not economics or industrial efficiency, nor even to deal with the growth of taxes. However, all of this is encapsulated by "Wagner's Law," which indicates that in developing countries the growth rate of government is greater than that of the private sector—government tends to increase its share of GNP. As noted in chapter 1, the presumably inexorable growth carries with it a highly correlated growth in personnel. Government remains labor-intensive, and public service implies public servants. So far, "Wagner's Law" prevails over periodic attempts to simplify procedures, to introduce automation, and to stimulate productivity growth. Public revenues and expenditures grow more rapidly than those in the private sector, and this has generally meant an increase in public officials vis-à-vis the work force. Logically there are limits on the process. Only on a short-term, temporary basis could such expenditures exceed the GNP, to state the most obvious point; and by definition, if not reality, public employees can never exceed the total labor force. (If one included the military, one could actually achieve that bit of legerdemain!) "Wagner's Law" gives no hint of the real world—as opposed to definitional and logical—perimeters of his observation. To date, too, those limits are untested and unknown. Growth and expansion are the key words, seemingly leading to what a contemporary German writer (Henry Jacoby) called "the bureaucratization of the world."

This expansion creates problems for supervision and control that are clearly different from, and perhaps more difficult than, those of the past. The enemies of supervision in the distant past were space and time; what *was* Caesar doing three provinces and two-months' journey away? Control could be achieved by antlike diligence. The meticulous inventorying of everything—all property, all people—that characterized several regimes in Egypt allowed control of the general public. It also made it easy to check up on officialdom and its behavior to the public. It required a huge bureaucracy, scurrying about, moving little crumbs of information into the account books of the system. But just as the simple and structured society lent itself to minute regulation—times of harvest and planting, dates when the population could move back to the periodically flooded lands—so the bureaucracy could be precisely held to channelized behavior. A huge public service was needed, but the types and skills were limited and the "worker ants" at the bottom were restricted in range of discretion and repertory of behaviors.

In contrast, modern governments create complex duties involving diverse expertise. A Securities and Exchange Commission regulator deals with intricacies of both the securities industry and the federal regulations. Only a few score people in an entire nation are capable of judging with precision how effectively he serves the public in a negotiation. A computer programmer can do interesting things unseen, including mopping up the trail of his exploits. An expert on drugs or epidemics or surgery costs or the effects of smoking is called "doctor" and regarded as a physician, but in fact these people may have precious little in common in skills, knowledge, and mode of thinking. Who supervises such people and who supervises the supervisors becomes a not-too-easy question. Variable duties and professional responsibilities and expertise are not the only problems; the type of structure and supervision changes.

Bureaucracies are legitimized in part by expertise and function. But they also are installed by, and acquire by osmosis or other means, the authority of the political masters, whatever the regime. In fact, the reflected authority is a result of the assumption that supervision by political authorities implies approval. Under conditions of relative uniformity of functions, supervision is a reasonable assumption; supervision of larger numbers can be accommodated most easily by steepening of the structure. But in a complex system the expansion cannot be achieved without supervision by inappropriate decisionmakers. The structure that evolves pushes much more authority to the lower levels, because it results in pseudo grouping or supervision by superiors with little firsthand experience. They, in turn, must account to distant political authorities who are not only generalists but also basically nonexpert and even averse to expertise. Thus, new and special pressures are put on a fragile system.

We have emphasized the significance of social invention. That, however, is a process more of finding new means for fulfilling old arrangements than of the totally new. Control of bureaucracy can be analyzed in terms of processes as old as the structures themselves. Among means of control are loyalty, selection and function, socialization, norms, supervision and routine, and punishment and retribution. Each of these deserves some attention, since they have been used through the ages. In this analysis it is worth noting that "control" is a term with many connotations. The primary purpose of the political operators may be simply to survive, or to provide services, or to assure social stability—all in quite different mixes and with different priority levels.

Loyalty is a first desideratum, particularly of personal regimes, whether kingships or autocracies of various kinds. In fragile regimes control of the military and secret police or other key units can be a question of survival in the most literal sense. In such circumstances family loyalty or some equivalent—childhood friendships, being comrades in arms in dangerous (and perhaps disreputable) situations—is often relied on. (The Long March in Maoist Chinese historiography is a good example.) Close personal ties are relied upon, and this probably is as good a strategy as can be devised for so complex a situation. Betrayals frequently occur because of the high stakes. Benito Mussolini's son-in-law, Count Ciano, tried to displace his father-in-law, and Saud grew tired of fronting for his brother. More recently the KCIA chief in Korea shot his boyhood friend, President Park Chung Hee, under unclear circumstances.

If personal ties do not exist, alternative modes of securing loyalty may be structured. Certainly loyalty is strongest when there is a joint fate involved; in a sense, emphasis on family ties asserts this. It is widely believed that Heinrich Himmler had proof of Reinhard Heydrich's Jewish origins and convinced the latter he would use it if needed, or see to it it was released should an "accident" occur to Himmler. The use of eunuchs as sultans' officeholders was designed to maximize loyalty, and the fact that they were generally despised in societies where they served made their dependency on the monarch abundantly clear. The Ottoman Empire used Christian slaves as its officeholders—young men selected as children for their talents, "adopted" by the ruling family, and given material rewards, including power, though remaining legally slaves and second-class citizens. The generosity of the system toward them was emphasized in their training and was in fact practiced. Within the system they could be almost everything; outside it they were nothing. In their empire the British clearly followed such a practice where they could, most notably favoring the educated Christian minority, the Copts, for administrative posts in Islamic Egypt.

It must be noted that emphasis on loyalty diminishes the effectiveness of a regime and, when carried to extremes, substitutes particularistic criteria—sometimes odd ones—for ability. Able rulers may have stupid siblings; Presidents Lyndon Johnson, Richard Nixon, and Jimmy Carter all had embarrassing brothers who had trouble with solvency or sobriety, or both. Iran under the Shah was so fiercely concerned with loyalty that wholesale corruption was permitted. In regimes such as the Shah's, or Ngo Dinh Diem's in South Vietnam, family corruption was countenanced because the premium upon family ties meant that replacement or punishment was not an option. Thus loyalty may drive out the ablest, and permit lax and even corrupt performance. The same tends to be true in dictatorships of a more extensive cast. Hermann Goering was notoriously venal, but his unswerving loyalty to Adolf Hitler kept his place secure. Nikita Khrushchev attributed his downfall to having foolishly allowed the ambitious Dmitri Shelepin to replace the ineffable Ivan Serov as head of the secret police. As Khrushchev saw it, the Stalinist excesses of

Serov were appropriately punished, but he later regretted agreeing to the replacement, noting that, unlike Shelepin, Serov was personally loyal. The moral derived from his downfall was that he had worried about trivial matters like savagery and illegality when his first concern should have been his own personal power.

In advanced governmental structures loyalty is primarily to the regime and not to any officeholders. (Compare the oath of office taken by Germans in the Nazi period—"I swear by God this sacred oath that I will render unconditional obedience to Adolf Hitler.") The primacy of this responsibility was dramatically highlighted in a series of confrontations during Watergate. Judge John Sirica indicated that as a judge he could not accept an "agreement" on the facts by the government and the defense. Since his obligation was to justice and the stipulations were unbelievable, Assistant Attorney General Henry Petersen indicated to the president, he would keep him informed and follow his instructions unless he were convinced the trail led—Petersen used euphemisms—to the president, at which point Nixon would be cut off from all information. In short, Nixon headed and personified the regime unless he breached his trust. In an action that amazed many people, military units were alerted after the Nixon resignation was announced, but before he actually left, to ensure that no action was undertaken to keep him illegally in office.

To continue with the United States as an example, only a thin stratum of policy officials is appointed by the president—perhaps 700 in recent years. These include some confidants and co-workers, but many are chosen for their expertise and have only gratitude and expectations to link them to the administration. In addition, there are 7,000 "supergrade" positions in the bureaucracy. Of these about one-third are noncareer positions. Because of special expertise required, they are not synonymous with political choice. Some freedom also exists in deploying career bureaucrats. Depending upon one's definition, Hugh Heclo (1977) concludes that from 9 percent to 25 percent of those 7,000 can be fairly identified as political choices. In the 1980s an administration exercises control through filling something less than 3,000 posts, perhaps as little as half that number. Furthermore, the selection of people for these jobs is complex, almost random, with few of the final choices, except for the inner circle, drawn from actively associated individuals. It is always, as Heclo suggests, a "government of strangers" linked more by the tasks assigned than by personal bonds (Heclo 1977, esp. pp. 36–44, 84–88). William Niskanen's observation is especially pertinent:

> In a few rare cases, a senior bureaucrat may conscientiously serve the interests of the President or some other representative of the middle-demand group, at least until his position is made intolerable by the

> bureaucracy, and the review committees. . . . My impression is that the Secretary of Defense in the first few years of each new administration has usually tried to serve the interests of the President, but that this is not the general or continuing case. (Niskanen 1971, p. 21)

By and large, strains between control loyalties and day-to-day loyalties average out and the more immediate pulls prevail, unless the authority lays it on the line or the challenge from the central power appears clear. Loyalty to the regime affects rather little of the behavior of individuals, since dramatic Watergate-type situations do not generally occur; in day-to-day situations regime loyalty reduces to exercising judgment or following directives. Office politics persist, but these are small games with little at stake and most of the personnel are not even involved.

SCREENING, CAREERISM AND DEVOTION TO DUTY

Although theoretically and in fact screening, careerism, and devotion to duty are separable, they are often combined. As weapons of control, they are designed to inculcate devotion through identification with the function of the office through process, rather than exhortation or personal influence.

Initial screening that is selective and difficult has long been a device that seeks exceptional devotion by immediate identification with the chosen few. "The Marines are looking for a few good men" encapsulates that service's approach, which has emphasized its tough role and meager material rewards. Through history, civil services have often tried to achieve that sort of identification with the job.

Oldest and most famous of the selection processes is the Chinese examination system (Menzel 1968). Emperor Wen required nominees to answer a set of questions at least as early as 165 B.C. His successor, Emperor Wu, followed the practice, and chose strictly in order of achievement on the test. Wu also founded a school for training civil servants. It became a university, and other regional schools were established. The system of examinations also was utilized for promotions. Individuals were made eligible by sponsorship of prominent officeholders, who were rewarded or punished in accordance with their protégés' later performance. The system was strengthened over time, and by the eleventh century was producing 250 successful candidates a year, enough to replenish a service of approximately 10,000. The system involved many in the effort to gain office—so much so that a lesser office could be obtained for those who failed to pass the final hurdle by the age of 50 or 60.

The rigors of the examination varied over time, as did its objectivity.

Opening up the examination to sectors of the population formerly not involved occurred in stages, and at times regional quotas were employed. At some points in history it produced unimaginative and uncreative administrations, yet on the whole it is the judgment of those who have studied Chinese history, and of contemporaries who came into contact with the system, that it served the Chinese well, attracting a disproportionate share of the country's best talents.

Obviously the success of a system lies not merely in the initial mode of recruitment, which instills price, but also in subsequent behavior and treatment, which maintain it and even give the initial selection meaning. Positions achieved must be of importance and give day-to-day satisfaction; they must also constitute compensating life chances, a reasonably good life—a career. There will be competitions for life prizes, for as Adam Smith pointed out, it is human to overestimate one's probabilities of winning. But the prize must be perceived as worth the risk. It can be seen that transfer of the source of reward from local coffers to the central treasury is vital in the concept of career control through the job.

GETTING THE RIGHT PEOPLE

Closed-entry systems maximize the sense of opportunity or career. They also limit the talent pool from which selection is made. This is true not only in the sense of filling a particular post—for there will be talent outside the system that is not even considered—but also in the sense that some talented individuals will refuse to join a stepladder system at the lower rungs. (Of course, private organizations also face the dilemma between promotion from within versus the "parachuting in" of high officials, a trade-off of efficiency through morale against efficiency through recruitment. The latter alternative often involves a greater difficulty in evaluating external potentiality against the known performance of candidates already in the system.)

American governments have emphasized open systems, while the British have created relatively hermetic structures. Interestingly, each has looked with envy at aspects of the other, and in recent years each has borrowed from the other. Oddly, at the higher levels the British emphasize movement from agency to agency, while the American system has been less flexible. Loyalty then inheres to the agency rather than to the job, and it has been common for the U.S. bureaucracy, in Hubert Humphrey's words, to act as if each department were sovereign and the U.S. government some sort of loose U.N. debating structure. President Carter's reforms, instituted in 1978, involved procedures permitting transfer of officials, by which it was hoped to transmute the occupants of discrete posts into a cadre higher civil servants. Of course, as the British example illustrates, this does not automatically solve the problem of political versus bureaucratic controls; it transmutes it by pumping in prestige. And it may well succeed in improving operations and initiative—as intended by the sponsors—but at the cost of further deterioration of responsiveness to political policy control—as feared.

SOCIALIZATION

Once selected, bureaucrats are trained to share common perspectives and to seek common objectives. This socialization to hold common perspectives may be unconscious, and a by-product of familiarization with the job and "the way we do things here." More often there are at least some overt efforts to indoctrinate and to shape—through orientation sessions, hortatory speeches, slogans, and exemplary figures. Socialization through example and role models is particularly effective.

Loyalty is inculcated through such notions and, with it, devotion to values. Seminars and meetings, and such nominal recognition as medals and certificates, act as "booster shots." Recognition from peers is utilized everywhere as a powerful tool.

These techniques are well-known, and are similar to those utilized in sports, business, and military units. Sophisticated societies tend to spurn the most overt form of such devices, the badges of success. Yet the Prussian civil service emphasized them, and secured tremendous loyalty. The British high civil service, through recruitment from a narrow stratum, effectively utilized the university and "public" school system as socialization devices: the work group was much the same social group as that at school. Generals who knew each other as "Bunkie" or "The Warbler" had strong incentives to live up to expectations, and to achieve in the eyes of their longtime associates.

The maintenance of professions through socialization is essential, since supervisory control of their activities is well-nigh impossible. The intensity of ethical exhortation and appeals to professional pride provide a clue to how such internal controls are generally sought. When so much of the actual performance is unobservable—"We bury our mistakes"—or vaguely deducible at a much later time—poor removal of decay under a filling, for example—such appeals to pride are virtually the only restraints. The evaluation by peers is a club, but it is also an internalized one, since these "detached professionals" maintain a virtual conspiracy of silence toward the outside world. The effectiveness of these invisible controls may be variously estimated; doctors, lawyers, and architects have been known to do strange things. Yet they also do surprisingly principled things. Under Josef Stalin the disappearance rate of procurators in the

Soviet Union—the people responsible for maintenance of legality—was exceptionally high. While people dwell upon the unethical conduct of lawyers in the Watergate affair, in fact most of them performed well—Petersen, Archibald Cox, and William Ruckelshaus were lawyers, too—or showed much more remorse than their counterparts among the politicians.

In any event the principle—and the problem—is the same. As Philip Selznick has shown, bureaucrats are constantly in the process of succumbing to "co-optation"—taking on the viewpoint of their clientele. This phenomenon is hardly limited to the independent regulatory commissions, where the persistence of the operation is well publicized. In point of fact, more interaction may take place with clients than with co-workers. Repeated interaction leads to familiarity, which breeds many things besides contempt. It leads to a happier relationship if the bureaucrat is seen as an ally. The bureaucrat looking for allies can most easily find them in the group he or she deals with administratively; indeed, that may be the only durable source of support. The involvement is particularly corruptive of organizational integrity when the bureaucrat is assigned to a nonheadquarters location, unobservable and in day-to-day contact with the clientele. In short, the bureaucrat needs socialization and pride in work as he or she becomes more and more a detached worker, operating under his or her own discretion and coming closer to the pattern of professionals.

In *The Forest Ranger* (1960), Herbert Kaufman has described how constraints operate upon members of the U.S. Forest Service. The ranger is a lone worker, covering a large area remote from headquarters. He has great powers over issuance of permits that assign valuable rights to private use. In short, the ranger is as vulnerable to corruption as the policeman or housing inspector. Yet the Forest Service has had an almost unblemished record, and scandal is a stranger. Kaufman explains this in terms of its elite image, its ability to transmit a tradition of pride, and the existence of detailed regulations and a requirement for elaborate logging, in minute detail, so that control is achieved to the degree possible. It is clear that the moral portion is primary, however. The environment had to be structured to reinforce attitudes and dispositions, but it was not rigorous enough to create the desired behavior in the face of obvious and easy temptation.

NORMS

If functions could be standardized, precise norms could be set out and controls achieved both through previous decision and subsequent audit. The need to exercise discretion arises because situations are unpredictable, and it is impractical or inefficient to constantly push decisions to higher levels. The model here is the military. U.S. and other armies have proved more capable when commanders are given flexibility within parameters than have comparable Russian units functioning under more primitive and invariant command rules. Thus, norms can be efficiently transmitted as the parameters of conduct to achieve limited flexibility.

Norms range from the formalized rule to the informal understanding. The concept of law as truly fixing relations is basically naive; life constantly confounds even what appear to be immutable and exactly specified relationships requiring no interpretation. Rather, law is a more formalized and more often enforced norm or parameter of acceptable or required behavior. Of course, it is not merely the precision of the written word—modern dictatorships often have elaborate provisions for liberties that put the U.S. Constitution to shame—but the precision of the enforcement. In the Forest Service the availability of a detailed manual and a daily logbook both implies and permits close control. It is the iterative process, not the initial promulgation of a policy, that constitutes enforcement.

Less formalized norms may in fact be more firmly entrenched. They may be so firmly imprinted upon behavior as never to be questioned. Reflexive behavior is, of course, the most consistent. There are cultural and institutional norms that control bureaucratic aspects both within and beyond the law. Bribery is almost invariably officially illegal but is, in fact, permissible in many societies, or in particular police forces or other organizations. How individuals are treated by bureaucrats, and how bureaucrats respond to directives, is also a matter of great variation. In their influential study of four countries, Gabriel Almond and Sidney Verba (1965) showed that expectation of fair treatment by bureaucrats was different in each country.

These values are complex and interwoven: what people expect determines what they get, and what they get is in part what causes their expectations. Government bureaucracies usually reflect the norms of their societies. If a little gift is standard in negotiating contracts in the private sector, government policy regarding its own contracts will not be substantially different; where the getting of a telephone is a product of personal influence, governmental decisions are not likely to be impersonal. In his 1976 campaign President Carter effectively used the slogan that he would give the United States a "government as good as its people." In point of fact, societies generally—for good or bad—have just that.

SUPERVISION AND ROUTINE

The crystallization of norms is found in prescribed routine and supervision. In modern societies the political branches are presumed to supervise the bureaucracy. The problems are immense, and have been so in various societies and at various times.

Essentially the dilemma of the supervisor is that power and authority inhere at his or her level, but day-to-day activity and the flow of events often place the lower-level personnel in a position to thwart, delay, or even ignore. The classic dilemma of Mao Zedong versus Zhou En-lai and Deng Xiaoping suggests the problem. Mao had the power, which he could rally to destroy the base of the machine—he could disgrace Zhou and Deng—yet he needed someone to conduct regular business. During much of the period the anti-Maoists survived by maintaining their posts and, during periods of purges, "misunderstanding" directives to suppress their opponents. In fact, both the Maoists and the anti-Maoists were loudly proclaiming their Maoism.

Political supervision of the bureaucracy has always been difficult. A good indication is that in English there are several terms for the small group of men who help the executive—chamber, privy council, cabinet—all meaning small rooms. Those structures start out small, and gradually expand. New small units are superimposed to coordinate what was once the coordinating unit. In time the new coordinating unit will get out of hand, and there will be a new stratum. There is strong evidence that the Executive Office of the President, created to lessen the burden on the president, has reached that cumbersome point. President Carter transferred a number of its members to other units, in a cosmetic attempt to keep a campaign pledge to cut its size, but essentially the staff grows and grows. This is not a small, flexible, easygoing structure. As George Reedy (1970) wisely suggested, its very size tends to create problems of adjustment and decision fatigue for a president, for the more aides, the more problems are likely to be called to his attention.

Throughout the world the twentieth century has witnessed the decline in the effectiveness of legislatures as supervisors of bureaucracy. A legislature is a mass structure with little capacity to expand its time for deliberation. It may meet more often, for longer periods, but there are temporal and physiological limits to that expansion. As the domain of government has grown, and more issues have been presented for legislative concern, some matters have necessarily been displaced. Legislatures have responded by delegating ever larger amounts of material to bureaucrats, and have expanded the function of the legislative committees. In the first instance they cede power to others; in the second, to a subdivision of themselves, or even to their own assistants or bureaucrats. In both instances some of the power is lost to the main body.

In the third quarter of the twentieth century, though, the executive has been showing signs of succumbing to the ravages of enfeeblement. The range of issues has had its effect on a political leadership divided among the craft of management, the craftiness of politics, and the calculations of foreign policy. While presidents have tried to solve their problem by creating an inner bureaucracy at the White House, there are limits to the size at which that operation is efficient. Further, like all devices of control not backed by clear power—the White House staff operates mainly through invoking the president's name rather than clear legal authority—familiarity and repetition weaken its shock value and power to compel. Resistance, too, grows in the bureaucracy when the presidency is at odds with, and visibly ineffectual in relation to, a Congress anxious to reassert its own powers.

REWARDS AND PUNISHMENTS

Supervision implies the ability to sanction desired behavior either positively or negatively. That power has been considerably limited since the time when rewards encompassed being elevated to the nobility (with all old and new prerogatives, not merely today's empty honorifics), and punishment might well be as severe as death.

The key battle between legislatures and monarchs in the modern era was over control of the "king's servants." To establish a regime of law, it was necessary to establish the proposition that the executive could not empower exceptions to the law. The legislature could, in short, establish limits to bureaucratic behavior and prescribe punishments. On the positive side, the legislature asserted authority over budgets, thus giving it the ability to reward both individuals and units. (A key ally of the legislature—in many instances the front line army—was the court system.) To the extent that Communist regimes have rendered legislative bodies rubber stamps, they have completely reversed this major modern accomplishment.

The notion of career lines and certainty of expectations limits the desirability of extreme variation in rewards and punishments. The substitution of the requirement of loyalty to the regime and legislated policies also suggests that day-to-day power of supervisors can be channeled. The rewards and punishments also should be graduated—calibrated to the achievements or misbehavior of the bureaucrat—rather than to the whims or needs of the superior. Expectations, in short, are structured in terms of the purposes of the public service, not of an individual or small group.

Punishments need not be severe to accomplish their goal. A good example is the Scandinavian custom of dealing with administrative misbehavior by means of small fines. The important factor in this, as in nonmonetary reprimands, is that it appears on the record of the bureaucrat. Transfer to a less significant job—with or without loss of pay—is a common technique. Assignment to a job without duties is for some people the greatest of tortures. (Care has to be taken with this punishment; for some people there would be no cost to the arrangement.) As an ultimate penalty, dismissal and loss of pension rights can be utilized. Other punishments presumably are not disciplinary, but are part of another system's responsibility—the legal order's prohibition of illegal actions, or the civil order's limit to misuse of authority. Where civil action is taken—for example, suit against a driver of a government car who causes an accident while intoxicated—it is not unusual for the government to bear the financial responsibility. The cost to the perpetrator may be—as it would be in our instance—internal discipline or merely the recording of the fact on the record.

Rewards are more obvious. Promotion, pay, and responsibility are easily available to the executive to dispense. In recent decades these have been heavily restricted in the U.S. system because of the power to abuse them. The Carter measures give the executive a somewhat freer hand in both promotion and demotion. Congress's willingness to allow this replaces a strong feeling that the civil service had been stagnating for want of incentives. Then, too, the loss of the excitement of new programs means that the internal reward and punishment structure must bear a greater burden for promoting desirable behavior.

EXECUTIVE CONTROL

In sum, the emphasis with respect to control over the bureaucracy has been to assume an accountability through political channels. The assumption of obedience of these servants is the bedrock of any past theory of control. Indeed, obedience was the presumption that permitted the rest of the system to grow unchecked, and rather unexamined, in most countries.

The theory of ministerial responsibility in England most admirably captures the essential theory by which bureaucratic operations have been traditionally justified. While day-to-day business is administered by the permanent undersecretary, who is a high-level civil servant, the Cabinet member has complete authority over policy, in name at least, and has been understood to be completely responsible for mishaps. If serious enough, the Cabinet may fall over a minister's failure. At any rate, the minister has been expected to be the scapegoat. In a sense all of this is a form of British parliamentary control. When Commons arrogated to itself the right to find a king's servant guilty of crimes or of misbehavior (misdemeanors), it asserted that it controlled the officials and held them accountable for outcomes. As Cabinet government has developed, the Parliament asserts no great authority over the lower levels of the bureaucracy, assuming that its delegated authority to ministers ensures parliamentary supremacy. The corollary of that delegation is ministerial responsibility. To be sure, the consequence of error is no longer having one's severed head stuck on a post at the Tower; now it is being removed, demoted, or at a minimum roughed up politically.

In a famous postwar contretemps that theory was put to test. In the Crichel Downs affair, bureaucrats bungled and suppressed evidence on a pledge given to the residents of that community, to return property taken for public use but retained by the government. Theoretically the Agriculture Secretary was responsible for his subordinates' misdeeds. In practice he had no knowledge of the letters in the files, and could not be expected to read each file to note the absence of a promise. The decision that he would not resign—primarily the decision of the prime minister—was based on that reality.

But after an inquiry recommended he not resign, the minister did so in the course of the parliamentary debate. In point of fact, his subordinates were not punished, but he was—over a matter he knew nothing about, and with which everyone conceded he should not have concerned himself. Still, he walked the plank when the matter became controversial. Subsequent legislation has vested many matters at lower levels in ministries, including Agriculture. It remains to be seen whether the fiction of ministerial responsibility will be maintained for such matters. Relations between ministers in charge of nationalized industries and boards expected to run programs with a modicum of efficiency have proved perplexing, and do not easily fit the political administration model. In general, the British have blinked at the obvious erosion, even in law, of what they insist is the operating norm that must be maintained, however silly all know it to be.

There is no better symbol of the decline of even the fiction of political control than the Crichel Downs incident. And, as we shall argue shortly, such an admission cuts into the heart of the notion of legislative authority. But the case should not be overstated. Crichel Downs, however serious in moral terms, was a minor matter in national terms, and it was not surprisingly handled—in this instance, atrociously mishandled—at a low level in a vast machine. In point of fact, most matters fit that description. A minister sets policy not over the routine, but over the expansive, the new, and the significant. The daily grind of a department is largely independent of ministers, who come and go, and are occupied in Parliament and elsewhere with national politics.

On basic issues, when the ultimate question is asked, the traditional answer must be given. It is the minister who commands, although his range in time and expertise must be small. Herbert Morrison (1954) assures us that the Labor Government had no difficulties with loyalty of the civil service even during the periods of nationalizing industry. But even that assurance must be tempered. The work of scholars since Morrison's writing have found his statements overly bland, perhaps even a fairy tale. Certainly Richard Crossman's irreverent diary (1976) of his time in the Cabinet indicates that the control delegated to the minister has to be fought for; it cannot be taken for granted. And that increasing complexity means that less and less mastery can be anticipated.

The American situation has been more confused from its inception. The founding fathers wrote the Constitution through Whig eyes, and at a time when ministerial relations and Cabinet supremacy in England were not apparent. Consequently, the direct involvement of Congress in all aspects of the bureaucracy is written into the Constitution. The small size of the fledgling civil service meant that presidential control could be coextensive with the structure. Any of the few Cabinet positions could become that of a political executive, and the role of Cabinet member was both ambiguous and ill-defined. The predominance of the presidency was guaranteed, as demonstrated by Andrew Jackson's replacement of the secretary of the treasury, and his appointment of Roger Taney to the position in order to assure that his policy was carried out. (As attorney general, Taney had already ruled that funds could be withdrawn from the Bank of the United States.)

Leafing through Leonard White's administrative histories of the early years of the American bureaucracy (1965), one finds numerous examples of both congressional and presidential intervention. What in England was a seminal issue, even a matter of life and death, was in the United States a problem of finding a boundary, a tug-of-war more than a conflict. The concept of limited authority constrained bureaucrats in a policy sense. The early history was largely therefore one of establishing controls over financial discretion—controls that have been maintained almost exactly for a century. Thus the pattern of development since the 1880s has seen greater and greater difficulty in control over the bureaucracies. Nineteenth-century administrations and Cabinets were often coalitions that reflected differences of various types, especially geographic. By careful selection of appropriate Cabinet members, presidents both allocated and controlled policies. Regions and states as a source of strength for the political official provided an opportunity to form a relationship with congressional forces and a partnership that could be two- or three-sided—that is, including or omitting White House control in the domain of any particular Cabinet member.

The expansion of the welfare-regulatory state in the United States has closely paralleled the insulation of large strata of public servants. The demand for program effectiveness has grown as the legal protection afforded subordinates has expanded. Further, the specialization of government has made control and supervision more difficult. The thinness of the appointive political stratum is remarkable. Heclo's study (1977) is as authoritative as possible, and his estimates are fairly liberal. As we have noted, one can glean the figures 700, 2,000, and 4,000 from his list of political appointments. And, as he points out, there are additional sources of political control. Civil servants, of course, are not eunuchs—even when their appointments are fixed—and there are possibilities for restructuring staffs and responsibility that permit more direction at that level. Yet the opposite is equally true; many of the so-called political appointees are chosen for reasons of expertise, and may not have strong programmatic commitments.

In sum, Heclo finds a very thin layer of political executives in office for a short period of time who have very little relationship with each other. They try to cope with large numbers of entrenched bureaucrats who have long periods of service, are thoroughly familiar with the agency, and often are more highly specialized than their supervisors. In short, political direction is spread thin, though it is dominant if it can concentrate its authority and resources on a specific issue.

All of this provides some parameters for bureaucratic dominance and for any trend toward its control. The American bureaucracy has to face few extreme dominance efforts from political executives. More than in most systems, the latter are temporary operatives with limited goals. While a few agencies, such as the Defense Department, have sophisticated internal control systems, most are loosely administered. And the bureaucracy itself is in an unusually secure position, which means that great effort is required to move it.

It would appear that the span of control of American executives is rather larger (therefore spread thinner) than in most systems of government. This is, however, probably only a matter of degree. The number of political executives replaced is relatively tighter than elsewhere, though the president is remarkably free in choosing his chief subordinates, at least by standards of Western democratic systems. Those countries with coalition governments—characteristic of Scandinavia—witness explicit bargaining for Cabinet posts, and the secondary parties often insist on specific people in specific posts. And a disciplined party in a Cabinet-type system generally has prominent leaders the prime minister cannot easily ignore. Such a really prominent figure in American politics—a charismatic rival hovering in the wings, yet demanding office—is rare in the American system.

But that thinness of control is highly significant for all systems, no matter how the top echelon is selected. Following Weber, writers on bureaucracy have reasoned that in an ever more complicated world, political executives would see their grip ever more loosened. Weber himself was impressed with Prussian and French bureaucracy, and believed its grip was "unshatterable."

That notion may not be totally in error, but Weber's confusion of the bureaucracy with its current incumbents and their authority has been repeated time and again. In the very short run, bureaucrats have impressive advantages, and in the long run they usually—but not invariably—have the staying power. In Western democratic systems, administrations are short-lived. The political executives get their way on matters not disputed, and on a limited range. If the bureaucrats dig in their heels, political executives have the means to loosen their heels, but there is a limit to deployment of those means. In a stable totalitarian or authoritarian regime, individual bureaucrats are easily dispensable—sometimes executable. Over time such replacements bring about remarkable adjustments in attitudes. The bureaucracy continues to have its interests and modes of opposition to political executives, but it may well have retracted completely on the issues once seen as requiring intractable opposition.

The error of Mao—the conspicuous failure in the struggle of politics against administration—was that there was no challenge to the notion of bureaucracy, or regulation of administration—not just to the particular incumbents on particular policies. In this sense the Weberian notion was demonstrated. The breaking of regularized control was inefficient and sporadic. To have smashed the bureaucracy, Mao would have had to create a rival one; the Red Guard and other irregulars were gadflies but not supplanters. Still, had Mao lived and been vigorous for 20 years longer, the results would have given us much firmer evidence.

Additionally, it must be remembered that span of control is a product of procedures and techniques of accounting. Complexity of the external world increases, but it is paralleled by the technology of securing compliance. Such techniques may alter the balance of expert scrutiny or tighten control in specific situations. Certainly the expectation that those in charge can't keep tabs on events is complicated by computers and modern communication in its instantaneous and multifarious forms.

GROWTH OF MERIT SYSTEMS

The problem is intensified by the decline of patronage in recent years—the thinning of the political executive stratum. As executive places become scarcer, greater central control from the White House is the rule. Thus executives are not likely to bring in their personal team. At most it is an administration team. At its worst, rivals for control of the organization are ensconced in office. More often a mixture of specialists and partisans is likely to share an office.

Cabinet members in the United States are much more parochially involved in their units than is true in most systems, and as a rule, the longer they serve, the more they become ambassadors to the White House. The expectation that they will concentrate on their units has been an almost universal one. Since the 1930s this view has been increased by the tendency of the Cabinet to become an obviously archaic unit, so that substitute units do most interagency work, and of Cabinet and other political executives to be drawn more often from nonpolitical, celebrity, or otherwise prominent groups rather than from a political base. Even when these appointments are conferred upon former administrative officeholders, they involve competence rather than independent political power or a relationship with the president. In the first half-century of its existence, a substantial portion of the Cabinet was composed of presidential rivals, close associates, and political operatives. The modern tendency is to exclude rivals or even representatives of other factions, and to concentrate associates in the presidential staff. Thus, political executives for routine matters constitute one stratum, and for supraunit or salient matters there is another. This, in turn, drives permanent officeholders even more resolutely into their agency shells, and minimizes their cooperation with the two sets of strangers with temporary control of the premises. It is, in short, a formula for inaction and frustration, leaving no one in control and no one very responsible.

Quite obviously major policy decisions continue to inhere in the top executive stratum. There is no challenge to top executives' legitimacy, and they can work their way decisively on clear-cut issues. Thus, the influence of the Office of Management and Budget (OMB) on short-range expenditure has remained crisp and sharp—perhaps has even been enhanced. Political decisions on military design systems or SALT agreements remain major considerations, though considerable administrative bargaining also takes place. At the same time, less than tight control is feasible on the totality of transactions. At the end of his first term, Richard Nixon felt he had failed to exercise dominance over a bureaucracy whose heart, he thought, still belonged to John Kennedy. At the time of Watergate, the effort had begun to control still more thoroughly the domestic policy agencies, especially those dealing with welfare. The flirtation with reform and a new start having come a cropper, older ideology was to be more strictly enforced through tighter control of personnel. This has been epitomized as "the plot against America." Though some of the methods have the Nixon stamp, it is difficult to see why an administration's effort to implement its own mandate is substantively deplorable. However, the fact that a full term had been inadequate for securing control indicates the relative ineffectuality of the superstratum. This was perhaps equally indicated by the continued operation of the machinery of government while its nominal epicenter was frozen into inactivity over a period of half a year.

What does all this do to any notion of representativeness in the action of political executives? The fact is that operations are only tangentially affected by anyone with any claim to electoral endorsement. Because the most intimately involved policymakers are functionally relevant to reelection, of the key officeholder, they are often high-level advance men, skilled in the arts of media politics and at putting the candidate at ease. The development of the political entourage so conspicuous in the past decade confounds the problem of governance.

Then, too, the percentage of the political posts that require technical skills—the administrator of the Food and Drug Administration or the surgeon general—makes any notion of representativeness or mandate artificial in the extreme. Finally, the thinness of the stratum in terms of both numbers and the time served makes the role of the remaining political appointees increasingly less significant.

The solution advanced for this by Heclo (1977) and others is the development of a higher civil service, a solution embraced by the Carter administration. It is, in fact, a universal solvent, the administrative panacea for critics of the American bureaucracy. Theodore Lowi (1969) suggests that what he sees as a tendency of American bureaucracy to bargain rather than to implement the rule of law will be cured by a higher civil service. Those who see decay and inertia in the civil service are confident a higher service will be the cure. It also has been suggested that the solution to the stratum's thinness is to create a new substratum.

The essence of the reform is to offer higher civil servants the option of moving into an elite, less secure, and nonagency-specific service. Bonuses based upon performance are possible, but job security is less assured. Predictions on the response of those eligible has been varied, but the overwhelming majority of those eligible to do so chose to move into the new ranks.

Hopes for this program tend toward the utopian. It is seen as a cure for the current profound inertia in the federal service and as a magnet for bolder, more creative types. It is touted as potentially securing loyalty to the administration, rather than to the unit, and ending the partnership among the agency, the regulatees, and Congressmen that has been labeled the "iron triangle." And by creating a cadre that can be rewarded for executing policy, it is hoped that the representativeness issue will be addressed through making the bureaucracy more responsive.

Cynics are confident that little has been changed—they believe that bonuses will be largely automatic (particularly in inflationary times) and that transfers and demotions will be rare and, as in the past, will occur for the wrong reasons. In short, the mechanisms will produce differing results, depending on how they are employed. Past experience is not encouraging, and expectations that small changes will blossom into large ones seem particularly unrealistic.

Time will, of course, demonstrate which view is correct. In the interim, the pattern is clear. For decades, political executives have not been effective in transmitting policy directives, except of the most urgent sort and over a small range of issues at any one time. This continues to leave enormous discretion at nonresponsive levels. The positions open to political discretion become increasingly limited in their demands on those eligible to fill them. The technical knowledge required of a secretary of defense today is quite different from the generalist's knowledge that permitted William Howard Taft and Henry Stimson to transfer their lawyer's skills to the duties of secretary of war. And the nature of political support has been transformed so that the loyalty of political followers is not generally bought by co-opting a leader.

Thus, in any of these senses of representativeness, political executives are inadequate personifications of any theory of mandated control. Except in the sense that it is mediated by presidential selection, much of the choice is not policy-oriented. Drawn from a highly constricted grouping for highly artificial reasons, these executives cannot be a broad microcosm of the population. And their lessening (though still present) grip on the reins limits any notion of control by representative functions.

REPRESENTATIVENESS THROUGH ACCOUNTABILITY: CONGRESSIONAL CONTROL

Essentially, control by political executives is comparable with directing a ship by small rudder or wheel adjustments. Its relative ineffectiveness is not a newly discovered phenomenon, but has been long lamented by such analysts as Woodrow Wilson, Harold Laski (1940), and Rexford Tugwell (1960). Even in the era when charges of an "imperial presidency" were rife, most of the critics, including Arthur Schlesinger, Jr. (1973), and James MacGregor Burns, distinguished between foreign policy, where the president's power was deemed excessive, anti-democratic, and dangerous, and his domestic powers, which were held to be dangerously insufficient and anti-democratic. Thus, the problem is old news, and one recent exacerbation was not so pronounced as to upset many.

The basic reliance for fundamental policy has been on congressional control through its undisputed powers over structure and the purse. Together with the presidential authority to "take care" that the laws be obeyed, this forms the constitutional rock upon which the U.S. government is based. The legislative power was seen as primary—the "great vortex," *The Federalist Papers* called it, threatening to pull all other powers into itself. The creation of minor offices, the approval of appointments to major offices by the Senate, and the control over financial matters made Congress central and capable of exercising as much control as it could grasp or was willing to pursue, subject to restraints from court and president. Congress's abuses could be much more sweeping and uncontrollable, tempered only by democratic principles: "The wisdom and discretion of congress, their identity with the people, and the influence which their constituents possess at elections are, in this as in many other instances . . . the sole restraints on which they have relied, to secure them from its abuse" (*Gibbons* v *Ogden*, 9 Wheaton 1 [1824]).

Alone among great nations, the United States retains a fundamentally legislative budget. This process, however, is now considerably affected by centralized executive budgeting, and actual expenditures are controlled by complex OMB regulations and release of funds. For a few years now the government has spent less than intended, partly because of the "lumpiness"—of defense expenditures—such as major weapons development—interacting badly through the screen of OMB procedures. Nevertheless, the authority and decisiveness of congressional control has made a comeback since the Budget and Impoundment Act of 1974. So long as Congress maintains its fragile resolve to contain the subject matter and appropriation committees within the budgetary shell set by e body as a whole, it will continue to regain the budgetary authority it most abandoned throughout the 1960s.

A bit of history seems necessary to clarify this point. From the beginning Congress found itself frustrated by excessive expenditures by departments. A series of measures was authorized to control expenditures, to make sure departments did not exceed their authorizations. This machinery remained creaky, and provided little or no coordination at the authorization stage. The crystallization of these problems and the demonstration of comparative ineptitude led to a major budgetary reform in 1921, reinforced by Brownlow Commission suggestions in 1937. The president was authorized to compile and present a budget document that became the basis for legislative action. That proposal was considered piecemeal by appropriate committees organized, like Congress, on a dual basis. Both the House and Senate committees, as well as both houses as corporate bodies, had to act on budgetary matters. This meant that the subject-matter committees—say education—dealt with the program authorizations involved in an expenditure, and the appropriate appropriations subcommittees acted on dollar amounts. Their work emerged as a recommendation usually, but by no means invariably, followed by the House or Senate. Fragmentation of the budget under those circumstances was incredible: there was no "budget" except as this process produced a series of bills with appropriations figures, which in turn had been produced via a complex route.

Under such complex conditions, lack of responsibility led almost inevitably to irresponsibility. Everyone tended not to make the tough choice, but the superficially "generous" one. No one except the president had responsibility for a balanced statement in the original budgetary document, which was months upstream from the final product. As each subject was acted upon, the tendency was to resolve disputes over appropriations on the high side. The habit of excess was like most addictions, requiring larger doses all the time. By delegating to the president and the Bureau of the Budget (now the OMB) the task of drawing together the consequences of these discrete indiscretions, and by imposing a limit on the national debt—the excess of expenditure over tax income—Congress compelled the chief executive and his agents to limit the total of expenditure and to program the pace of different bits of expenditure.

The effect of this was to create a rather curious miniature appropriation in which the roles of the participants were reversed: Congress proposed while the executive disposed. This gave the presidency a third shot at expenditures—in addition to the "budget" process and the veto—and a free hand at setting priorities that was both largely invisible and extremely flexible. It was in essence a nonpublic, or pocket, item veto. So long as the president was a maximalist—driving the Congress toward more social programs—the process of impoundment operated as an additional sieve allowing the president's men to test his priorities and to favor programs deemed most productive at any point in time. Under an activist who wished to roll back some programs, the remarkable power that had accrued became more visible. Under a leader not known for a light hand, the previously subterranean authority was brandished as an inherent power. Reaction was inevitable, even had Watergate not occurred. Nixon's naked use of the power was a call to action.

Congress recognized that its own failings had promoted the challenge, and that self-discipline was its only recourse. We have already noted that the Joint Budget Committee negotiates a target expenditure for all major bills, and then attempts to bring the final picture into balance. To date, though, it has backed down here and there, and engaged in sleight-of-hand from time to time; the process has appeared shaky in the extreme. Congress has stuck to its resolve, and has reclaimed some of its abdicated authority. And both before and after Watergate, the courts have strengthened congressional authority by making clear that where funds are specifically earmarked by the legislature, the executive has no magical veto. In general, the authority of the president can be controlled by good legislative draftmanship. If this power is coupled with fiscal courage—a more difficult prescription—Congress can be more effective than it has been for decades.

But it would be quite mistaken to think of this overall responsibility as establishing congressional control of policy in any minute or exact sense. This power-in-the-large is essential and nontrivial. But it is less impressive when efforts to deal with detail are required. This, too, has been augmented by the establishment of the Congressional Budget Office (CBO), directed by the formidable Alice Rivlin. But even so, all but a handful of financial matters never come to the attention of the full House. Detailed control may result from a hard-working and informed committee, buttressed by a tough staff, and committees and staffs are improving all the time. But it is much more likely to be a hit-or-miss exhibition of personal hobbyhorses by individual congressmen, often subcommittee chairmen. Important congressmen and significant committees often have enormous influence over specific agencies. In most instances it is a highly personalistic policy stance that prevails rather than any reasonably well-established congressional view. Few congressional leaders show signs of acting only on the basis of an evident mandate from the body as a whole.

This creates odd problems about control by Congress. While it is not terribly representative in a microcosmic sense, it is elected and has the clearest public mandate of any branch of government. But chairmanships and other key posts of influence are still largely the product of accident of circumstance and of longevity. Individual congressmen and senators can act with the force and in the name of the entire body, but more usually represent, at most, their constituents—and on many matters not even their constituents' interests are involved. We have already referred to the "iron triangle" partnership of congressional committee (sometimes the staff), agencies, and the regulated industry or group. This is a natural partnership of relatively enduring elements.

It is still perhaps novel to regard service in Congress as long-term. But the past few elections have demonstrated that incumbents are safer today than any other period in history. To a large extent this is the unexpected dividend of reforms intended to achieve the opposite. The Supreme Court decision making redistricting mandatory led to the carving out of electoral precincts favoring incumbents. The occasional disciplining through "upheaval"—for example, an 80-year-old congressman is finally dispossessed after 45 years of service (generally in his party primary)—should not obscure the fact that politicians have structured most districts so that they are no longer party-competitive, and a good many of the remainder are not competitive so long as the incumbent remains the candidate. Campaign expense reforms give incumbents access to both public and private funds to such an extent that only extraordinary wealth, or exceptionally organized initial backing, is likely to turn out a sitting member. Under these circumstances, the House has proved quite stable in its orientations in the face of erosion of basic Republican strength.

On the other hand, reform has had great impact on the internal structure of the House and, through that, on turnover. Making the seniority system only semiautomatic—some senior members are passed over for chairmanships or even removed, usually for extreme nonadherence to party policy—multiplying subcommittees while limiting multiple chairmanships, and encouraging informal groupings like the Democratic Study Group or the Saturday Club have all contributed to a sharp diffusion of power.

The further buildup of technical staff—not only the CBO but also the more than doubling of committee expert employees and personal staff—has resulted in an information explosion on Capitol Hill and has elevated standards of performance. It has also, to some extent, involved sharing of power. This should not be exaggerated. Most personal staff members are spear carriers or troubleshooters, and handle constituency service more than they advise on policy. But committee staff members, particularly in complex areas like defense or ways and means, are highly professional, sometimes have much detailed experience, and contribute input on major policies.

All in all, the rewards in Congress are increasingly uncertain and smaller. Seniority and luck are insufficient guarantees of power. Performance is constantly demanded under increasingly difficult conditions. It seems that this state of affairs is responsible for much of the turnover. Record numbers of congressmen do not seek reelection, explaining public service that it just isn't the fun it once was.

In any event, the conjunction of these events heavily discounts any claim of Congress to representativeness and to effectiveness in pressing that claim. The growing entrenchment of incumbents presents problems for any theory of democratic responsibility. The diffusion of power within Congress has progressed very far indeed, greatly outweighing any of the centrifugal force of the Budget and Impoundment Control Act of 1974. Such dispersion means that the links of specific legislators or committees are ever more significant, and less likely to be reviewed or controlled. Legislative policy is less a product of any real aggregation of interests than a rather strange, accidental outcome of a diffuse, amorphous, and increasingly unplanned process. On all but the trendy, highly publicized matters, those relationships are much the most decisive.

Symbolic of this is the declining importance of the General Accounting Office (GAO). This fascinating institution originally was designed to handle all government accounts. As the number of those accounts became so large the GAO could not properly exercise its authority, its functions were transferred in essence to the Bureau of the Budget. Yet the latter was an executive agency, while the comptroller general and his GAO were congressional—the legislature's, not the Treasury's, watchdog. The logic of the transfer was apparent, but the dimensions of its remaining operation were not—and are not—clear.

After futile and criticized efforts to control fiscal flow, the GAO has been limited to post-audit rather than pre-audit control. That is, it reviews and deals with expenditures after they occur, in order to evaluate general operations and policies. But again the process is beyond reasonable capacities and judgments. The GAO has yet to develop a notion of sampling or other techniques for systematically assaying the government's total operations. It has been successful in saving far more than its costs, a not very difficult task, but nevertheless a success. It has also been effective in publicizing its role, and has shown considerable shrewdness in choosing the objects of its investigations (and, often, in timing the publicity of its findings). Yet its findings often turn out to be exaggerated or only technically true, not sufficiently grounded to be fully accurate or to indicate remedies or solutions. It suffers from the difficulties of the casual investigator needed as a gadfly but not coming from or getting to the heart of the matter.

Congress, like the GAO, has no trouble attracting attention when Three Mile Island dramas occur. Its effect on matters requiring long-range implementation is less consistent. From time to time, for example, Congress has ordered limits on the size of the bureaucracy. These announcements are always made with a great fanfare; a freeze on new appointments is stated; and attrition, it is said, will soon effect reductions. Within a few months, policies for exceptions are announced. Within a year the new size limits are all but forgotten.

Yet Congress's attitude is hardly without consequences. To avoid political criticism, the size of the federal bureaucracy has grown at a very small rate since World War II—less than the rate of population growth. Some of the vastly increased functions have been absorbed by mechanization of routine white-collar work—computers as record keepers for Social Security—or the elimination of blue-collar jobs, as in Mint or the Government Printing Office. But the bureaucracy has partly solved the problem by contracting out some of its functions. Even payments can be issued by private firms on behalf of the government. In point of fact, it is impressive, and sounds as efficient as a tiny staff operating a huge program. Through an outside contract an inside administrative function is transformed into "operations." The effect is to appear trim and efficient, when in fact the costs may be equal—and be topped off by a profit. The number of hidden governmental employees may well equal the number of known workers, according to some estimates. A survey published in The *New York Times* on December 24, 1978, found 12 major agencies had three to four times their official staff. Where the function is temporary, such contracting may well be called for; the government gains from not having to duplicate existing facilities. The fact that contracting out is a legitimate device makes it hard to tell when it is being used for the wrong reasons.

In short, congressional efforts to keep numbers down have hardly succeeded in the form desired. In many ways they have driven real operations partly underground and made accountability more difficult. Interestingly, it was the candor of HEW Secretary Joseph Califano, not congressional inquiry, that developed the true state of affairs. Because its review is so cursory and episodic, and its attention span short, Congress is a highly limited instrument of control.

Yet it must be remembered that, all in all, this is a success story. Of all the national legislatures in the world, the U.S. Congress has maintained more power over fiscal policy than any other in the face of a trend toward decline; it has reasserted its authority and laid claim to more, not less. But whether or not it is successful in its budgetary aspirations, the limits to its policy control have been clearly charted.

COURTS AND THE BUREAUCRACY

The relationship between administration and law is complex. In the simplest form it is a rivalry and direct competition. Frank Goodnow (1900) suggests there are only two processes of government: rulemaking and rule application. Clearly the two function in the same arena and complement each other.

During the late nineteenth and the twentieth centuries, as the administrative state developed, the judiciary in most countries reacted to the new agencies with resentment. This attitude was strongest in common-law countries with the tradition of judges who, using historical principles, innovate and deal with changes as situations unfold. Thus, administrators who acted solely with legislative mandates were clear rivals; they were seen as a vicious lot, trampling the law. A. V. Dicey's celebrated criticism (1959) is a classic, later echoed by many others. Contrasting administrative proceedings with the "rule of law," he suggested that rights and property should be taken only "for a distinct breach of the law established in the ordinary courts of the land." In the discretion and vagueness inherent in regulation, he found aspects that defined both administration and despotism.

American law was, if anything, more hostile than the British. Dicey's notions seemed to fit the constitutional prescription that no property be taken without due process of law. The constitutional courts insisted upon highly restrictive standards. Thus courts, in reviewing administrative decision, were to consider each case de novo—that is, with their own eyes—rather than defer to findings from an agency. Again, the ruling that "he who decides must read" insisted that due process required an administrator to read the whole record and sift all the facts. Imposing court procedures upon the process of decision is a disease to which lawyers have little resistance as they ignore the reality that even the bulk of litigated cases don't follow the exhaustive and exhausting adversary system. And as the New Deal fought the Great Depression through expansion of regulations, administrative agencies proliferated and the courts had ample opportunity to strike down departures from the principles of Dicey's "rule of law." The effect was to place the courts on a collision course with the temper of the times and to lead to direct confrontation—almost to a constitutional amendment to clip the Supreme Court's wings in President Franklin Roosevelt's famous "court packing" plan of 1937. Ultimately, too, contradictions between what courts did and their claim to permit popular government were pressed particularly effectively by leading jurists and jurisprudential specialists.

In the wake of the court fight, a reappraisal of that relationship was inevitable. Rather in shell shock, the courts deferred to administrative agencies to the extent that if there was any rational basis for a decision, it was assumed that the agency should be sustained. This attitude of the 1940s provoked almost as negative a reaction from those not completely enamored of the modern welfare state as the anti-agency attitude of the courts of the 1930s did in its admirers.

The resulting synthesis was the Administrative Procedure Act of 1946, a major legislative effort, codifying the basic legal standards applied by federal courts in reviewing appeals from agencies. Essentially, that arrangement remains an acceptable—perhaps because ambiguous—disposition, adequately flexible and subject to further refinements or structuring by duly enacted legislation. Essentially, except where enactments specifically provide otherwise, the standard for review is that a decision will not be overturned by the courts when there is "substantial evidence on the whole record" to justify the outcome. The judge is not supposed to act as an independent policymaker presenting his own decision; the effort should, rather, be to see whether the original policymaker had gone beyond reasonable inference from what is known. Deference is thus paid to the expertise and authority of the bureaucrat while making that person reviewable and, on occasion, reversible. The formula is clearly intended to be tougher on the administrator than the old "warrant in the record," but to permit some scrutiny of the facts and conclusions.

Lawyers place a great premium upon such formulas. In this instance the instructions in the statute are aimed at judges, and so perhaps the shoe fits. Still, it is more likely from the evidence that the judges do something both simpler and more complex. They tend to defer to agencies they respect and to reverse less well-regarded administrative units. Studies show quite different reversal rates for different agencies at different times. Of course, agencies with bad decisions are likely to have a bad reputation and those with good decisions, a good reputation. But the relationship that has been found is too strong to be easily attributed merely to application of local formulas to agency lapses. It seems clear that judges derive their decisions on cases before them partly from their knowledge of an agency's operations. The "standard of warrant on the whole record" presumably excludes such external factors but permits judges to have an expansive eye, at least in an unofficial way.

On the whole, the evidence also suggests that administrators are generally less constrained in what they do than in how they do it. Law and the courts do limit policy thinking somewhat, but generally administrators and lawyers recognize that "creative thinking" will find a legal way to accomplish much that on first sight is not permitted. On the other hand, some things simply will not do, or are doubtful and will involve an agency in costly litigation. Thus, some decisions clearly become too expensive.

How an agency operates is much more clearly affected by legalisms. Violation of rules of procedure is clearly more probable, and legally more lethal, than lapse of judgment or lack of performance. Elaborate records imply—but often counterfeit—care and thoroughness. Voluminous records exact a price that judges must pay to exercise judgment. It is, in short, safer to play it by the book, and even guard against requirements being found between the lines.

And in administration, as elsewhere, "the letter killeth but the spirit giveth life." Multiplication of formal requirements and duplication of efforts, forms, and memos are singularly depressing to the administrators hip-deep in trivia and to those being administered. "Red tape" historically has been a synonym for bureaucracy precisely because it is a malaise to which it easily succumbs.

Judges have never felt themselves absolutely constrained by legislative wordings, which are almost always as ambiguous as possible. As Kenneth Davis (1975) has written, outrageous cases involving bureaucratic excesses are easily controlled by the judiciary though they sometimes create bad precedents.

In recent years many of the old restraints that judges had imposed upon themselves have been relaxed, and commentators have even suggested that their pretensions are those of "an imperial judiciary." Utilizing in particular their authority to create remedies in equity, judges—especially federal judges—have intruded into the processes of regulatory administrations and also of front-line administrative structures. The courts are carrying out mandated civil rights standards, following new and expansive interpretations of the constitution—especially the Fourteenth Amendment. They are also responsive to growing litigation, the bringing of cases by individuals and groups, often on behalf of large segments of the population for whom they claim to speak. Such cases—"class actions"—and more traditional actions often come about in response to new statutes establishing both standing to sue and causes of action. Also, the new legislation often contains provisions giving potential litigants encouragement to sue through the right to recover costs if the case is successful and such bounties as triple damages. In that way

Congress has unmistakably evidenced a desire to encourage remedial statutes being enforced, not just through normal Department of Justice procedures but also through private and group initiatives.

At least as long ago as the 1930s, the American courts began to liberalize the rules of legal standing and participation in proceedings to accommodate the greater social role of the courts. This expansiveness and increase of access have gone hand in hand with congressional attitudes. They also have led to wide-ranging remedies and to adaptation of judicial techniques to deal with broad problems through intervention.

These two developments involve the judiciary both more often and to a greater degree than formerly in the administrative process. Critics are wont to point to court intervention in schools—principally on desegregation matters—and their involvement with prison conditions and treatment in mental institutions. Depending on one's view, Judges David Bazelon, Frank Johnson, and Skelly Wright can be the epitome of the social realist or the overweening interloper. Such involvement includes the areas of welfare recipients, rights of residents in public housing, and federal expenditures.

And these cases have been brought by myriad organizations and activists. The civil rights area has long been established, with the NAACP and the American Civil Liberties Union active in litigation for most of this century. Their successes in the 1930s and 1940s encouraged the growth of other liberal, labor, and ethnic organizations. The 1970s have seen the emergence of consumer-oriented groups, welfare interests, Common Cause, and many more esoteric ones.

These developments raise other questions relevant to our original inquiry. Does the opening of doors make the judicial process, and through it the administrative process, a flexible instrument of the public and its base structures? And do the processes of law, either separately or in conjunction, contain and restrain the administrator sufficiently to constitute checks and accountability, as suggested in constitutional theory?

There seems to be little doubt of the courts' greater availability to a broader social spectrum for policy purposes, though establishing this is well-nigh impossible. The range of questions adjudicated involves a broad spectrum, including vindicating the rights of those formerly treated as nonpersons. (Illegitimate offspring for example, or recipients of governmental welfare were not, at one time, in a position to raise meaningful issues.) A rich variety of organizations have their day in court. The administrative structures often permit and encourage such group participation. It has been shown that higher state courts, like the federal courts, increasingly draw their cases from broader social issues, and are less involved in traditional business and property issues than in the nineteenth century.

Still, courts have clear restraints—not to say blinkers. The modes of proceedings, the nontrivial costs, and the expertise involved limit who can litigate and—even more significantly—who is likely to benefit from, and therefore engage in, litigation. It is, for example, difficult to maintain standing in environment cases, since it is often impossible to pinpoint a specific or unique or even substantial stake that one person or a few people have. At the same time, courts could be swamped if Christopher Stone's imaginative proposal (1973) that physical objects—trees or rivers, for instance—be given standing. The difficulty, of course, is not in the legal recognition, though it has a faintly medieval cast; after all, actions *in rem* persist in the law, and we still get wonderful case names like *United States v 42 Kegs of Whiskey* and *United States v the Schooner*. It is, rather, the question of who speaks for the nonperson in court, when everyone has an equal right to assert the "interest of the rock or grove." One is reminded of Ethan Allen's feat of capturing Fort Ticonderoga "in the name of the Continental Congress and the great God Jehovah," but as a historian pointed out, without a commission from either of them. At present the only obvious solutions to this dilemma of standing—either total exclusion or the opening up to each and every person—are actions by the legislative or the administrative unit, or self-help. Each is unsatisfactory, although in combination that dissatisfaction is not so pronounced.

Legislatures have historically defined those who speak for others in the judicial process—parents for children, the attorney general for illegal aliens who technically have no voice, the setting up of administrators or conservators. In recent years they have played a greater role in the defining of classes permitted to litigate jointly. The traditional definition of "class action" had confined it to those with a clear joint fate or expected return as participants in a fund (such as stockholders). The expansion to those who might have diverse, but sufficiently conjoint, interests began in the 1930s, but for nearly two decades thereafter it was common for such legally approved actions still to be referred to as "spurious class actions." As the form of action became more popular in the 1960s and 1970s, the line of distinction between traditional and "spurious" class actions was not found useful; it is now a virtually forgotten term even among law professors.

The problem has been identifying the boundaries of a group or position, and in finding within it a representative voice. Here Congress or another legislature can, and does, speak, particularly on the first question, with some authority and perhaps objectivity. Often in establishing a domain of regulation—environmental policy or equal employment, for instance—Congress may express a direct or indirect preference for some group as having standing. Thus the Civil Rights Act expressly mandates the attorney general to bring cases on behalf of women discriminated against in basic rights. But this has been interpreted by the courts as also enabling private suits without elaborate proof that women may constitute a class. Similarly, agencies may directly or inferentially create representation through whom they consult or in the course of what are often complex hearings with multiple steps.

Such authorizations or entitlements can be quite effective in securing and expanding representation. But in fact and in appearance they raise questions of the objectivity of the original entitlement. To the extent that the original authorizations meet the Buchanan-Tullock constitutional requirements—that is, they are set prior to and independent of the particular issue involved—they appear, and may well be, more objective than if they are ad hoc.

The bias of the common law is toward self-help and self-definition of one's interest; and that remains, though diluted, in cases in equity. Self-starting groups represent the opposite end of the dilemma. Studies have shown that most of the "new" public-interest groups have few members and are run by partisans with their own private sense of right; usually they are not dependent upon the members for either financing or policy. In many instances, members have no real way of influencing policy except by withholding contributions, and the bulk of funds come from some combination of legal fees, government grants, and sources other than membership fees. Thus the bulk of these organizations may be fairly described as representing their leaders' concept of a group interest rather than the broad spectrum. This is not a new phenomenon, but its extent is. Mancur Olsen (1965) has generalized in economic terms what E. E. Schattschneider, as a political scientist, and Roberto Michels, as a sociopolitical economist, had noted: that in practice, groups tend to be dominated by a leadership elite, even if the structure is nominally democratic and open. But these groups are in fact often not open, even nominally.

The effect, then, of the broadening that has taken place under legislative, administrative, and judicial auspices is real but limited. Like the famous review of Tallulah Bankhead's dramatic range, it has witnessed a growth of the gamut of interests from A to B.

Paradoxically, the courts constitute the most open branch in theory, and to some degree in practice. It is possible to come to speak, and to conquer in a way highly unlikely for one to begin to mount a political effort. A handful of litigants and lawyers can move mountains with laughable sums—sometimes less than six figures. Yet, the circumstances necessary for individual action—the information costs, the establishment of channels, and the risks involved—make it, like the stock market, a luxury for those who can afford any of the losses, and who can bear the consulting and other expenses of engaging in an essentially esoteric insiders' game. Even the pooling of the right to litigate in mass terms—to carry the image one step further the "mutual funds" of litigation—that the new groups represent has not become widely diffused. It requires too much sophistication and commitment for it to become a household occupation.

If there has been some increase, though not much greater representativeness, in litigation, it might appear that the greater involvement of the judiciary still represents confinement of administrative discretion, vindicating the dominant theory of control through law, which ultimately rests upon legislative authority. No doubt there would be conceptual problems even if this were simply seen as an intensification of traditional court action. However, the view both of critics and of supporters has been that the courts are taking bold constitutional or logical steps that intervene beyond the normal pattern of legislative deference. The fact that judges are drawn from the slightly broader spectrum of lawyers would not alter the fundamentally unrepresentative nature of the judiciary any more than the previously discussed expansion of group interests has. Certainly, insofar as the judges get further along on this limb, the logic of their control seems more anomalous in a democracy.

But these considerations are less demanding in the light of evidence and argument that the intrusion of the courts is a mark of weakness, not of strength, and has been basically unproductive. On conceptual grounds Lowi (1969) has argued that the welfare-administrative state has betrayed the rule of law. Motivated by "interest-group liberalism" that has few or no fixed principles, it reduces the ascertainment of welfare to a measurement of differing interest demands. In effect, administration (and presumably courts) is reduced to a group of bargainers rather than interpreters. Presumably the courts are forced to intrude upon administration when the bureaucrat makes an egregious miscalculation, or perhaps when the balance of power has shifted. In short, on this theory courts are corrupted from their true purpose as they review decisions that should be based upon law.

More shifting still are the evaluations of the results of court efforts on empirical grounds. It is generally conceded that the Warren Court's efforts to control the police through requirements as exemplified by the search-and-seizure rule have engendered political hostility and little more. (An exception to this is Brad Canon's [1979] interesting, though inconclusive, empirical argument, with a sophisticated understanding of the difficulties of showing what the state of affairs would be if something that has happened had not occurred.) The courts have neither secured police support nor been consistent or precise enough to enforce automatic compliance.

In attempting reform of prisons and mental health facilities, the court record is more mixed. A review by attorney-researchers of the impact of four court decisions found vaguely positive consequences. The most significant effect, in three of the four instances, was greatly increased appropriations, which permitted improvement in the grossly inadequate facilities. In one of these cases, interposition of clear legal standards for treatment and punishment had a decided positive effect. In one instance clearly (and one possibly) outside intervention lowered the sense of efficacy, and led to turnover and morale problems. In all instances the processes were time-consuming, extended, and expensive. In one case virtually no results ensued, except some negative costs.

Donald Horowitz (1975) has made the most penetrating and sophisticated critique of court interventions in terms of efficacy. He distinguishes between "legal facts" and "social facts." Legal facts are the relevant particulars having consequences for the concrete dispute before the court. Social facts are the entrained results that follow upon the particular case and constitute the basis for a prediction (and later an assessment) of the effects of a policy. Courts, Horowitz suggests, are not well-equipped to deal with the latter. (A more subtle form of much the same issue is presented in the Herbert Packer's *Ex-Communist Witnesses* (1962), in which he attempts to deal with the problem of the limits of fact-finding in courts and in administrative and legislative proceedings. The court proceeding in the Alger Hiss case adjudicated his alleged perjury. It did not, except indirectly, deal with Hiss as a spy or with the vital question: How deeply entrenched were Communist sympathizers in government? In Horowitz's terms, even in dealing with "legal facts" the judicial enterprise has limited horizons.)

As Horowitz points out, the interventionist cases, by definition, involve the courts more and more in social facts, an area where they are less competent. In a sense, then, the recent developments illustrate an institutional "Peter Principle." (This mock-serious law states that functionaries rise in rank to "their level of incompetency.") In these instances—school desegration in Washington, control over police search processes, the Model Cities program in Philadelphia, and juvenile court reform—Horowitz suggests a set of common problems. Acting in areas unfamiliar to them, the judges often misinterpret the evidence. This is often exacerbated as cases are appealed, for crudities intrude on this shift, much as headlines often contradict the main body of the story. Those aspects of decision beyond judicial control cannot be tackled even indirectly. For example, housing segregation haunts integration proceedings, but courts have no effect on it at all. The orders or decisions of the judges often betray lack of experience, or have unanticipated, unintended, or perverse ramifications. The specificity required in judicial orders often introduces rigidities, as well as justified complaints about them. Change can be introduced and secured only with effort. Allegations of evasion become complex bits of litigation in their own right.

The Boston effort to deal with school segregation supports Horowitz's view. Judge Arthur Garrity, Jr., eventually issued orders detailing building use, made personal selection of principals, and controlled admission not merely to specific schools but also to specific programs. He utilized not only his own skills but also those of educational experts to deal with specifics. (However, he often overruled them.) In spite of this, the consequence has been to create "white flight" to the suburbs and tense, underattended, unsuccessful schools, with the most highly "integrated" schools strong candidates for closing.

This is, of course, only partly relevant to the particular social policy and resistance to it. However, it would appear from these events and from the literature that courts are generally most effective in dealing with administrative or other governmental units when they can speak with the analytic, global vagueness that characterizes legal presentation, and can get a positive response—the working out of details by the resident professionals. The court's need to become ever more precise with an administrative unit results from the latter's failure to respond to more global cues. In one sense an overly detailed order is a finding of semi-contempt of court; put another way, it is a confession of court weakness rather than a profession of strength. The "judge as administrator" emerges, in Horowitz's terms, as a judge who is near the end of his or her powers to cope with a decision that was too far-reaching in the first place.

In short, these interventions generally are not signs of court control, and are almost publicity-seeking forays, except where they are linked to general principles or structural changes that are easy to implement. A few years ago courts were deeply involved in faculty tenure decisions, but quickly decided to have minimum involvement, provided the institution involved had reasonable procedures and followed them. "Are we going to be involved in prison punishment?" Judge Clement Haynsworth rhetorically asked a small group a few years ago. "Yes, we will, until they set up a way of dealing with prisoners that has the basics of due process. And then we are going to get out of the act so fast it will make your head swim." In criminal matters, control by the police has made the courts unable to deal effectively with evasion tactics, short of overspecification to the point of the ineffectiveness. At that point, opponents of the vague policy can come forward, not in opposition to the broad goal but to the poor implementation of the policy. The analogy is to guerrilla warfare, where a prime objective is to force an opponent to take such extreme measures that it will lose the respect and support of the marginally committed in the population.

Because of the growth of governmental complexity, courts are increasingly unable to understand a broader and broader domain of administration. In 1979, for example, a DC-10 crashed in Chicago, with signs the tail assembly had broken off. Inspection of other DC-10s revealed similar cracks. "Passenger representatives" went to court to prevent the planes from flying. Judge Aubrey Robinson was, in the end, at the mercy of the findings of the Federal Aviation Agency (FAA) and the National Transportation Safety Board as to the safety of the DC-10. He might have kept the planes grounded, as his order that was preempted by FAA action suggested, pending review by the Board. But once the evaluations were in, he had little choice but to permit the agency to use its judgment. The courts are very much in his position in thousands, not to say millions, of instances.

The number of instances alone constitutes an obstacle to control. It is estimated that the number of Social Security payment decisions made within the system outnumbers all cases in all U.S. courts, and theoretically all are appealable.

The curious permeability of the courts—hardly a system in any rigorous sense—also plays into the hands of the administrative unit. A good example is the Internal Revenue Service (IRS), whose policy is not to appeal a Court of Appeals decision rejecting a claim based on policy, but to continue making that claim in the rest of the United States. Effectively, then, it will permit two (or more) policies to exist. Only if two or more circuits find against it, will it appeal to the U.S. Supreme Court. Many other agencies now are said to be adopting this arrangement. In effect, the agency (IRS) chooses to quarantine a policy that might cost revenue, obeying it solely where a court says it must, and refusing to generalize if it chooses not to.

While these matters are illustrative and conceptual, they reflect the fact that courts have not been able to develop any sort of patterned review of administrative relations. The fundamental approach to cases arising out of the agencies is the same as their approach to court business in "real life": they take the business brought to them, sifting those conflicts for what should be handled in court. It is a reasonable way to maximize courtroom time, given a system where courts are a last resort for trouble in society. It is a terrible way to monitor another system, however, and the chance elements in the arrangement minimize the potential impact.

In one area there is both a growth of administrative review by the courts and effective and satisfactory service: the domain of interagency disagreement. The development of an extensive regulatory state often will pit two agencies furthering different regulatory purposes against each other—or perhaps a regulatory agency view against an operating agency view. Thus, the Interstate Commerce Commission may wish to maintain high shipping costs for vegetables while the Department of Agriculture, as a farmer-interest agency, and the Department of Defense, as purchaser, may be on the other side. Again, the Maritime Commission has collided with the Antitrust Division of the Justice Department. These disputes may be settled administratively, through agency or White House resolution; quasi-legally, through ruling by the attorney general; or through the courts. At one time, impressed by concepts of unitary government, courts found the notion of U.S. v. U.S. conceptually difficult. Today, such differences between agencies are perceived as normal reactions to different responsibilities imposed by statute. Court decision is appreciated as a best solution where there is ambiguity in the law, and especially when the Department of Justice is one of the parties in the dispute. In this respect the courts function as troubleshooters, resolvers of administrative problems, and not as supervisors or enforcers of externally imposed policies.

At the present time courts hear appeals from administrative decisions where someone thinks it worthwhile to bring a case, and finds the appropriate legal "handle" to do so. Those able to find the "handle" by no means exhaust the universe of interests in our society. For one thing, as we have noted, the technical conditions for legal standing—the right to bring a case—are still reasonably restrictive in any given fact situation. Even if a person or group has the requisite legal attributes, the particular issue, slant or point of view desired to be urged may not be legally relevant to a specific dispute. And it must seem worth the financial commitment—five or six digits in dollar terms—to pursue the litigation. But that calculation depends on the type of issue and how much money is involved. Where legislation provides a bounty for the lawyers or where lawyers are already hired by companies—or unions—for other purposes, and thus are already available, litigation is easier organizationally, and less costly in every sense.

"Repeat players," to use Mark Galanter's (1974) label, have low start-up costs for cases falling in their domain. They "police" an administrative area well, but from their own point of view. "One-shot players" have to start from the beginning, learning the legal game and lining up legal skill, and are less likely to be fully represented in legislative appeals. The unevenness of likelihood of litigation means that sophisticated administrators can have uneven responses in different domains. It is safer—less likely to produce litigation—if the IRS has extremely tough auditing procedures for dry-cleaning establishments but less tough ones for auto manufacturers, for example. In this environment courts can function as a brake upon bureaucratic calculation only to a highly limited extent.

All of this is exacerbated by the pace of the judicial system. Violations take time to be presented through normal channels, though through the power to cite for contempt and the right to issue supplementary orders, courts are hardly helpless. But follow-up cases may or may not develop in any given period. The dependence of the courts upon the parties to generate follow-up, to see whether the policy works, or whether the decision is followed, makes "control" a highly limited term.

Indeed, an approach to administrative law is developing that takes as its premise the notion that current review by litigation is a failure, and by its nature cannot succeed. In its place, it is suggested, an automatic review of some sample of cases should be implemented. (In Social Security and some other agencies such a procedure is already followed for administrative reasons.) Such a review would transfer the function of the courts from mediating troublesome cases to supervising quality control. A court can become a court of automatic review (federal criminal cases are approaching 100 percent review at the Court of Appeals level). But sampling would inevitably have consequences for court-administrative relations. From our standpoint the significant point is the basic understanding that permeates the attitude or proposal: the highly limited effectiveness of courts in this domain. As with the executive and the legislature, its control over bureaucracy has proved less than pervasive.

OTHER EFFORTS AT CONTROL: POLITICAL PARTIES AS RESTRAINT

Political parties' imprint upon the bureaucracy has largely paralleled the power of the political executive, but is sufficiently different to justify a brief treatment of its own. Its heyday was, of course, the period of spoils, and its influence has been diminished with the growth of the civil service and the professionalization of careers. Yet, in another sense political parties operated as restraints and catalysts upon the bureaucrat; this sense also is in decline, but has not completely disappeared. Bureaucrats, in theory, are programmatically neutral, but obviously they have preferences. Certainly specific structures have flourished under presidents from one party and done less well under the other. Social Security, for example, is still a faintly illegitimate term to Republicans, while the Federal Reserve Board, never constituted with nonbanker dominance (as Woodrow Wilson wanted it to be), has been seen by Democrats as a nonconforming spinster aunt with stock holdings sufficient to disrupt the family business. Republicans see it as the last stronghold against chaos. The Labor Department under the Democrats is virtually an AFL-CIO franchise, and a dead-letter office under Republicans. The National Labor Relations Board is another agency that still experiences vast and abrupt changes with party shifts.

Even the decline in patronage does not cut the programmatic consequence of party shift or eliminate bureaucratic catalytic changes. Agencies adjust their behavior to friendlier or more hostile political environments. The "alphabet agencies" created by Democrats hibernated under Dwight Eisenhower, their red-taped hearts beating for friendlier White House incumbents. We have noted Richard Nixon's perception that Washington regarded him as a temporary inconvenience, and that this form of his paranoia was not without some considerable reality. Even Jimmy Carter tried to cope with a perception that he was not a true, vigorous believer in Democratic policies.

Beyond the increase in structured independence and the inertial growth of the bureaucracy discussed earlier, the atrophy of party as a true political force has operated to minimize even this aspect of bureaucratic control, which never was very precise or measurable. Since Lyndon Johnson and Carter correctly perceived that they had much the same problem as Eisenhower and Nixon, the party variable cannot be taken very seriously. Indeed, since Johnson was programmatically a believer in agency government—perhaps even more than President John Kennedy and/or Robert Kennedy—even this self-interest aspect may be subordinate to image and media politics.

The pattern of that politics is increasingly "every candidate for himself." The Jerry Brown syndrome of virtually no fixed alliances—"nothing to everyone," as one critic has labeled him—exaggerates but delineates the modern politics. Parties are the chief losers in this dominant personalism. Carter's weak hold even on the formal apparatus of the Democratic Party was matched by Nixon's basic contempt for Republican structures not completely subservient to him. As this is written, the differences between the two parties on administrative issues have become less significant even in the area of monetary policy, though that could change in the Reagan administration. That Carter could appoint Paul Volker—a former Nixon administrator—head of the Federal Reserve Board reflected his concern with inflation and the support he felt necessary from the business community. But that an appointee could also be a Democratic choice for so key an economic role meant that less than total disagreement on such policies characterizes our political environment. Yet it is probably in the economic arena that the most enduring differences between the two parties have been found.

The decline of these party ties means a further weakening of bureaucratic discernment of potential differences between parties and involvement therein. Personal qualities of the candidate are more significant, and these are more difficult to assay. Consequently, policies designed to aid nonincumbents are hazardous. Since incumbents are poised for election only 50 percent of the time under the two-term rule, no partnership develops.

There remain links between bureaucrats and committee chairmen. These are tied to party control of the house of Congress involved. Chairmanships are less certain under the flexible congressional standards now prevailing, and the increasing independence of party by congressional candidates is drastically changing the nature of those links. No longer grounded in party government notions, the links emerge as less easily justified in democratic theory and, even in the views of the participants, take on a more complaisant, nonprogrammatic, cozy, and sometimes sleazy tone.

The extent to which party has declined as a check is underscored by the relatively unnoticed and strictly conceptual decision in *Elrod* v *Burns* (1976). In spite of the rather imposing historical evidence that could be amassed for "spoils" notions in conjunction with government service, or for a concept of party responsibility, as having been intended by the framers of the Constitution or their immediate successors, the Supreme Court made short work of the entire matter, reasoning that political affiliation could not be the basis for dismissal. Thus, First Amendment rights—not properly understood by framers of that provision—precluded removal and replacement. It is possible that had the sheriff of Cook County specifically based his action upon policy differences appropriate to the position, the result would have been different. However, in *Branti* v *Finkel* (1980) the Supreme Court clarified *Elrod* by allowing patronage dismissals only where ". . . the hiring authority can demonstrate that party affiliation is an appropriate requirement for the effective performance of the public office involved."

"Sunshine" Laws

The evidence of the failure of direct control has spurred efforts to find new or even exotic control systems. These take many forms, and have their own peculiar advantages and disadvantages.

In keeping with populist impulses of recent decades, one emphasis has been upon "sunshine" laws—requirements that matters be pursued in open meeting. These are particularly aimed at boards, regulatory commissions, councils, and the like. In general, enacting bodies exempt themselves from the most stringent provisions, have found it difficult to prescribe informal evasions of the letter of the provisions, and have generally avoided the thorny problem of reconciling "sunshine" and freedom of information concepts with their usually fierce insistence on privacy.

Enacting bodies understand for themselves the limits of "sunshine." Some matters can be worked out only in flexible, nonpublicized give and take. Even public trials have moments where the lawyers "approach the bench" and, with varying degrees of privacy, seek accommodation and compromise.

Similarly, some matters are most efficiently and ruthlessly pursued in private. Personnel discussions generally are more equitably conducted in private, and will often change in tone under different conditions. Public land purchases become more costly if intent to buy is publicized. Litigation strategy traditionally is confidential. "Sunshine" laws could, in theory, permit greater flexibility, on such matters providing also that the final position be made public. In practice, exceptional language will be seized upon and expanded. Thus, precise outlawry of practices would prove necessary, making flexibility more urgent and, in a classic vicious circle, pushing the public bodies to find ways of evading the controls.

The "sunshine" laws arose almost simultaneously with the emphasis on privacy. But the two simply do not mesh as operating principles. If the public has the right to know, privacy is diminished. Reconciling the two is obviously a key issue, and principles to set boundaries are badly needed. In general, legislatures have deliberately ignored the obvious contradictions. In Minnesota there was explicit recognition of the contradictions, but the task of delineating was delegated to the commissioner of administration. At the federal level, a commission on privacy is authorized to develop regulations, while the Freedom of Information Act is enforceable by individual action. In that area most proceedings have been by businesses intent upon gaining information about rivals or (more rarely) agencies they deal with.

In only a few instances has the effort been to control bureaucracies, though some of those have been of considerable significance. In a conspicuous instance, revelations about IRS operating procedures were instrumental in changes in its subsequent modes of conduct. The intelligence community has also experienced shock waves from revelations developed by these means, often as a result of inquiries by journalists and scholars. While the record is mixed, it is nonetheless significant that Congress expanded the coverage of the Freedom of Information Act in its major revision of 1974. The climate of the times was that disuse of the act by the public was attributed to poor mechanisms rather than lack of interest. Still, the relatively small number of inquiries and the predominance of business requests make it clear that it is at most a useful supplement rather than a major control mechanism.

"Sunset" Laws

"Sunset" laws are proposals, advocated by both ultraliberal critics and ultraright critics of the welfare state, that suggest a statute should cease to exist after a specific time period unless duly reenacted. It is claimed that this is analogous to zero-base budgeting, which forces legislatures to reexamine agencies so that they do not perpetuate themselves without at least some affirmative gesture by the legislature. In some jurisdictions, periodic review by a commission or other expert body brings recommendations to the legislature. This arrangement at least recognizes the fact that sweeping assignment of new supervisory duties to an agency that does not utilize the powers it has, is throwing a bucket of water at a drowning man. To date, even the more carefully structured efforts have been disappointing. Legislatures are overburdened, not underarmed. They have difficulty assessing new needs.

One basic premise of "sunset" laws seems reasonably demonstrated. It is argued that governmental institutions, once created, persist no matter how useless they become, and that these agencies grow incrementally over time, largely or completely by a process of mitosis. This thesis is brilliantly captured in "Parkinson's Law," a semiserious satire that builds from the axiom "Work expands to fill the time alloted to its completion" to the conclusion that government growth is self-created. Both aspects of this notion are somewhat exaggerated. Herbert Kaufman (1976), viewing a period of 50 years in the history of the U.S. government, found 27 agencies had in fact been abolished, out of a total of 175. Efforts to apply "Parkinson's Law" to actual organizations have shown it to be both highly exaggerated and oversimplified. But government does in fact grow in much that pattern. We have noted "Wagner's Law," which suggests that government constantly absorbs a large share of the gross national product.

It is the minor premise that has proven faulty. The assumption is that agencies grow by neglect, and without regard to size. Rather, they seem to be adept at developing support groups and carving out a niche for themselves. "Sunset" laws do not threaten agencies of even reasonable efficiency and modest political proficiency. The more sweeping the scope of review, the less real attention is paid to any particular agency. Review for existence in fact is not much different from budget review, and the hope that it would be has thus far proved to be a forlorn one.

Ombudsmen and Other Advocates

Continental Europe has long had a tradition of both general review and specific complaint agencies of the type found in the military's Inspector General Corps. In Scandinavia such procurator functions have been crystallized in a complaint agency centered on the ombudsman (literally "grievance man"). Effective publicity and a sense of frustration with modern bureaucracies have glamorized the ombudsman, who reviews citizens' complaints and seeks redress in most instances of bureaucratic wrong. The desire for protection of individualism has made the ombudsman the remedy-of-choice in most Anglo-Saxon jurisdictions, and often for nongovernmental structures as well. (Thus, many Roman Catholic orders have discussed an ombudsman for priests—a chaplain's chaplain, as it were. Prisons often have ombudsmen, and so do a number of universities, usually for student grievances.)

These structures have proved important, perhaps as much for symbolic and morale as for policy purposes. Invariably they find heavily for the bureaucrats, since their leverage with the bureaucracy virtually requires that they demonstrate awareness of the complexities of decision. Throughout the world they tend to find against the complainant about 90 percent of the time. The number of cases processed by such offices is generally small—several hundred a year in most countries. Even when they persuade an agency to accept their decision in a particular case, they usually lack the power to force the agency to change a basic policy. In this respect they resemble newspaper or other media complaint operations. (A refund is relatively easy to get for a publicized complainant. Real change in policy and practice is much more difficult.) However important they are in a frustrating and complex world, and as significant as they may seem to a victim of governmental machinery, they are clearly designed to mediate the troublesome case and, on the whole, cannot channel or control the bulk of the bureaucracy.

Initiative, Referendum, and Recall

Populists of the right and left have found new hope in the use of the products of the populist-progressive era, the family of political home remedies known as initiative, referendum, and recall. The recall permits a stated number of voters to force a new election on the status of an incumbent, the referendum forces a popular vote on a measure already enacted (but in some instances only if it is not yet in force), and the initiative allows voters to place a new measure or one rejected by the delegated lawmakers directly on the ballot. There is a clear East-West pattern on these matters, with the "newer" western states much more enamored of these devices. Furthermore, this pattern has been fixed for several decades. While the package of devices in various forms expanded to the Midwest in the first two decades of the twentieth century, the 1930s saw expansion halt. Since then those with such instrumentalities have retained them, but no new converts have emerged.

In recent years, however, a strong group of advocates for national populist devices has appeared. At times they have advocated the halfway measure of implementing the device in Article V of the Constitution—calling a Constitutional Convention—thus obviating the need for congressional action. Since it has never been employed, precedents do not exist. Generally, advocates have favored such a convention to draft some tax-and-spend limit for the national government, a radical enough proposal. However, most constitutional authorities feel the convention would not be limited by the call of the meeting and, on analogy to the Annapolis and Philadelphia conventions, could range into any aspect of the Constitution. The convention proposal, which moved rapidly to gain state legislative approval, has ground to a halt in the light of this objection and the fact that approval is no longer a symbolic gesture against government spending, but might really result in drastic change.

By and large, recall has proved very useful for minor offices and those areas with a homogeneous electorate. Impeachment is, after all, a complex, legalistic device and is seldom employed at any level. Calls for impeachment of President Nixon resulted in the Reuss Amendment. As originally drafted, Congress would have been able to call for a new election of a president. Experts agreed this would shift power to Congress to a drastic degree. The final proposal would have stipulated that action by Congress would force an election involving the presidency, House, and one-third of the Senate. The proposal, thus carefully hedged, has drawn little popular or political support, and has been most notable for the careful discussion it has provoked on the nature of political balance in the American system.

The referendum is a subspecies of the initiative, having the advantage that the legislature has already gone through the process of bargaining and refining the drafting of the proposal. The problem of drafting is a major one for the initiative, not for technical reasons but for political ones. Legislators are not really specialists in the drafting of good, technical provisions, and most bodies have specialists available for that purpose. On the other hand, in any area of legislation a great variety of proposals is possible. A legislature has give and take, rational discourse, and a sifting of alignments and possibilities that can, at its best, simulate what the community reaction would be. The art of being a good legislator is finding the form of legislation that will not be amended, that maximizes one's purpose.

Initiatives are sponsored by those who have a clear commitment and who are generally willing to pay a heavy price to secure adoption. A good proposal, from their standpoint, is one that will be enough better than the status quo to secure votes, and not so slanted in their own direction that others will feel forced to offer a rival proposal or to vote no. The costs of a rival proposal are much greater than those of offering an amendment, both in the obvious sense of cost and in that a frequent consequence of rival, complex initiatives is voter rejection of both. Thus, the first one to present an initiative has enormous leverage on others wanting a change. The lack of amendment and compromise is a grievous fault in a process in which—as we know from public opinion polls—working is extremely important, and popular reading and legal interpretation may be quite distinct.

To date, the record of the initiative has been neither as successful as its advocates hoped nor as alarming as its opponents feared. In reviewing the record through the first half of the twentieth century, careful students generally have found the device a moderately useful one. Surprisingly, few policy thrusts have been sought or achieved by such procedures. Taxes and political machinery had dominated the concern of sponsors and, on the whole, the voters had been discerning in what they backed or defeated. There was also evidence of some small educational benefit to voters in campaigns.

However, these generalizations were based upon early and less systematic and dramatic campaigns. The techniques involved in modern efforts have been forged in the California experience and the pioneering effort of the husband-wife team of Whittaker and Baxter. Built upon knowledge that few voters are concerned with detail or precision, they have sought dramatic themes for their efforts, and concentrated on arousing simple emotions to bring out the uninterested voter. The principles they employed have been utilized in a number of campaigns that have generally been characterized by extreme but effective appeals to stimuli often remote to the real issue. To most observers the results have been unfortunate most of the time. Appeals to racial animosities have carried the day; hysterical campaigns against fluoridation of drinking water have been successful in arousing fears, particularly among the elderly; police review boards and other "civilian" controls have been rejected in campaigns that have emphasized fear of crime, and not the merits or demerits of the effort to bring community control over the police; social issues such as "gay" rights, regulation of obscenity and pornography, and location of jails and halfway houses have been decided in an atmosphere of hate, and generally have repudiated previous policies regarded as "advanced."

These efforts have usually had little impact on general policies. Even in California, voters have passed only a handful of initiatives, though those had considerable influence even before the bombshell of Proposition 13, which sharply limited local government levies in the form of the property tax. (An earlier test would have limited state spending, and gave some indication of growing voter dissatisfaction with exceptionally high taxes.)

It is in the area of taxes and expenditures that the initiative has had the most consistent results. Voters generally respond favorably to a firm "no new taxes" or even a rollback. The tactic of the pro-Proposition 13 forces was blandly to assure voters there would be no curtailment of services, while opponents claimed police stations and libraries would have to be closed. Truth has been somewhere in between, which one suspects most voters must have expected.

Are such revolts effective limits on the bureaucracy? Undoubtedly they have some impact, creating a mood and providing a brake where, theoretically, few exist. Such revolts, like the threat of migration of businesses and people, or systematic defeat of "spenders," construct a weapon for voters who feel bureaucracy is expanding at the expense of the citizen. It is, however, a crude and undiscriminating weapon with no specificity of which programs to cut. It serves the purpose of gaining the attention of politicians and bureaucrats, both tough audiences. It still leaves the political and bureaucratic forces in charge of how to interpret why their attention was sought and what to do about it.

Some initiatives have, therefore, sought to develop very precise rules about taxes and finances in order to eliminate discretion. The difficulty is that when those restraints really pinch, if the mood is to circumvent the provisions, people who can concoct an evasion are easily found.

Traditional controls over American bureaucracy eroded drastically over the first six decades of the twentieth century. Recent efforts to find new devices or to resuscitate old ones have brought forward means that provide occasional brakes on the bureaucracy and transmit public attitudes, but by and large they have failed to develop strong, regular, and effective controls over the administrative agencies of the U.S. governmental system.

REFERENCES

Almond, Gabriel, and Sidney Verba. 1965. *The Civic Culture.* Boston: Little, Brown.

Branti v *Finkel.* 1980. U.S. Supreme Court no. 78–1654 (March 31).

Buchanan, James, and Gordon Tullock. 1962. *The Calculus of Consent.* Ann Arbor: University of Michigan Press.

Crossman, Richard H. 1976. *The Diaries of a Cabinet Minister.* New York: Holt, Rinehart and Winston.

Canon, Brad. 1979. "The Exclusionary Rule." 62 *Judicature* 398.

Davis, Kenneth. 1975. *Administrative Law and Government.* Second edition.

Dicey, A. V. 1959. *Introduction to the Study of Law: The Constitution.* London: Macmillan.

Elrod v *Burns.* 1976. 49 L. Ed. 2d 547.

Galanter, Mark. 1974. "Why the Haves Come out Ahead." *Law and Society Review.*

Heclo, Hugh. 1977. *A Government of Strangers.* Washington, D.C.: Brookings Institution.

Horowitz, Donald. 1975. *Courts and Social Policy.* Washington, D.C.: Brookings Institution.

Kaufman, Herbert. 1976. *Are Government Organizations Immortal?* Washington, D.C.: Brookings Institution.

———. 1960. *The Forest Ranger—A Study in Administrative Behavior.* Baltimore: Johns Hopkins University Press.

Laski, Harold. 1940. *The American Presidency.* New York: Grosset and Dunlap.

Lowi, Theodore. 1969. *The End of Liberalism.* New York: W. W. Norton.

Menzel, Johanna, ed. 1968. *The Chinese Civil Service: Career Open to Talent?* Boston: D.C. Heath.

Niskanen, William. 1971. *Bureaucracy and Representative Government.* Chicago: Aldine/Atherton.

Olsen, Mancur. 1965. *The Logic of Collective Action.* Cambridge, Mass.: Harvard University Press.

Parkinson, C. Northcote. 1957. *Parkinson's Law and Other Studies in Administration*. Boston: Houghton Mifflin.

Reedy, George. 1970. *The Twilight of the Presidency*. New York: World.

Schlesinger, Arthur, Jr. 1973. *The Imperial Presidency*. Boston: Houghton Mifflin.

Stone, Christopher. 1973. *Should Trees Have Rights*. Los Altos, Calif.: W. Kaufmann.

Tugwell, Rexford. 1960. *The Enlargement of the Presidency*. Garden City, N.Y.: Doubleday.

Weber, Max. 1968. *From Max Weber: Essays in Sociology*. Translated and edited by H. H. Gerth and C. W. Mills. New York: Oxford University Press.

White, Leonard. 1965. *The Federalists. The Jeffersonians. The Jacksonians. The Republican Era*. New York: Free Press.

5

REPRESENTATION THROUGH INTERACTION WITH THE PUBLIC

Bureaucratic representation is a subtle process that can take many forms. Bureaucracies can be representative in a social sense; they can be actively representative through the views of their employees; and they can be representative through their organizational structures and interaction with interest groups. In each of these cases, the extent of representation is related to the degree of legitimacy accorded to the bureaucracy. Legitimacy, in turn, is related to the public's compliance with administrative regulations. A final, and equally subtle, form of representation and legitimation results from public bureaucrats' interaction with the public. Such interaction can take several forms, including the face-to-face relations of bureaucrat and client, various formal mechanisms for increasing public participation in bureaucratic policy formulation and implementation, lobbying by "public-interest" groups, and the interaction brought about through litigation.

FACE-TO-FACE INTERACTION

The rise of the contemporary administrative state makes it necessary for the individual who would be a part of the society's mainstream to interact with public bureaucracies. Even in a "capitalist" society such as the United States, economically, as Charles Reich points out:

> One of the most important developments . . . during the past decade has been the emergence of government as a major source of wealth. Government is a gigantic syphon. It draws in revenue and power, and pours forth wealth: money, benefits, services, contracts, franchises, and licenses. Government has always had this function. But while in early

> times it was minor, today's distribution of largess is on a vast, imperial scale.
>
> The valuables dispensed by government take many forms, but they all share one characteristic. They are steadily taking the place of traditional forms of wealth—forms which are held as private property. Social insurance substitutes for savings; a government contract replaces a businessman's customers and goodwill. The wealth of more and more Americans depends upon a relationship to government. Increasingly, Americans live on government largess—allocated by government on its own terms, and held by recipients subject to conditions which express "the public interest." (Reich 1964, p. 733)

In more bureaucratized societies, the individual's dependence upon administrators is more acute. For instance, it has been observed that "The USSR is best understood as a large, complex bureaucracy comparable in its structure and functioning to giant corporations, armies, government agencies, and similar institutions. . . . The Soviet Union shares with giant organizations everywhere the urge to organize all human activities rationally, from professional life to consumption patterns and leisure activities" (Meyer 1965, pp. 467–68).

The individual's dependence on public bureaucracy is not confined to economic life; it is also important to political participation in the administrative state. Rinehard Bendix observes:

> Access to influence upon the administrative process is a problem of increasing importance. . . . As rights are universalized and governmental activities proliferate, it is less problematic that the uneducated citizen is barred from public employment because he cannot qualify, than that he may not possess the aptitudes and attitudes needed to obtain reasoned consideration of his case by the public authorities. (Bendix 1964, pp. 129–130)

Consequently, a substantial group of citizens of the contemporary administrative state may be hampered in participating in political and economic life unless public bureaucracies can be representative of their interests during face-to-face contacts.

The notion that representation along these lines can take place is not new. Herbert Storing contended that ". . . many civil servants have, in their particular fields, a kind of direct contact with the people and experience of the problems of government which even the politician whose ear never leaves the ground cannot possibly match" (1964, p. 152). Elihu Katz and S. N. Eisenstadt (1969, p. 236) observed how, in the context of Israeli public administration, this direct contact was turned into a representative process. In dealing with immigrants from Middle Eastern nations, who were not familiar with the impersonality of contemporary bureaucracy, public bureaucrats found it desirable to "teach a client something about his (the bureaucrat's) expectations concerning how the client role is to be played. In other words, the bureaucrat teaches the client how to be a client so that he (the bureaucrat) can go on being a bureaucrat."

Although there are serious limitations on this kind of representation, there is also substantial indirect evidence that it occurs and can become an important part of a nation's bureaucratic culture. The most pronounced limitations are twofold. First, it has been observed that some individuals have a pronounced distaste for, and reluctance to interact with, bureaucracy. Victor Thompson theorizes that

> The bureaucratic culture makes certain demands upon clients as well as upon organization employees. There are many people in our [American] society who have not been able to adjust to these demands. To them bureaucracy is a curse. They see no good in it whatsoever, but view the demands of modern organization as "red tape." This kind of behavior is external to the organization. . . . Its source will be found within the critic himself, not within the organization. (Thompson 1961, p. 170)

Thompson calls such people "bureautics," and argues that because of their "low powers of abstraction" and "need to personalize the world," the "bureautic can rarely enter successfully into an impersonal, functional, or bureaucratic relationship. The world is peopled only with friends and enemies; it does not have impartial, impersonal functionaries" (1961, p. 173). Bureautics feel powerless in relation to bureaucracy, and have "no confidence in securing justice through an impersonal, abstract system of norms and routines . . ." (1961, p. 174).

Alvin Gouldner studied the same phenomenon empirically. He found that individuals were likely to consider bureaucratic processes to be "red tape" when

> . . . the individual's ego is challenged on two counts: (1) A claim which he believes legitimate is not taken "at face value." He must either supply proof or allow it to be investigated. He is, as one remarked, "treated as a criminal"—he may feel his worth is questioned, his status impugned. (2) Not only are his claims and assertions challenged, but other details of his "private life" are investigated. The individual enters the situation on "official," "technical," or "public" business, and feels that he ends up by being investigated as a person. (Gouldner 1952, p. 413)

Gouldner also found that those who are critical of the "red tape" associated with bureaucracies are sensitive to the disparities of power, suspicious, and unable to defer gratification.

The existence of such a pattern of reaction to bureaucracy was further evidenced in a study of Israel's bureaucratic culture (Nachmias and Rosenbloom 1978). It was found that about 30 percent of the Israeli citizenry could appropriately be called "bureautic." As a group, their reactions to the Israeli national bureaucracy differed from those of other citizens. They were much more critical of the bureaucracy's role in nation-building, they felt a lower sense of efficacy in dealing with it, and, overall, they evaluated bureaucratic performance more negatively than did other citizens. Importantly, from the perspective of face-to-face contact with bureaucrats, Israeli bureautics were substantially less likely than others to use bureaucratic channels to influence the bureaucracy, preferring instead to enlist the support of outside audiences through newspapers and political parties.

Although bureautics can be found among all social classes, lower-class populations have been identified as having particularly acute difficulty in interacting with public bureaucracies. Indeed, it has been said that ". . . bureaucratic systems are the key medium through which the middle-class maintains its advantaged position vis-a-vis the lower class" (Sjoberg et al. 1966, p. 40). In part, this is because bureaucracies tend to be overrepresentative of middle-class values and interests. In part, however, it is due to the lower class's difficulty in dealing with bureaucratic structures and norms.

Four reasons for this have been identified. "First and foremost, the lower-class person simply lacks knowledge of the rules of the game. Middle-class persons generally learn how to manipulate bureaucratic rules to their advantage and even to acquire special 'favors' by working through the 'private' or 'backstage' (as opposed to the 'public') sector of the bureaucratic organization" (Sjoberg et al. 1966, pp. 46–47). Second,

> This situation is complicated by the fact that the problems the lower-class person faces are difficult to treat in isolation. The lack of steady employment, of education, and of medical care, for example, interlock in complex ways. . . . [N]o official is able to view the lower-class client as a whole person, and thus he is unable to point up to the client how he might use his strengths to overcome his weaknesses. (Sjoberg et al. 1966, p. 47)

Third, ". . . . lower-class persons typically relate to one another in a personal manner. Middle-class persons are better able to relate to others within an impersonal context" (Sjoberg et al. 1966, p. 47). Finally, these elements interact with each other, making ". . . it more difficult for a lower-class person to acquire knowledge of how the system operates. It is not surprising that under these circumstances members of the lower-class often experience a sense of powerlessness or alienation" (Sjoberg et al. 1966, p. 48).

The relative inability of members of the lower class to use public bureaucracies effectively has been identified as a major difficulty in the implementation of public policies in some political communities. Governmental programs to help the poor, for example, often fall far short of their goals. Consequently, some attention has been paid to remedying this situation, including emphasis on participation by the lower class in administrative policy formulation and implementation.

Despite these important limitations on bureaucratic representation through interaction with the public, there is much indirect evidence that such representation does occur. It takes place fundamentally because some bureaucrats depart from the Weberian model of strict impersonality, and identify with their clients. Thus, systematic empirical research has found the existence of a type of public administrator who can be appropriately referred to as a "service bureaucrat." Leonard Reissman describes the "service bureaucrat" as follows:

> He is oriented in terms of the bureaucratic structure, but seeks recognition for the job he does from a group outside of it. He entered civil service primarily to realize certain personally-held goals which center about rendering service to a certain group. The bureaucracy offers a frame-work through which he can best function and his task is one of utilizing that mechanism to achieve his goals. (1949, pp. 308–09)

A study of Israel's bureaucratic culture further confirmed the existence of this type and found that, as a group, "service bureaucrats" were frustrated by the bureaucracy's shortcomings in rendering service to the community (Nachmias and Rosenbloom 1978).

Case studies of bureaucratic operations also indicate that bureaucrats sometimes identify with individuals who constitute their clientele. Katz and Eisenstadt's study of Middle Eastern immigrants in Israel has already been mentioned. Examples of prison guards identifying with prisoners, teachers with students, and social workers with the poor are not uncommon. However, it is probably also true that "street level bureaucrats"—bureaucrats who interact constantly with the public, have a large measure of independence on the job, and have an extensive potential impact on the individuals with whom they deal—tend to adopt a hostile attitude toward their clientele, especially when the latter is involuntarily in that relationship (Lipsky 1976, p. 135). Teachers, police officers, and housing inspectors have been found to fall into this pattern (Nivola 1979, p. 61). It should be remembered, however, that, as Lipsky argues, "It may not be that street-level bureaucracies are *generally* unresponsive, as is sometimes claimed. Rather they have been responsive in the past to constellations of reference groups that have excluded a significant portion of the population with whom they regularly deal" (Lipsky 1976, p. 144).

If public bureaucrats identify with or otherwise represent their clients in face-to-face interactions, the public should be more favorable in its evaluation of concrete interactions with public administrators than in their general view of bureaucracy. This is especially true where the overall societal attitude is not supportive of bureaucracy, as is so frequently the case. Daniel Katz and associates found much evidence in support of this proposition in the United States:

> . . . when specific experiences are compared with such general evaluations, one finds that people's specific experiences are more positive than their general attitudes. For example, 80 percent of respondents felt that they received fair treatment in their contact with government agencies, but only 42 percent rated government offices in general as being fair. There seems to be a clear separation of generalized attitudes from the specific attitudes derived from an individual's direct experiences.
>
> . . .
>
> These seeming inconsistencies can be reconciled if we assume that people are characterized by cognitive complexity rather than cognitive consistency and that we have tapped two modes of response: the ideological and the pragmatic. Thus general evaluations of bureaucracy may tap the ideological level, and the specific evaluations of experiences may tap the pragmatic level. (1975, pp. 185–87)

Negative experiences with bureaucracy, by contrast, do seem to lower an individual's general evaluation of bureaucracy. Thus, "Evaluation of specific experiences transfers to the general level when the evaluation is negative, but not when it is positive" (Katz et al. 1975, p. 186).

These findings point to the complexity of bureaucratic representativeness. It is apparent that in the United States, public bureaucracies seem unable to improve their image through satisfactory face-to-face interaction, but may damage it through unsatisfactory contacts. To the extent that representation, in the sense of identifying with a client, teaching a client how to interact effectively with bureaucracy, and helping a client, does not take place, support for public bureaucracy, and presumably its legitimacy, will suffer. Thus, the relationship between representation and legitimacy in face-to-face contacts may be asymmetrical; a decrease in representativeness begets a decrease in legitimacy, but increasing representation seems not to cause an increase in legitimacy. Commenting on the implications of their findings, Katz and associates observe:

> Somehow people need to become more involved in policy formulation if they are to have an understanding of program objectives and their implementations. How to encourage such involvement has long been recognized as a problem critical to the survival of political democracy. Various mechanisms have been suggested, and even put into practice, to

> bridge the gap between people's limited specific experiences with government and their knowledge of public policies. We have witnessed such attempts as the Town Meeting of the Air, local forums for the discussion of issues, more systematic communication between elected representatives and their electorates, some granting of local autonomy in the administration of national programs, and special organizations to involve citizens in common problems. . . . Future studies of public bureaucracy should explore progress toward citizen involvement, the efficacy of different mechanisms of involvement, and the conditions which facilitate their development. (1975, p. 189)

Of all the mechanisms for such involvement, "citizen participation" has been the most ambitious.

INDIVIDUAL PARTICIPATION

The bureaucratization of political life militates against meaningful individual participation in governance. Citizen participation in democratic nations having well-developed administrative components tends to center on voting and elections. However, as pointed out in chapter 1, bureaucratization brings with it a decline in the ability of elected officials to control the course of government. Thus, even where elections convey mandates, it is difficult to translate these mandates into concrete actions concerning bureaucratic implementation or nonimplementation. Moreover, as Morris Fiorina (1977) and R. Douglas Arnold (1979) argue, in the United States the rise of the federal bureaucracy and the nature of bureaucratic politics have a tendency to reduce the vitality of electoral competition and to favor the reelection of incumbents. In such a system a majority of the electorate may actually agree that elected leaders have lost control of government to public bureaucrats, as in the United States (Harris 1973). To the extent that one believes this is a systemic problem, there is little reason to attempt to elect new officials. Consequently, it should not be surprising that a majority or near-majority of citizens in a bureaucratized polity may abstain from voting. Indeed, in the United States nonvoters are much more likely than voters to believe that the political system needs more fundamental change than can be brought about through the ballot box (*New York Times* 1976, p. 33). The decline in citizen participation in bureaucratized democratic polities has generally been considered a major political problem.

Nonparticipatory democracy is often thought to contain two crucial weaknesses. First, it is considered by some to be potentially highly unstable. Since the system operates on a relatively low level of participation, increased participation, which is always a possibility, may bring about radical changes. Depending upon the values of typical nonparticipants, these changes may not stress a commitment to democracy. For instance, with reference to the United States, it has been argued that "Political apathy and nonparticipation among the masses contribute to the survival of democracy. Fortunately for democracy, the anti-democratic masses are generally more apathetic than elites. Only an unusual demagogue or counter-elite can arouse the masses from their apathy and create a threat to the established system" (Dye and Zeigler 1975, p. 184). But, should nonparticipants decide to exercise their rights to participate in politics, the consequences for democracy could be disastrous: "The masses are less committed to democratic rules of the game than elites and more likely to go outside these rules to engage in violence. Mass activism tends to be undemocratic, unstable, and frequently violent" (Dye and Zeigler 1975, p. 183). To the extent that these conditions prevail, political elites can thrive only in the presence of mass apathy. However, nonparticipation is generally thought to be a cause of antidemocratic attitudes. Consequently, democratic governance based upon mass apathy has a built-in cycle promoting instability.

Second, nonparticipation reduces the capacity of a political system to represent its citizenry. It has been argued by some that nonparticipation in elections is not a severe problem because there is little difference between voters' and nonvoters' views on most policy matters (as opposed to faith in the rules of the democratic game). However, even voters are likely to be misrepresented if the extent of their participation in political life is confined to the act of casting ballots. For instance, in the United States it was found that members of the House of Representatives substantially misperceive their constituencies' attitudes and that their legislative votes are not good reflections of their constituents' preferences (Miller and Stokes 1963). In large part this is the case because communication between congressmen and their constituents is distorted. Only about 15 percent of the population has ever written a letter to a congressman, and approximately 3 percent of the population writes two-thirds of all congressional mail (Dye and Zeigler 1975, p. 328). There is also a tendency for congressmen to hear most often from those who agree with them, and for these officials to assign greater weight to the opinions of newspapers and economic and social leaders than to those of ordinary citizens.

It is apparent that nonparticipation poses a threat to democratic political systems. By contrast, participation is often viewed as an intrinsically positive good. Classical political philosophers have sometimes valued participation highly. Jean-Jacques Rousseau, for example, argued that participation was desirable for three primary reasons. First, it enhances freedom by providing every participant with some measure of control over his/her life. Where all participate equally, none is the master of others. Second, participation promotes the rule of law by depersonalizing government and freeing every member of the political community from absolute dependence upon the will of another. Third, participation is seen as promoting the integration of individual and community. Through participation each individual becomes part of a larger collective unit in both an objective and a subjective sense. This line of thought was also reflected in the work of John Stuart Mill, who stressed the educative benefits of participation.

Today arguments in favor of greater participation in political life are cast in related, but nevertheless distinct, forms. At the base of many of these arguments is the view that bureaucratization reduces participation, and that consequently bureaucracy must be modified to allow more meaningful participation if democratic government and individuals' well-being are to be promoted. These views can be summarized as follows:

Participation promotes individual growth. It plays an educative role by making participants more cognizant of the needs and values of others, and of the complexity of political questions. Through participation one can clarify one's own values as well as learn to appreciate those of others. Individual growth is also promoted through a greater sense of political efficacy that may be associated with participation. Participation may also have some therapeutic value in reducing alienation and a sense of anomie.

Reduction of alienation. Bureaucratic government, as noted in the first part of this chapter, can be alienating. Individuals may feel that they are powerless to control or even influence their environment. They may feel that the political system fails to represent their interests and welfare. A pronounced gap between a dominant political philosophy stressing democracy and a government based on bureaucracy may generate deep political cynicism. Participation, it is often argued, can help overcome these feelings by providing a greater measure of influence, representation, and congruence between theory and practice.

Political integration through individual change. Participation, it is sometimes argued, can promote the creation of a political community based upon individual consent. In some societies, such as the United States, where the political system is based to a large extent on organized conflict, this is a revolutionary idea. Competitive, conflictual organizations are seen as promoting competitive, conflictual individuals (Thayer 1973). Participatory organizations, by contrast, may produce participative, cooperative individuals. Such individuals will be better equipped to develop a consensual political community, as opposed to one based on an ever-shifting balance of power among competing, hostile groups.

The assertion of new demands. As noted above, nonparticipation is related to misrepresentation. Those who do not participate may be misrepresented because the political system is unaware of their demands. This is not solely a question of "apathy," because even nonapathetic individuals may not believe that there are any significant channels for participation open to them. Thus, Theodore Lowi (1972), a leading American political scientist, has argued that "abstentionism" in elections would be a useful mechanism for political reform that cannot be brought about through participation. By contrast, meaningful participation would allow individuals to raise new demands. These demands can provide valuable perspectives on public policy, since it is often the ordinary person who can best judge where government programs are not functioning well.

Ideological "rehabilitation" of the individual. Participation, it is argued, can promote democracy on an ideological level as well. The central notion here is that the rise of bureaucracy and contemporary social science has damaged the belief that the individual has a valuable role to play in political life. For example, some political scientists have argued that, as voters, individual citizens can no longer satisfy the needs of democratic government. Through participation not only could the individual be revitalized politically, but his/her reputation could be enhanced accordingly. Government could then be reconceptualized as a means of reflecting individual preferences.

Legitimacy and compliance. A final argument in favor of greater individual participation in political life is that such participation promotes governmental legitimacy, which increases compliance with offiicial policies and directives. The central idea here is that if citizens feel that they have a significant input in policy, they will be more apt to comply with governmental decisions. Participation promotes a sense of proprietorship, even for those who oppose the final policy direction chosen.

Overall, it is reasonable to conclude that

> Whether one finds these arguments persuasive, there is little doubt that, contemporary politics . . . has been marked by a revolution seeking more direct participation by citizens in policy-making. In contrast to the tendency for institutions to represent organized interests, this resurgence of participatory democracy seeks direct access to decision centers and involvement in decision-making regardless of any connections or affiliations that the participants might have with organized interests. In fact, the participation movement has stressed representation of unorganized publics that have been given only casual concern in policy arenas. (Morrow 1975, pp. 189–90)

This has been true despite anti-participatory arguments stressing problems associated with the tyranny of the majority; the need for expertise in public policy decisions; the needs of would-be nonparticipants for freedom, privacy, and solitude; the impossibility of participation in crisis situations; and the time-consuming nature of participation. Thus, major experiments have been undertaken to incorporate direct citizen participation in bureaucratic government, in an effort to reduce the incompatibility between democracy and bureaucracy while enhancing the capacity of both. The United States presents a good illustration.

It should be remembered that in the United States, citizen participation in public administration is not a new phenomenon. Advisory groups, as pointed out in chapter 3, have been a major aspect of national bureaucratic politics for some time, and are especially well developed in some departments, such as Agriculture. Citizens' committees also have long been involved in actual governing, as in the case of school boards and other local governmental boards. William Morrow observes:

> Citizen's committees have had more policy impact in situations where they are afforded direct policy-making authority. Such a practice is rooted deeply in public school government in the United States. This practice has insured local control in all but the largest cities, and the result has been one of encouraging wide diversities in teacher qualifications, curriculum, and extracurricular activities. In cases where city-wide school boards have nearly plenary authority, attempts have been made to decentralize school administration, to grant local school boards more policy authority. (1975, p. 192)

These arrangements for participation, however, tend to result in the election and dominance of local elites, thereby "making the operation less than the ideal envisioned by theorists" (Morrow 1975, p. 192). Consequently, these types of participation have not generally been considered an effective mechanism for representing the mass of citizens in a bureaucratic age.

A far more controversial and potentially more effective mechanism of promoting citizen participation in bureaucratic government was attempted by the Economic Opportunity Act of 1964 and the Model Cities Act of 1966. The Economic Opportunity Act was the main vehicle for fighting the "War on Poverty." It provided for the funding of community action programs to be administered by community action agencies. The latter could be public or not-for-profit private, but could not be political parties. A year after the act was passed, the Office of Economic Opportunity, noting that the poor had not yet organized, sought to organize them through administrative action. It issued guidelines for the formation of the community action agencies, seeking tripartite participation by public officials, representatives of private social service agencies, and representatives of the poor. The latter were to be elected by the poor themselves, who in this and other ways were supposed to have "maximum feasible participation" in the development, conduct, and administration of community action programs.

Participation of the poor along these lines, however, may not have been anticipated by those who wrote the statute (Moynihan 1970, p. 87). Emphasis upon "maximum feasible participation" was closer to a bureaucratic ideology, developed to serve the needs of a particular agency, much as the participatory activities of the Agricultural Extension Service and the organization of the American Farm Bureau Federation by the Department of Agriculture provide examples of an earlier effort to generate support for an agency's desired programs. In any event, the anticipated participation was much criticized as an inapplicable "middle class notion":

> In a classic case of elitist condescension and the perversion of democracy by some of its most vocal advocates, the middle class decided that what the lower class needed was participation, and the maximum feasible amount of it to boot. They needed not money, but identity; not jobs, but self-respect; not decent homes, but a sense of community; and finally, not better schools with more funds to make education effective, but control over their destiny. (Norman Hill, quoted in Moynihan 1970, p. xxi)

Not surprisingly, the poor chose not to participate. As Daniel Patrick Moynihan observes:

> It may be that the poor are never "ready" to assume power in an advanced society: the exercise of power in an effective manner is an ability acquired through apprenticeship and seasoning. Thrust on an individual or a group, the results are often painful to observe, and when what in fact is conveyed is not power, but a kind of play-acting at power, the results can be absurd. The device of holding elections among the poor to choose representatives for the CAP governing boards made the program look absurd. The turnouts in effect declared that the poor weren't interested: in Philadelphia 2.7 per cent; Los Angeles 0.7 per cent; Boston 2.4 per cent; Cleveland 4.2 per cent; Kansas City, Mo. 5.0 per cent. Smaller communities sometimes got larger turnouts, but never anything nearly approaching that of a listless off-year election. (If theory held the poor to be apathetic, why proceed as if this were not so? . . .). (1970, pp. 136–37)

Experiences under the Model Cities program were similar. The program's purpose was to pump money into deteriorating urban neighborhoods, and "wide-spread citizen participation" was sought in the administrative machinery (Community Action Agencies) to be used to implement this end. Again, the poor did not participate in numbers approaching administrative expectations. Moreover, in some cases where such participation was substantial, the local and federal governments sought to reduce the power of Community Action Agencies by preventing them from playing an initiatory role.

On the basis of these events, it would not be difficult to conclude that mass participation in public administration is not feasible, at least in a political culture like that of the United States. Yet, it is possible to argue that the War on Poverty and Model Cities programs did not provide a fair test. Urban riots, the Vietnam War, and Richard Nixon's election to the presidency in 1968 drastically changed the U.S. political constellation. Moreover, the experiments did not have much time to run their course, and in the view of some, participation along these lines is still a viable and desirable means of strengthening representation in a bureaucratized government. Robert Aleshire is a proponent of this view:

> The simple conclusion of a comparison of the costs and benefits of participation of the poor in the Community Action and Model Cities Programs is that democracy would not and will not survive without such participation; that a basic reallocation and decentralization of power is required; and that the necessities as well as the benefits outweight [*sic*] the costs, some of which are produced by the fact that the system itself is not designed to encourage or facilitate participation. (Aleshire 1972, p. 442)

The apparent failure of these participatory programs should not divert attention from the extent to which participation generally can convey legitimacy to bureaucratic agencies, if not make them representative. It may be that the participatory device is most effective in its application to certain social classes and economic interests. Even so, it has been observed that citizen participation serves some bureaucratic needs, including those of building clientele. For instance, it has been said that "Participation in a cooperative sense has thus led in most cases to the acknowledgement [*sic*] and approval of bureaucratic activities that may have benefited the urban renewal program's clientele group—the city businessmen—but not the program's target—the poor living in the central city" (Eliot Kraus, quoted in Morrow 1975, p. 198).

Other cases of participation benefiting bureaucratic agencies include the pacification of clientele and citizens' groups, the ability to abdicate authority in controversial areas or in those in which the problems facing an agency are insoluble, and the co-optation of various groups, including members of the poor in the Model Cities and War on Poverty programs who ". . . when chosen to represent the poor, are pleased to be accepted by middle-class leadership and function with docility" (Morrow 1975, p. 200).

Consequently, participation in bureaucratic governance presents a considerable dilemma. Where participation is confined to elites or effectively represents their interests, as is generally the case with advisory committees, it can be an effective device for promoting individuals' interests. Bureaucracy in this context does tend to be highly representative and to have a good deal of legitimacy, at least among its clientele. In such instances, participation can serve both the needs of interest groups and those of the bureaucratic agency. However, when participation is extended to nonelites, it may be more likely to serve the interests of the bureaucratic agency than those of any given target group. An agency can derive the benefits of pacification and co-optation along with the legitimation they are likely to bestow. However, when this takes place, the agency cannot be said to perform a representational function, except in a symbolic sense. Thus, we are still left with the question of the means by which bureaucratic agencies can be representative of individual citizens through interaction with them. Public-interest groups present another possibility.

"PUBLIC-INTEREST" GROUPS

It has already been observed that public bureaucracies can be highly representative of special-interest groups. Indeed, such representation may be incorporated into the structure and process of public administration, as in the United States and much of Europe. Thus, the question arises whether "public-interest" groups can also play a representative role in bureaucratic government, and thereby act as an antidote to the decline of public participation in bureaucratized democratic political communities. This question is especially crucial for members of the middle class, who may well find themselves largely excluded from both the participatory mechanisms afforded the poor and those available to the large corporate interests.

At the outset it is necessary to address the issue of whether the distinction between traditional interest groups and "public-interest" groups is tenable. Although it is undeniable that traditional interest groups may work for the common good, what appears to distinguish them from public-interest groups is the extent to which their members seek to benefit directly and selectively from the promotion of their material interests. Jeffrey Berry defines a public-interest group as "one that seeks a collective good, the achievement of which will not selectively and materially benefit the membership or activists of the organization" (quoted in Ornstein and Elder 1978, p. 46). Nevertheless, the line between traditional and public-interest groups may sometimes be vague.

In any event, political analysts have employed the distinction and have argued that the recent rise of public-interest groups in nations such as the United States has created a new force in politics. As Andrew McFarland (1980, pp. 132, 133) observes, "What is new is the amount of influence that public interest groups have acquired in a relatively short time. . . In the last few years, public interest groups, and the type of public opinion that they express, have been more influential in American politics than at any time since the entry of the United States into the First World War ended the so-called Progressive Era." Table 5.1 presents some examples of public-interest groups, their founding dates, and approximate membership.

In the United States the membership of public-interest groups appears to be overwhelmingly middle-class. With reference to Common Cause it has been found that

> From the beginning . . . fifteen-dollar subscribers tended to be upper-middle-class whites, well educated, middle-aged, financially secure, with a disproportionate number of Northeastern seaboard and Pacific coast residents. . . . A careful study of the Massachusetts members in 1974 . . . indicated a typical family income of about twenty thousand dollars per year. (McFarland 1978, p. 320)

Not only are these supporters of public-interest groups middle-class, as one might suspect, but they are given to participation in politics and may be among those segments of society most frustrated by the bureaucratization of political life:

> Available evidence indicates that supporters of public interest groups generally fall into the 11 percent of the public designated as "complete activists." . . . [A] majority of the supporters of Common Cause in Massachusetts were found to be active in partisan politics. Contribution

TABLE 5.1: Examples of Public-Interest Groups

Organization	Year Founded	Staff	Membership
Consumers Union of the United States	1936	410	2,300,000
Common Cause	1970	85	225,000
People's Lobby	1968	*	20,000
Consumer Federation of America	1967	10	220 consumer associations
League of Women Voters	1920	55	125,000
American Civil Liberties Union	1920	330	200,000
Sierra Club	Before 1961	130	183,000
Water Pollution Control Federation	1928	48	30,000

*Data unavailable.

Source: Margaret Fisk, ed., *Encyclopedia of Associations*, 15th ed. (Detroit: Gale Research, 1977).

> to one or more public interest groups—multiple contributions are a frequent phenomenon—indicate [*Sic*] a particularly high psychological involvement in politics, unless the contribution is to one of those groups who repay their members with financial savings, such as Consumers Union. It seems safe to say that the majority of contributors to Common Cause, Nader, and the environmentalist movement also vote, occasionally try to persuade a friend to vote for a favorite candidate, and communicate with a government official about some matter. (McFarland 1980, p. 134)

Although it cannot be pinpointed in a systematic fashion, there appears to be little doubt that the rise of public-interest groups is related to the bureaucratization of political life. The rise of the administrative state reduces the significance of the individual's vote in its relation to the resolution of political issues, and also diminishes the power of elected officials. At the same time, bureaucratization may enhance the power of traditional interest groups or of special interests that may be given direct representation through bureaucratic structures. Therefore, to the extent that political activists seek to promote the common good, as they see it, in a bureaucratic age they must act through the bureaucracy. This accounts for one of the seeming peculiarities of public-interest groups: that many of their proposals are pro-bureaucratic in nature. Common Cause and the various Nader operations present clear examples.

Common Cause conceives its organizational mission to be "representing the people against the special interests" (McFarland 1978, p. 318). In making this mission operational, the organization developed a consensus that "'structure and process' reforms are the number one priority" (McFarland 1978, p. 319). Such reforms can affect any of the institutions of government, but as defined by Common Cause they heavily involve bureaucracy. For example, Common Cause's greatest victory was perhaps the enactment of the Campaign Reform Act of 1974. The major purpose of the act is to reduce the dependence of candidates for federal elective office on large contributions by wealthy individuals and special-interest groups. It establishes limits on campaign contributions and a system of matching federal funds for presidential candidates.

The act, however, is enforced by the Federal Elections Commission (FEC), which serves as a regulatory agency for elections. Like other regulatory commissions, its activity is highly bureaucratic. In fact, the FEC threatens to bureaucratize elections themselves. Thus, its reporting requirements add to the costs and staff of election campaigns, and can be characterized as "red tape." In addition, the FEC has issued a number of rulings on such matters as whether trips by an incumbent president should be considered campaign activities. Overall, there can be no doubt that regulation in this area, as in others, has increased formalization and other bureaucratic attributes.

Another example of Common Cause's attempt to use the bureaucracy concerns its activities in the Department of the Interior. As McFarland (1978, p. 321) notes, ". . . executive lobbying activities have emphasized 'accountability' in the Interior Department by forcing prospective Interior secretaries to publicly commit themselves to proenvironment policies during confirmation hearings and by getting Interior executives to 'log' contacts with extraagency people as an index to special interest power."

Ralph Nader's various public-interest group activities also have occasionally concentrated on bureaucracy. In fact, Nader has sometimes been a strong advocate of increased regulatory power for public bureaucracies. He has even criticized agencies for not using their powers to the hilt. Thus, upon conclusion of a study of the U.S. Civil Service Commission (CSC), he stated: "Unlike some other Federal programs, there is no doubt whatsoever about the adequacy of the Commission's authority to do its job. It has ample authority, leverage, and disciplinary power vis-a-vis other Federal agencies, but it has been reluctant to use these tools" (*New York Times* 1972). Robert Vaughn, who was a major participant in Nader's study of the CSC, concluded that the shortcomings of that agency could be partly remedied with structural reforms. He specifically avoided the anti-bureaucratic approach; "Some critics call for the abolition of the Civil Service Commission, but it would be far better for citizens to call for the creation of a true Civil Service Commission instead" (1975, p. 153).

Public-interest groups seek to use bureaucratic power, structure, and process to promote their vision of the common good. As in the cases noted above, this may lead them to call for further bureaucratization and a greater use of bureaucratic authority, or they may seek to gain a measure of control over the selection of political executives. These groups have also sought to make the use of bureaucratic authority more representative by calling for "sunshine" and "sunset" legislation. The former could allow outsiders to monitor bureaucratic policymaking and could enhance their ability to oppose bureaucratic decisions. The latter could tend to prevent bureaucratic intransigence and entrenchment (see chapter 4).

These approaches tend to be the more glamorous ways in which public-interest groups have sought to make the exercise of bureaucratic power responsive to their constituents. A more routine approach has been to monitor the promulgation of bureaucratic rules and to participate in their development. In the United States, the Administrative Procedure Act (1946, as amended) requires agencies to publish notice of proposed changes in rules and ". . . the agency shall give interested persons an opportunity to participate in the rule making through submission of written data, views, or arguments with or without opportunity for oral presentation. After consideration of the relevant matter presented, the agency shall incorporate in the rules adopted a concise general statement of their basis and purpose" (sec. 4 [b]). Statutes such as the Freedom of

Information Act (1966) and the National Environmental Policy Act (1970, called "of 1969") further facilitate the ability of public (and traditional) interest groups to keep abreast of bureaucratic policymaking by requiring the release of various kinds of information, including the anticipated environmental impacts of agencies' regulations.

It is precisely by monitoring, challenging, and participating in the adoption of agency policy formulation through such devices that public-interest groups can routinely bring their vision of the common good to bear upon policymaking. It is also in this arena that the information and values represented by traditional interest groups can be most effectively counteracted. From this perspective public-interest groups can take advantage of established bureaucratic processes designed to provide representation. And, to the extent that such groups actually do represent the "public," they can use these processes to make public bureaucracy more representative generally. In this sense, these groups simply supply the other half of the equation for interest-group representation.

Thus, public-interest groups in a bureaucratic system such as exists in the United States can be effective proponents of their vision of the public interest. To the extent that they faithfully represent either the desires or the interests of their members, they can make public bureaucracy more representative of another segment of the political community—in this case, the politically active middle class. But to what extent can such groups be representative of their membership? Although the information remains sketchy, it does appear that when they are based on voluntary contributions, public-interest groups can be potentially solicitous of their memberships' preferences. With reference to Common Cause, McFarland observes:

> Fighting to keep members meant an increased concern to please members. In the period of declining membership, the staff and board did not want to irritate sizable numbers of members by lobbying for too many controversial issues. Questionnaires sent to members about their preferences about Common Cause issues were watched carefully. (Such questionnaires were a matter of great concern in the founding period of the organization, but in the 1972–74 period, as Common Cause settled into its antiwar and good government issues, these questionnaires were treated in a somewhat perfunctory manner by the staff.). . . It is clear from the construction of [a] sample survey, and from the attention which was paid to the results, that CC leadership really cared what their membership thought about tax reform, gun control, nuclear power plants, and military spending—issues on which membership opinion appeared to be split, at least in comparison to the virtual unanimity on "structure and process" reform issues. John Gardener commented at a governing board meeting in April 1976: "we should have done this years ago. . . ." (1978, pp. 325–26)

The quest for consensus, however, limits the issues upon which the organization can take a forceful stand. Some of the public interest research groups have sought to avoid direct dependence on individual contributions by establishing "check-off" arrangements on college campuses, and in New York, unsuccessfully attempted to obtain funds through the establishment of a "check off" contribution system attached to utility users' bills.

Overall, then, it appears that, depending upon the nature of prevailing bureaucratic processes, public-interest groups can play a substantial role in making public bureaucracies cognizant, and even representative, of their members' desires or interests. Even if their membership is not representative of the population at large, another dimension is thereby added to representative bureaucracy. To the extent that public-interest groups actually represent the public, the interest-group process, which has long afforded representation to special interests, can be used to make public bureaucracies responsive to the population generally.

LITIGATION

Litigation is the final type of bureaucratic interaction with the public to be addressed. In the United States it is possible for individual citizens to sue public bureaucrats personally for civil damages for abuses of their legal or constitutional rights. It is also possible to sue municipalities for similar breaches. Such litigation can be considered "interaction" because it places the individual's challenge to the public bureaucrat and the latter's response virtually on a face-to-face basis in the same forum. Importantly, suits against public bureaucrats as individuals are a mechanism by which the citizen can hold the agents of the administrative state directly accountable for unconstitutional transgressions. As such, even the potential of such suits being brought can serve as a deterrent that forces public bureaucrats always to remain fully cognizant and supportive of the individual citizen's rights. This requires the public bureaucrat to be representative, in the sense of seeking to afford the individual citizen the full constitutional protections to which he/she is entitled. Hence, it is a kind of legal representation in which the bureaucrat acts to protect an individual's rights, and perhaps also to inform the individual of those rights.

In the United States the erosion of public administrators' official immunity from civil suits for damages is a recent and far-reaching development. Though found nowhere in the Constitution, in 1896 the Supreme Court first created such an immunity, based on the rationale that:

> In exercising the functions of his office the head of an Executive Department, keeping within the limits of his authority, should not be under an apprehension that the motives that control his official conduct may, at any time, become the subject of inquiry in a civil suit for damages. It would seriously cripple the proper and effective administration of public affairs as entrusted to the executive branch of the government, if he were subject to any such restraint. (*Spalding* v *Vilas* 1896, p. 498)

Department heads, of course, could be held accountable by the president, and consequently the ruling was not a drastic blow to governmental accountability. However, in *Barr* v *Matteo* (1959) the same principle was extended to career bureaucrats, who were afforded both legal and some measure of constitutional protection against dismissal. A plurality of the Supreme Court now subscribed to the premise that

> To be sure, the occasions upon which the acts of the head of a department will be protected by the privilege are doubtless far greater than in the case of an officer with less sweeping functions. But it is because the higher the post, the broader the range of responsibilities and duties, and the wider the scope of discretion it entails. It is not the title of his office but the duties with which the particular officer sought to be made to respond in damages is entrusted—the relation of the act complained of to "matters committed by law to his control or supervision". . . which must provide the guide in delineating the scope of the rule which clothes the official acts of the executive officer with immunity from civil defamation suits." (*Barr* v *Matteo* 1959, pp. 573–74)

On the basis of this reasoning, a host of public administrators were afforded immunity, including an acting director of the Office of Rent Stabilization (in *Barr* v *Matteo* 1959), a deputy U.S. marshal, a district director and a collection officer of the Internal Revenue Service, a claims representative of the Department of Health, Education and Welfare, and a secret service agent (Davis 1972, p. 487).

In the two decades following *Barr* v *Matteo*, the Supreme Court recognized the potential consequences of absolute official immunity for public administrators, and sought to redress the citizen's right to hold the administrative state accountable for its actions. That the Court was reacting precisely to the consequences of the rise of the administrative state is suggested by Justice William Brennan's question in *Barr* v *Matteo*: "Where does healthy administrative frankness and boldness shade into bureaucratic tyranny?" (1959, p. 590). Ultimately, the Supreme Court afforded the citizen-antagonist of the administrative state a new avenue for challenging its alleged unconstitutional abuses.

The standard of public administrators' official immunity was adjusted to protect the citizenry of the administrative state. Rather than an absolute immunity, or even an immunity based on traditional concepts of good faith or the reasonableness of an administrator's actions at the time they were taken, the Supreme Court has opted for a standard that requires public administrators to be fully cognizant of the constitutional rights of the individuals affected by their actions. In the context of school board members, this standard was articulated as follows:

> The official himself must be acting sincerely and with a belief that he is doing right, but an act violating a student's constitutional rights can be no more justified by ignorance or disregard of settled, indisputable law on the part of one entrusted with supervision of students' daily lives than by the presence of actual malice.
>
> . . .
>
> [A] school board member is not immune from liability for damages . . . if he knew or reasonably should have known that the action he took within his sphere of official responsibility would violate the constitutional rights of the students affected, or if he took the action with the malicious intention to cause a deprivation of constitutional rights or other injury to the student. (*Wood* v *Strickland* 1975, pp. 321, 322)

Although there might be some rationale for limiting this standard to situations involving schoolchildren or extending it only to institutionalized populations, in *Butz* v *Economou* (1978) the Supreme Court treated it as the proper standard of immunity for public administrators generally. However, in that case the Court created an absolute immunity for public administrators exercising adjudicatory functions, such as hearing examiners, administrative law judges, and agency attorneys exercising "prosecutorial" functions. This limitation on the ability of the citizen-antagonist to hold the agents of the administrative state accountable was considered by the Supreme Court to follow directly from the absolute immunity enjoyed by judges and public prosecutors generally.

Civil suits for damages by citizen-antagonists of the administrative state against state and local officials for breach of constitutional rights are authorized by 42 USC 1983. Where such rights are abridged pursuant to the policy of a political subdivision, it is now possible to sue the subdivision directly, and the latter can no longer raise a "qualified good faith immunity" (*Monell* v *New York City* 1978; *Owen* v *City of Independence* 1980). In establishing this principle, the administrative state was very much on the Supreme Court's mind:

> The knowledge that a municipality will be liable for all of its injurious conduct, whether committed in good faith or not, should create an incentive for officials who may harbor doubts about the lawfulness of their intended actions to err on the side of protecting citizens' constitutional rights. (*Owen* v *City of Independence* 1980, p. B1768).

In politically related developments, the Supreme Court created a new right for the citizen-antagonist to sue federal administrators for breaches of constitutional rights, even in the absence of a statute explicitly authorizing such suits.

This right was first created for citizen-antagonists whose Fourth Amendment rights had been violated. In *Bivens* v *Six Unknown Named Federal Narcotics Agents* (1971), the Supreme Court reasoned that expecting an individual whose Fourth Amendment rights were violated by federal agents to seek to recover by bringing an action in tort under state law, the traditional remedy, was unrealistic in the contemporary administrative state:

> Respondents seek to treat the relationship between a citizen and a federal agent unconstitutionally exercising his authority as no different from the relationship between two private citizens. In so doing, they ignore the fact that power, once granted, does not disappear like a magic gift when it is wrongfully used. An agent acting—albeit unconstitutionally—in the name of the United States possesses far greater capacity for harm than an individual trespasser exercising no authority other than his own. (p. 392)

The possibility that such suits would be confined to Fourth Amendment rights was foreclosed by their authorization for breaches of the Fifth Amendment's equal protection aspects (*Davis* v *Passman* 1979) and for violations of the Eighth Amendment's prohibition against cruel and unusual punishment (*Carlson* v *Green* 1980). Suits of this nature permit the citizen-antagonist to have a jury trial and to seek punitive damages. Consequently, as the Supreme Court pointed out in *Carlson* v *Green* (1980, p. B2033), ". . . the Bivens remedy, in addition to compensating victims, serves a deterrent purpose" that should reduce abuses of individuals' constitutional rights by administrative officials. Moreover, in *Butz* v *Economou* the Court suggested that federal officials' immunity in such cases would be the same as that of state and local officials in 42 suits under U.S. Code section 1983 because "the 'constitutional design' would be stood on its head if federal officials did not face at least the same liability as state officials guilty of the same constitutional transgression" (*Carlson* v *Green* 1980, p. B2034, interpreting *Butz* v *Economou* 1978).

In practice, the erosion of public administrators' official immunity can promote a kind of bureaucratic representation. It provides the citizenry with a means of holding administrators accountable for breaches of their constitutional rights. But since "constitutional law," as Justice Lewis Powell observes, is "what the courts say it is . . ." (*Owen* v *City of Independence* 1980, p. B1787), the liability of administrators also encourages them to keep abreast of changing constitutional standards and interpretations. Consequently, judicial decisions concerning individual rights must be integrated into administrative decisionmaking and action if administrators hope to minimize suits and judgments for damages. This requires the public bureaucrat to protect the individual's rights in the fashion of a legal representative, even where the individual is ignorant of those rights or fails to assert them.

CONCLUSION: BUREAUCRACY AND THE PUBLIC

Although the rise of the administrative state militates against the individual citizen's ability to participate in governance in democratic political communities, bureaucracy can nevertheless afford some new avenues of representation and participation. Most obvious is the representation that comes about through face-to-face interaction between bureaucrat and client. As Seymour Lipset (1952) pointed out, public bureaucrats are part of a larger social structure and culture. They reflect the norms of bureaucracy, as Weber observed. However, these norms are tempered by others stemming from the societal context. Arnold Heidenheimer (1970) has shown how various styles of bureaucratic corruption in face-to-face interactions between administrators and their clientele are associated with different types of political cultures. Gerald Caiden (1970) and Katz and Eisenstadt (1969) explain how Israeli bureaucrats have adapted to the complexities of that nation's political and social conditions. Bureaucrats may generally try to turn the client into a case, as Ralph Hummel (1977) suggests, but at other times they identify with the client and seek to represent his/her interests.

Such representation is akin to the "casework" representation provided by legislators. However, in the bureaucratic setting it takes place on a much more widespread and haphazard basis. Still, it is a kind of representation approaching advocacy that would be unattainable in a large, nonbureaucratized political community. The multiplicity of government agencies and programs operating on a decentralized basis also makes possible a kind of direct participation in government that is unavailable at the legislative level in large democratic nations. The fact that turnouts were so low and participation so sparse in the War on Poverty and Model Cities programs should not be taken as evidence that citizen participation is not feasible. For various reasons addressed above, such participation may be unworkable in the short run, where the poor are concerned. However, citizen participation defined along occupational lines has proved workable over the years in various agricultural and natural resource programs. Indeed, the operation of agricultural programs in the United States is formally dependent upon farmers' participation.

Ironically, then, the rise of the administrative state tends to negate traditional mechanisms of representation, such as mass elections, but at the same time carries with it the possibility of reactivating the pre-republican democratic ideal of individual participation in public policymaking. Whether this potential can be achieved depends upon factors pertaining to political culture. However, that it may not work perfectly, or even at all, in the short run simply suggests that, as in the case of other civic obligations, the citizenry may need further training in order to capitalize on the potential for making government representative. Bureaucracy and democracy are less incompatible in this context than in others.

Public bureaucracies can also be highly representative of the public to the extent that the citizenry has formed pressure groups to represent its general interests. There is no doubt that traditional interest groups are often well represented in public bureaucracies. Indeed, it is not unusual for public power to be "captured" by private interest groups in their interaction with bureaucratic agencies (McConnell 1966). A similar, though perhaps somewhat lesser, potential exists for public-interest groups. In political systems such as the United States, bureaucratic politics and administrative procedure allow for a great deal of interaction with interest groups. Such groups, including those claiming to represent the public interest, are afforded various formal channels of access to bureaucratic policymaking. They have a formal right to express their views on proposed agency regulations and to receive various kinds of information from the bureaucracy. Public-interest groups can supply the perspectives of their membership in an effort to counteract the pressures brought by traditional interest groups and as a means of making public bureaucrats more cognizant of broader, less specialized interests.

In this fashion, public-interest groups can partly overcome the tendencies of small constituencies to express narrow demands (McConnell 1966), and those of "single issue" groups to be unconcerned with the public welfare generally. However, it is crucial to this kind of representation through interaction with public bureaucrats that the public-interest groups actually reflect the public's interest. To date, in the United States at least, the most that can be said on this point is that such groups do seem to represent their membership on structure and process issues. Their membership, though, is heavily skewed in favor of the middle class and the politically active citizenry. Nevertheless, the potential for such representation to be expanded and effective is evident.

Finally, public bureaucrats can be representative of the public in a more legalistic sense. They can be required to protect the fundamental political rights of citizens when interacting with them. Since many of these citizens are ill-prepared to assert or exercise their own rights, this role can be of great value in harmonizing democratic citizenship with bureaucratic government. In the United States, representation of this kind has become a requirement as a result of the erosion of public administrators' official immunity. Under the contemporary standard, the public administrator who seeks to avoid a suit for damages must avoid breaches of individuals' constitutional rights. In practice, since these rights are constantly changing as the result of judicial decisions, public administrators must be cognizant of the continually evolving constitutional law. Thus, they may become the "first line" defenders of individual constitutional rights, and thereby become representatives of the individual's interests in civil rights and liberties within the context of bureaucratic government.

In sum, the rise of the administrative state, though largely incompatible with traditional democratic values and practices, need not entirely subvert either the individual's ability to participate in politics or his/her political rights. Bureaucratization forecloses some avenues of participation, but it creates others. Although it tends to reduce individual rights, under certain kinds of legal circumstances it can be turned into a vehicle for protecting those rights and even educating the citizenry with respect to them. We return to the first sentence of this chapter: "Bureaucratic representation is a subtle process that can take many forms."

REFERENCES

Aleshire, Robert. 1972. "Power to the People: An Assessment of the Community Action and Model Cities Experience." *Public Administration Review* (September): 428–43.

Arnold, R. Douglas. 1979. *Congress and the Bureaucracy*. New Haven: Yale University Press.

Barr v *Matteo*. 1959. 360 U.S. 564.

Bendix, Reinhard. 1964. *Nation Building and Citizenship*. New York: Wiley.

Bivens v *Six Unknown Named Federal Narcotics Agents*. 1971. 403 U.S. 388.

Butz v *Economou*. 1978. 438 U.S. 504.

Caiden, Gerald. 1970. *Israel's Administrative Culture*. Berkeley: Institute of Government, University of California.

Carlson v *Green*. 1980. 40 CCH S. Ct. Bull. B2026.

Davis, Kenneth. 1972. *Administrative Law Text*, 3rd ed. St. Paul: West Publishing.

Davis v *Passman*. 1979. 442 U.S. 228.

Dye, Thomas, and L. Harmon Zeigler. 1975. *The Irony of Democracy*. North Scituate, Mass.: Duxbury.

Fiorina, Morris. 1977. *Congress: Keystone of the Washington Establishment*. New Haven: Yale University Press.

Gouldner, Alvin. 1952. "Red Tape as a Social Problem." In *Reader in Bureaucracy*, edited by R. K. Merton et al. Glencoe, Ill.: Free Press. pp. 410–18.

Harris, Louis. 1973. *Confidence and Concern: Citizens View American Government.* Washington, D.C.: U.S. Congress, Committee on Government Operations, Subcommittee on Intergovernmental Relations.

Heidenheimer, Arnold. 1970. "The Context of Analysis." In *Political Corruption,* edited by Heidenheimer, pp. 3-28. New York: Holt, Rinehart and Winston.

Hummel, Ralph. 1977. *The Bureaucratic Experience.* New York: St. Martin's.

Katz, Daniel, et al. 1975. *Bureaucratic Encounters.* Ann Arbor: Survey Research Center, Institute for Social Research, University of Michigan.

Katz, Élihu and S. N. Eisenstadt. 1959. "Bureaucracy and Its Clientele—A Case Study." In *Readings on Modern Organizations,* edited by Amitai Etzioni. Englewood Cliffs, N.J.: Prentice-Hall. pp. 231-40.

Lipset, Seymour M. 1952. "Bureaucracy and Social Change." In *Reader in Bureaucracy,* edited by R. K. Merton et al., pp. 221-32. Glencoe, Ill.: Free Press.

Lipsky, Michael. 1976. "Toward a Theory of Street Level Bureaucracy." In *Bureaucratic Power in National Politics,* 3rd ed., edited by Francis Rourke. Boston: Little, Brown. pp. 135-57.

Lowi, Theodore. 1972. "A 'Critical' Election Misfires." *The Nation,* December 18.

McConnell, Grant. 1966. *Private Power and American Democracy.* New York: Knopf.

McFarland, Andrew. 1980. "The Rise of Public Interest Groups, 1965-75." In *Points of View,* edited by Robert Diclerico and Alean Hammock, pp. 132-143. Reading, Mass.: Addison-Wesley.

———. 1978. "Third Forces in American Politics: The Case of Common Cause." In *Parties and Elections in an Anti-Party Age,* edited by Jeff Fishel, pp. 318-32. Bloomington: Indiana University Press.

Meyer, Alfred. 1965. *The Soviet Political System.* New York: Random House.

Miller, Warren, and Donald Stokes. 1963. "Constituency Influence in Congress." *American Political Science Review* 57:45-56.

Monell v *New York City.* 1978. 56 L. Ed. 2d 611.

Morrow, William. 1975. *Public Administration.* New York: Random House.

Moynihan, Daniel P. 1970. *Maximum Feasible Misunderstanding.* New York: Free Press.

Nachmias, David, and David H. Rosenbloom. 1978. *Bureaucratic Culture: Citizens and Administrators in Israel.* New York: St. Martin's.

New York Times. 1976. November 16, p. 33.

———. 1972. June 25, p. 28.

Nivola, Pietro. 1979. *The Urban Service Problem.* Lexington, Mass.: Lexington Books.

Ornstein, Norman, and Shirley Elder. 1978. *Interest Groups, Lobbying and Policymaking.* Washington, D.C.: Congressional Quarterly Press.

Owen v *City of Independence.* 1980. 40 CCH S. Ct. Bull. B1738.

Reich, Charles. 1964. "The New Property." *Yale Law Journal* 73: 733-87.

Reissman, Leonard. 1949. "A Study of Role Conceptions in Bureaucracy." *Social Forces* 27 (March): 305-10.

Rourke, F., ed. 1978. *Bureaucratic Power in National Politics.* 3rd ed. Boston: Little, Brown. pp. 40-53.

Sjoberg, Gideon, et al. 1966. "Bureaucracy and the Lower Class." In *Bureaucratic Power in National Politics,* edited by F. Rourke. Boston: Little, Brown.

Spalding v *Vilas.* 1896. 161 U.S. 483.

Storing, Herbert. 1964. "Political Parties and the Bureaucracy." In *Political Parties, U.S.A.,* edited by R. A. Goldman, pp. 137–58. Chicago: Rand McNally.

Thayer, F. C. 1973. *An End to Hierarchy! An End to Competition!* New York: New Viewpoints.

Thompson, Victor. 1961. *Modern Organization.* New York: Knopf.

Vaughn, Robert 1975. *The Spoiled System.* New York: Charterhouse.

Wood v *Strickland.* 1975. 420 U.S. 308.

6

CONCLUSIONS

The texture and pattern of the American bureaucracy, unlike its other political institutions, was neither set nor even outlined at the dawn of the system. Great Britain, in 1789, had not really set out in coherent form even the principles for selection or for controlling its operations. The American Constitution refers to administrative problems and processes in subordinate clauses, almost in afterthoughts, and there are only a handful of these.

As a late bloomer, the bureaucracy has been something of a child of old age. It has been allowed to develop in its own fashion, without the strict concern and exacting demands for accounting characteristic of our intense preoccupation with the other branches of government. The analogy to later parentage breaks down with respect to regard and affection, however. In the American system the bureaucracy is never regarded with fondness, though in its finest hours it may achieve respect.

There are much more precise ways of understanding the curious position of bureaucracy in the system. Most basic is the fact that it is not, as the term implies, a monolithic structure in any respect. Additionally, it is neither a branch nor a function in its own right. Nor does it really fit well into the mythology of American constitutional ordering. This lack of fit is not just a question of semantics and symbols, but also of processes, attitudes, aspirations, and time perspectives.

The complexity of the American bureaucracy is apparent in the official flow charts. Special kinds of structures abound. The various plans and relations of its employees to the government are compound and perplexing. Congress has, with lapidary concern, rendered each agency so special as to require separate study.

There are the obvious and usual classifications we have already discussed, such as the independent regulatory commissions. Even those are independent to different degrees, both in law and in fact. Many agencies not considered classic independent commissions have in part or in whole exemptions from standard presidential control. Specialties like the Census Bureau and the Bureau of Labor Statistics, or such structures as the Nuclear Regulatory Commission and the National Institute for Mental Health have peculiar needs for isolation from political control. Even regulation of international airline routes is substantially different from and more presidential than that of domestic regulations.

Differences are inherent in function and in complexity. But the legal differentiation need not have been so great or unmodeled. Except for the increasingly fictional commonality of "departments" and the never fully equal, even in law, "commissions," structures are largely sui generis. We have no way of measuring, and no one has even tried to seriously think about, whether this is good, bad, or indifferent. But it does mean that when one writes about the nature of the bureaucracy, or attempts to develop a theory of the relationship of bureaucrats in our system—whether that theory is empirical or normative—one is almost doomed to distort vital parts of the reality. This makes it hard to develop new and appropriate modes for relationships that might more easily have developed in simpler times and have provided guidance and strength. The British and Continental systems are benefiting from—though using up—social capital in the form of clearer, albeit archaic, notions of bureaucratic power and responsibility. (As we will argue more fully later, Eastern Europe suffers from an exaggerated form of our problem: implanting new concepts of accountability in a system where these norms are visibly unrealistic.)

The usual concept of the bureaucracy is that it is part of the executive, of administration. But what are we to make of claims that the independent regulatory commissions are not (as appears in the charts) part of the executive, but are "arms of Congress" or quasi-judicial and quasi-legislative or even essentially judicial? Truly they are, as Edward Corwin has suggested, like Mohammed's tent, suspended between heaven and earth. Nor are other agencies much more integrated. The State Department's relations with the White House staff seem at most times to resemble those of a foreign ally: chilly and suspicious. The Nixon tapes reflect downright hostility extended to the administrative agencies. We earlier paid considerable attention to Hugh Heclo's discussion of American administration as a "government of strangers." Even stronger is the evidence that after some half-dozen years in power, a president and his intimates should still see a domain nominally under his control as dominated by enemies, an arena for outright struggle, a set of battles to be won. Observers of the scene admit, too, that while exacerbated by Nixon's paranoia, there was substance to the White House unhappiness.

Certainly the response to changes in the White House is inevitably less than 100 percent. Bureaucrats there, as elsewhere, are tempted to sit out changes in program emphasis to which they are not sympathetic, not so much opposing as foot-dragging. The two-term limit on the presidency provides encouragement for this even as it encourages first-term presidents to gear their programs to the short run.

The limited control by the president is matched in other systems. Indeed, in many ways, what is most distinctive in the American system is the lack of distance between administration and policy. Again Heclo's discussion (1977), emphasizing the peculiar politicization of American civil servants and the need for technocrats in some nominally politically posts, obscures such differences. It is not unusual for civil servants to resign or "take leave" to occupy political posts, or in effect to become programmatically partisan, beyond obedience or enforcement, while retaining their bureaucratic protection. Similarly, the appointment of, for instance, the director of the census by each new administration is (if anything) an effort to control patronage, not a need for policy perspectives on sampling theory.

Not fully integrated into the executive, yet easily penetrated by its influence, American bureaucracy presents an unpretty picture. It has nowhere near the autonomy or the élan of the French civil service. The latter is dominated by an elite corps educated in its own program. It is presided over by the Council of State, which combines legislative, juridic, and administrative powers with intellectual power and frosty Gallic pretension at its most intimidating. Nor does the American service have the clear structural accountability of British civil service, a clear arrangement that is increasingly seen by knowledgeable writers as a fiction by which the bureaucracy can exercise an acknowledged and unauthorized power.

But, whether fiction or no, "ministerial responsibility" and "civil service neutrality" have shielded the bureaucracy for decades. In contrast with France's sharp, separate, autonomy, with its own training school and its own court and legal systems unaccountable to the regular legal order, or the British screen of exemption, the American civil servant is "naked to his enemies," accountable to all. Political, budgetary, and civil service regulations, court orders, media criticism—virtually exempt from legal limits—pull in many different directions. Congress, the president, the "constituency interest groups," the courts, and the public all assume a right to direct and control in a sovereign manner.

This complexity is a product of ambiguity, an evolution lacking clean, directional movement. As we have indicated, neither the Constitution nor the early history of the republic charted a clear course. To the extent that the first century of the Constitution threw up a principle of bureaucratic legitimacy and control, it was articulated in terms of partisan control. "To the victor belongs the spoils" in its most vulgar form, the approach suggests that popular dominance is clear, and achieved through the presidential control of patronage.

But since the 1880s this guiding principle has been in rapid erosion. With occasional, infrequent exceptions, Congress has been sustained in efforts to hem in presidential removal and appointive power. The latest decisions of the Supreme Court have totally and decisively taken away from the executive the right to remove officials on simple partisan grounds, even without congressional action. Seldom has a long-standing constitutional practice been so interdicted without a direct constitutional amendment. Yet those decisions have been accepted without murmur, reflecting a sharp difference from nineteenth-century attitudes toward parties. Whether "the party is over" in the White House and Capitol, as David Broder (1979) and others suggest, it is at least overtly so in the halls of administration. Presidents (and other top officials) may exercise removal to bring in people they can work with, but may not use party affiliation as the reason. And even in that type of situation, the office involved must be sufficiently significant to suggest the appropriateness of such a need for policy and personal compatibility.

If partisanship has clearly been outlawed, new principles or guidelines have not significantly expanded to occupy the vacuum. On the contrary, the other evolved principles have also been under attack and the situation has become ever more murky.

The development of the bureaucracy that came gradually after the Civil War and ballooned during the New Deal was, as we have noted, rather free from historic or rigid precedent. As agencies expanded in number and in internal complexity, the shapes and forms drew upon French and Prussian patterns and experience, as well as those of Great Britain. The latter, however, was the principal guide, and most Continental practice was adopted when the British gave it their own imprimatur.

The foundation of early European bureaucratic authority was office, the entrustment of the post by the monarch. As we have noted, many such posts were livelihoods, not policy responsibilities. For the major positions, evolving bourgeois-democratic legislatures demanded, and got, powers of removal and a share in appointment, though to considerably varying degrees. In Great Britain, of course, the crown lost all effective control, while in Prussia it retained dominance. In a France vacillating between different regimes, the bureaucracy developed autonomic controls.

These patterns did not resolve the issue of control or satisfactorily meet the tests of performance. The emergence of merit and competence as standards for the right to office was in part a matter of efficiency. But, as with most reforms, it was also perceived in power terms, and backed or opposed by different groups in those terms, as much as or more because of its impact on quality. In Prussia, civil service mitigated autocracy and was a measure of pluralistic development. Islands of policy could develop to counter the king's (later the emperor's) singular authority over the chancellor and Cabinet. In Great Britain the rising middle class curbed the power and the perquisites of the waning aristocracy. In France merit was a check on the social nature of the bureaucracy, but one that helped preserve its elitism and insulation from political power.

In a world that no longer blindly accepts the power of the authorities, that does not believe in divine right of kings (or ministers, or presidents), appointment to office needs some buttressing when important matters are at stake. Other factors both call for new concepts and methods and make them possible. The fact that most modern governmental posts potentially have broad social leverage makes appointment for personalistic reasons inappropriate. The stability of regimes makes personal loyalty less significant; in only a few modern societies is retaining power a matter of life or death for political leaders. Removal power has always been a cumbersome method of control—ill-suited to control subtle resistance to policy (as opposed to defiance) or to deal with low-grade performance (as opposed to significant misdeeds).

Selection by merit thus enhances office in the modern world, and confers not only the sanction of authority but also a certificate of ability issued by sanctioned authority. The Scarecrow's quest for a brain was solved to everyone's satisfaction in *The Wizard of Oz* by the Wizard's "officially" granting a Ph.D. to him. "Brain" was inferred from presumed achievement. Under the merit system public officials are appointed under a presumption not merely that they have the right to office, but also that they are right for the office. This coupling of merit with authoritative selection restores some of the divine perfection of authority when "the powers that be . . . are ordained of God." Under the rule of merit, they exercise office by virtue of God-given talents. Even an atheist must accept such an ordering.

The sophisticated attack upon the merit standard has many strands. A mordant look at the actual performance of bureaucrats raises questions, and it is the conviction in the United States especially that the quality of such position holders is in decline. More important, the intellectual underpinnings of the testing approach have not proved fully convincing under examination for racial or social bias or for relevance to performance. The dissatisfaction with civil service did not begin with the civil rights movement; its essentially negative nature had long been noted. Not only was the merit standard unable to insure top-flight talent, but it often served to prevent recruitment of the best. It is complex and unwieldy, and is too often evaded by the top managers. All of these doubts about quality had already been registered when the racial issue emerged. While little of the claim of race-related bias has been established, neither has it been totally shaken.

With merit as a questioned basis, reliance upon the selection and removal power as a means of control and validation becomes much less impressive. An expanded bureaucracy means low-level selection and little awareness of performance; procedural elaboration makes removal more costly and less likely.

Thus, we are driven to the basic structure and nature of the relationship with the body politic and even with public opinion. The constraints—budget policy directives, performance review, discipline, transfer, and removal—are real, live, but only partially effective. Cumbersome government proliferates autonomic policy. The more transactions a government is engaged in, the more difficult coordination becomes. As Thomas Cronin (1975) points out, U.S. presidents invariably promise that Cabinet officers will become more significant figures in their administrations, but eventually tame them well before the end of the first term. Presidents learn the bureaucracy is like the universe, ever expanding away from their center, away from their control. Having no choice, they create and expand coordinating mechanisms that gradually also move beyond presidential control at a slow, but definite pace.

The erosion of patronage exacerbates all of this by making the few thousand "plums" dumping grounds for White House obligations as much as posts for assignment of responsibility and mobilization of talent. White House legacies are often not judged by normal standards of the need for policy implementation. Their ability to help carry Idaho may be more precious than their willingness to implement Social Security reform. With a team of appointees having access to the White House, power squabbles among the managers often take precedence over the "taming of the natives."

The problem is seldom one of outright defiance. It is one of remoteness, different priorities, and a lack of enthusiasm. Particularly strong agencies like J. Edgar Hoover's FBI, or Admiral Hyman Rickover's atomic submarine project, try to learn as little as possible of the president's world, but seldom cross swords with the political units. Continuous monitoring of a dreary and usually (not invariably) unworthy sort is necessary for an executive to gain compliance from a subordinate who is sitting out the term, well aware of the time limits set by the Constitution. Here, as elsewhere, executives must choose their battles.

Court controls also operate, and can hamstring agencies. Courts have the same tenacity and sense of timelessness that often prevail in the bureaucracy. Cases may go on seemingly forever. In bureaucratic terms such proceedings usually are a detriment to effective action, though on occasion they may in fact represent quasi victories, no matter what the outcome. (Regulatory cases costing the challenger dearly may induce general compliance, regardless of a particular outcome based on narrow circumstances.) Courts, however, are poorly equipped for systematic follow-through, and are even less inclined than the executive or legislature to monitor broad policies.

Bureaucrats are hypersensitive to the official, prescribed restraints. They respond quickly, even abjectly and sycophantically, to calls from the other branches, especially their political masters. In the nature of things, those calls are increasingly less systematic, more arbitrary, and idiosyncratic rather than genuinely programmatic.

It is difficult to track bureaucratic behavior. Modern management techniques, such as the advent of the computer, aid a bit. But they are better at evaluating quantities than quality of performance or programmatic integrity. The civil service in the modern world is continuously upgraded into the realms of discretionary management that are most difficult to map and grade. Sampling or other methods of review, common elsewhere, are difficult to implement because legal challenges to subjective evaluation are easily mounted. We have less and less knowledge of how well (or even what) bureaucrats do as they do more and more to affect us.

The vector of all these forces is an uncertain and wavering one. The bureaucracy is buffeted by influences of varying types, of a system in transition. Writers like Theodore Lowi (1969) argue that we have completed a transition to "interest group liberalism" in which the building blocks of political and legal analysis are groups and their claims, rather than individual rights. Yet certainly in the judicial system we maintain the preeminence of individual claims and reluctant acceptance of group participation. Many presidents—including Jimmy Carter—have viewed interest politics with suspicion (though Carter consummated affairs-of-convenience with labor and the National Education Association).

And while specific administrative agencies have close relations of varying kinds with differing clientele groups, these are hardly of the systematic nature of European corporative societies. This active, built-in representation of interests effected in a regulated sector occurs through meaningful formal participation or, more frequently, through systematic consultation of those groups. Decisions are reached as much as possible through consensus, achieved after marathon iterative discussions. In contrast, American agencies build limited constituencies, and agencies are more likely to move in idiosyncratic paths, colliding with other agencies moving in their own limited orbits. Part of the problem is the sheer magnitude of American society, so that determining an appropriate and comprehensive list of spokesmen is a Herculean and politically dangerous task.

Nearest to that state of affairs are the "cozy triangle" arrangements or clientele-controlled agencies discussed in earlier chapters. Additionally, the major regulatory agencies hold open hearings at which a wide (sometimes wild) variety of individuals and groups appear to present their points of view. This is a far cry from active representation in many ways. The volunteer aspect resembles a congressional hearing, and the regulators may value the views expressed or ignore them. Testimony is taken. Nothing like consultation or bargaining takes place. Presentation, not representation, is involved. If the system is moving toward either corporatism or active participation, neither the extent of current participation nor the trend is readily apparent.

The proliferation of organized groups, as is apparent from any perusal of the Washington telephone directory, might appear to contradict this and suggests a trend. But this growth has the opposite effect. The emergence of small numbers of peak organizations dominating a sector promotes corporatism. The continuous emergence of autonomous specialized groups or clusters of formerly unrepresented clienteles makes minimizing, formal, and noncommital contact imperative. Since the AFL-CIO is the only "three-ring circus" in town, the secretary of labor has been (especially, but not only, in Democratic administrations) the White House ambassador or liaison officer to the head of organized labor. But in areas like environmental controls, where businesses of different types have different interests and governmental concerns are equally complex, it is asking for trouble even to deal with the total set of existing groups, since others are likely to emerge in short order. The larger the number of potential groups, the more likely the regulator is to adopt an adjudicative rather than a negotiating style of conflict resolution.

The pattern, then, is largely crazy quilt. Every agency tries to find sustaining forces and relations in its complex environment. Abrupt changes and inconsistencies abound, as does stalling for time until it is known which way the wind blows. While presidents complain about inability to achieve control, bureaucrats seldom feel they are captains of their souls. Excessive obedience to a president may be frowned upon by a subsequent administration. It may be criticized by Congress or some relevant section thereof (including influential subcommittee chairmen or oratorial senators), even in a Congress controlled by the president's party.

As suggested earlier, this formlessness is a product of evolution, of ideas that administration is an unimportant or secondary extension of some other process of government. When this is combined with disagreement over which branch the extension of power is to enhance, problems are inevitable. The expansion took place in fits and starts, and different designers implemented their blueprints for change. European models were used to suggest devices, but significant changes were made. As often as not, political compromises were made without great concern for how tinkering with the structure of an agency would really affect operations or constrain policy choices. Even in those few instances where the lines of battle were precisely over that issue—as on the problem of the relation of banks and bankers to making Federal Reserve policy—concern was limited largely to the question of the number of seats controlled by bankers compared with the "public," although scores of intricate relationships have proved to be sticking points quite as significant as this basic one.

What emerges is that Americans have decided on personal authority as the chief means for bureaucratic control, then have drastically curtailed it. Reflecting a business, control mode of thinking, we still see tidal waves of change coming with a new administration. Politicians have visions of jobs from the "plum" book, a list of major positions available for patronage, now published by the Government Printing Office with each new administration and, in the Washington area at least, a best seller. In American business thinking, a new executive needs a new team. In fact, as we have noted, White House leadership and new agency leaders struggle over who will assign the plum. All too often the new agency executive gets only the pits.

Europeans have thought in different terms. They have emphasized internalized modes of control, supplemented by transfer of personnel, not waves of "new people." Dismissal or transfer is a black mark against the bureaucrat, and also a reflection on the managerial ability of the political chief.

Internalized controls, as Herbert Kaufman has shown, require considerable initial indoctrination and continued operational voice or comment. In most European systems the higher civil servants have moved in from higher social strata. All too often they have shared a common education and have similar social aspirations. Under this umbrella élan and enthusiasm can be fostered, and agreement—more or less as to what constitutes success or failure in life—is fostered. An adult version of the schoolboy's code dominates and contributes to ambition and drive and avoidance of improper behavior (including overstepping of authority). Those bureaucrats' self-image has some of the attributes of P. G. Wodehouse's Jeeves—a fictional butler who by cool astuteness saves his muddle-headed master from disaster. But Jeeves, and they, know that not only must the master's external power and authority never be compromised, but the master's self-esteem must not be diminished. The European civil servant thus has strong ideas about whom to serve, and the need to preserve certain facts and fictions of power. The American civil servant, faced with multiple claims and little guidance as to authority, follows one of the cardinal rules of bureaucratic life: "When in doubt, mumble."

To deal with these problems, reformers have urged the transformation of the upper ranks of the civil service into a higher civil service. As pointed out in Chapter 14, this is everybody's solution to all bureaucratic problems. Since many of the cures sought are diametrically opposed, someone is destined to be disappointed. In terms of our analysis, two expectations are of importance. First, it is presumed that such a structure will enhance the prestige, self-image, and initiative of bureaucrats. Second, by emphasizing service in the government as a whole, some of the separatist, dysfunctional conflict and ignorance may be diminished. Each of these goals requires separate analysis.

The implantation of éclat and élan through crude devices such as bonuses misses the essence of the problem, and is unlikely to solve root conditions. This is not a statement of absolute pessimism or of criticism for trying—merely one of little optimism. That Congress has already reneged on its commitments to provide such extra pay for good performance is a sample of the problem, and a manifestation of basic issues even earlier than had been expected.

The development of higher civil service attitudes in European systems is a product of centuries. It is a result not just of the civil servants' attitudes, but also of the needs and attitudes of the officeholders (Cabinet governments, for example, have special and complex needs). Already there are signs of breakdown in those understood relationships in the British system. Whether or not deterioration persists in the wake of welfare state pressures, it is doubtful that such a tradition can be interpolated into a huge system already under great pressure. The minimal reforms might have some effect upon the bureaucrats, but the political forces are not shaped for change in spirit, tone, or need. Nor is there a change in selection or training of the bureaucrats that suggests the reforms are much more than cosmetic.

To be sure, the more specific and limited goals have the potential for attainment. Some diminution of department loyalty is possible, but mobility on one's own initiative has always been feasible, so peonage has never been the problem. Some increase in use of removal power has been evident, and estimates are that a 10 percent increase in removals took place in 1979. Of course, the tiny base means that such increases represent no greater number and are unlikely to change the mode of governmental activity in any drastic way. Finally, congressional fickleness makes the promise of flexible pay unlikely to be kept to any degree commensurate with the level necessary for significant alteration in patterns of expectation and behavior.

In short, solutions preferred and enacted do not seem to change any basic fact of life. Bureaucrats are highly vulnerable to any and all of a range of influences. At the same time, the sheer volume and complexity of their operations frustrate those trying to achieve external control in an orderly and more or less comprehensive way. The effect is to discourage creative and active executives from going into civil service, and usually to frustrate those who wish to implement straightforward, well-publicized programmatic efforts for the subjects of regulation.

In most areas of the bureaucracy, covert strategies are the most rational, as little as that fact of life comports with our theories of constitutionalism and administration. This, in turn, inhibits our ability to get the brilliant, driving, creative bureaucracy some people hope for. The academic reformers borrow practice from Great Britain, but their dream bureaucrat is—though few know it, and fewer would acknowledge it—the Italian and (especially) the French technocratic, elitist, know-it-all rationalist planner.

We suggest that realities must be faced, and that by understanding the nature of our polity, the real strengths of our system can be recognized and built upon. At a time when other systems are trying to ascertain how they can reap some of the benefits our system possesses in terms of responsiveness to public pressure, it seems odd to be concerned with creating an insulated bureaucracy. Eastern Europe gives enough evidence of its undesirability, but liberal Western states that are further advanced in welfare policies also point the finger of discontent at bureaucratic abuse, as much as or more than bureaucratic inertia. Excessive zeal is often as much an issue in the United States as it is throughout the world. Something is badly wrong with an analysis that focuses only on problems arising from lack of initiative and creativity, that ignores the call for less interference in everyday life by highly intelligent know-it-alls who are smugly sure that they can engineer a better society, who wish to play God without risking rejection by running for lesser posts.

The American system is embedded in limited populism, and this has been true of appointive as well as elective officials. When J. Donald Kingsley (1944) coined the term "representative bureaucracy," he put forth notions of the advantages that a broadly recruited, open, nonelitist civil service had over restrictive, taut, narrowly based bureaucracies. In contrast with British bureaucracy, this service, drawn from all elements in society, could be expected to be motivated by much the same forces and attitudes as others are. It would be more in harmony with its environment, responsive to changes and nuances in opinions, as well as more effective in disseminating and in securing compliance.

These sweeping assertions, raised as much as indictments of the British system as in praise of the American, have been influential for many scholars of the administrative process. Both followers and critics have tried to develop the conditions under which the statements are either true or not applicable.

Some close observations have drastically altered Kingsley's notions. As many have observed and V. Subramaniam (1967) has proved, we are at most talking about bureaucrats whose backgrounds are broadly based.

Bureaucracies themselves are, as Subramaniam has documented, predominantly middle-class, with a probability that the more advanced the society, the larger that predominance. Of course, the difference between open and closed recruitment nevertheless remains significant, though not in the same degree. We do not know how a middle-class bureaucrat perceives the fact of humbler origin; many may become more "royalist than the king." Still, just as one can expect a hereditary army to be quite different from one recruited through universal conscription so will the two types of bureaucracies.

A second significant modification is closely related. Bureaucracies have not found it feasible to permit active representation or formal designation of a segment of the civil service. Even legislatures, where there has been an attempt to have active group representation, have found this paralyzing. Even in societies that permit "colonization" of an entire unit by a specific group require fundamental allegiance to the society as a whole, "active representation" has generally signified a polity in the process of disintegration, a "dual polity" (as distinguished from the sharing in power, a "pluralistic polity").

We are thus confronted with the imponderables of "passive representation." These are the advantages accrued through the inherent facts of diversity, not through a sense of obligation or accountability to groups. This, of course, presents the problem of whether diversity per se leads to administrative pluralism. There is strong but not conclusive evidence that it does. Both in the positive sense that scholars of public structures have found ranges of behavior by differing types of bureaucrats (analyzed on the basis of social background) and negatively, through evidence of obtuseness and default by narrowly based structures, Kingsley's intuitively appealing expectations have been generally sustained. The advantages established, however, have not been dramatic or overwhelming.

Studies of American civil servants amply demonstrate the breadth of social backgrounds, and seem to show some concomitant to a diversity of views. This has, however, been challenged. To date, no one has tested the proposition with respect to salient issues for the groups represented. Behavior of such appointive officials as judges, which has amply shown correlates with social origin, suggests that American bureaucracy is not immune from facts of human behavior that are well established in most domains of action.

Of course, representativeness is not by itself sufficient to provide a responsive, controlled bureaucracy. A bureaucracy drawn from all walks of life, but all-powerful and unaccountable, would be, practically speaking, as dangerous as any other uncontrolled group. Internalized responsiveness needs reinforcement, as do other social patterns. Without constraints, other behaviors will be easily learned.

In some isolated passages, enthusiasts of the discovery that bureaucracies could be broadly based wrote as if this discovery could substitute for the entire constitutional structure. We doubt they ever meant us to assume that they were aware that representativeness is an augmentation of, not a substitute for, traditional constitutional restraints. Certainly the frozen-into-place bureaucracies of Eastern Europe undergird the message, for they are living proof.

In his book, which is a somewhat inadequate hybrid between a novel and a treatise, Michael Young (1961) treats the rise of the meritocracy. He suggests that a group selected for competence will, in the future, gain control of society and attempt to seal off access to power for others than their children. This more or less undercuts his theme; a hereditary group is no longer a meritocracy. But it underscores our point; representative meritocracy must be responsive and accountable in any democratic society. A sense of identity with the populace is claimed by most despots; large tyrannical groups are not necessarily more pleasant than single despots. The notion of representative bureaucracy in the American system must be pursued in accordance with traditional American models of behavior. The needs of the system of democratic balances require more than faith in the goodwill of any branch. Indeed, the system is suspicious of goodwill without a move to structure. Augmented sources of goodwill, of "identity with the people," are, however, welcomed and acclaimed.

Efforts to strengthen the bureaucracy at its source must take into account and be built upon its structure and its strengths, as well as on alleviating its weaknesses. Most successful agencies have historically had a strong sense of self-identity. The core of that has been a sense of service, not of exclusivity. Operating agencies—TVA, the Social Security Administration, the Public Health Service—have been most effective when their sense of mission was strongest and their identification with constituent roots was highest. Regulatory groups need more standoffish attitudes, but they respond to those same base elements. Competence and drive are, of course, essential in initial phases of formation and revitalization, but that spirit of pride has momentum of its own.

In recent decades unsuccessful experiments with mass popular participation—in our view, inherently overdone and doomed to failure—have led to lack of interest in more moderate forms of integrating bureaucratic and community behavior. Overlooked are successes in agriculture, banking, and labor.

Similarly, the emphasis upon affirmative action to obtain "pieces of the pie" has exacerbated, rather than eased, group conflict and tensions. Concern with real tasks, taking advantage of talents and assets, could help alleviate this. Few quarrel with a need for black community specialists to deal with racial tension. Defining the criminal justice role to deal with potential crimes at an earlier point in the process would create posts for which minorities would have a presumptive advantage. Remolding missions would revitalize rather than dispirit workers. Thus, conceptualization of tasks would turn affirmative action into an ally of a better civil service rather than a rival of quality performance.

Continuing emphasis on decentralization, on flexible regulatory policies, and on review of existing structures will help restore the sense of accountability. The call for zero-base budgeting or automatic "sunset" laws also is not so much misplaced as overdone. More moderate forms of the same process might be taken seriously, and thus accomplish more. The General Accounting Office, for example, might be given the task of identifying agencies whose mission no longer seems justified, and suggesting abolition, adjustment, or rearrangement.

Above all, a sense of purpose and integrity, a sense of mission within the agencies, is needed. Congress has proliferated its staff at a rate well beyond any other arm of government. It has done so in a commendable attempt to reassert legislative authority over administration. Its proliferation of committees and experts now serves to keep Congress from acting with dispatch or decisiveness. The imperial presidency is giving way to an imprecise Congress.

The symbol of this is the extraordinary inability of the Congress to manage any resolution of the budget by any of the deadlines it has set during its heroic effort to regain budgetary control. This process has, in fact, multiplied tensions and has left a string of booby traps: authorizing legislation by the specialist committees, appropriations by the appropriate subcommittee of the Appropriations Committee, reconciliation by the Budget Committee, coordination with the other house of Congress, fear of the White House. Whatever strain it puts on the legislators—and it is considerable—the pressure on administrators is greater.

The uncertainty, capriciousness, and often contradictory nature of such decisions are made worse by a procrastinating, vacillating, and late end product. The costs of so handicapping administrators and preventing them from planning must vastly exceed those of peculation and graft. The problem of developing initiative within policy constraints requires a restoration of discipline and a sense of continuity in politics generally. A sense of the significance, difficulty, and creativity in administration, embedded in popular sentiment, would aid in this achievement, and might well be a necessary (though it is clearly not a sufficient) condition.

The place of bureaucracy in any political order is a complex one, and its rise or lowering in esteem is a product of many small things. The revitalization of the federal service will require a strengthening of its representativeness and its quality. Today these are still seen as contradictory trade-offs. But, to our dismay, we have found that an assumed "trade-off" of unemployment and inflation is not necessary—we can have both. The basic evolutionary tendencies of the American polity suggest that for the bureacracy, quality and representativeness must be constituted so as to go hand in hand.

REFERENCES

Broder, David. 1979. *The Party's Over*. New York: Harper.

Cronin, Thomas. 1975. *The State of the Presidency*. Boston: Little, Brown.

Heclo, Hugh. 1977. *A Government of Strangers*. Washington, D.C.: Brookings Institution.

Kingsley, J. Donald. 1944. *Representative Bureaucracy*. Yellow Springs, Ohio: Antioch University Press.

Lowi, Theodore. 1969. *The End of Liberalism*. New York: W. W. Norton.

Subramaniam, V. 1967. "Representative Bureaucracy: A Reassessment." *American Political Science Review* 61 (December): 1010–19.

Young, Michael. 1961. *The Rise of the Meritocracy*. London: Penguin.

INDEX

Accountability 4, 15, 16, 17, 22, 113, 123

Administrative Procedure Act (1943) 137, 173

Advisory bodies 64, 93-97, 101, 166

Advisory Committee on Hog Cholera Eradication 97

AFL-CIO 64, 92, 100, 147, 192

Agricultural Extension Service 272

Agriculture, U.S. Department of 14, 25, 26, 46, 64, 82, 84, 95, 97, 145

Aleshire, Robert 169

Algeria 79

Allen, Ethan 140

Almond, Gabriel 120

American Civil Liberties Union 139

American Farm Bureau Federation 14, 26, 91, 168

American Medical Association 91

Annapolis Convention 152

Aristotle 31

Army, U.S. 67

Army Corps of Engineers 8

Arnold, R. Douglas 13, 163

Arthur, Chester 40

Atomic Energy Commission 65

Austria-Hungary 38, 40

Bank of the United States 125

Bankhead, Tallulah 141

Barr v *Matteo* (1959) 176

Baxter, 154

Bazelon, David 139

Belgium 60, 61

Bendix, Rinehard 158

Berlin, Edward 96

Berry, Jeffrey 170

Bivens v *Six Unknown Named Federal Narcotics Agents* (1971) 178

Blacks, in United States 47, 51-52, 55, 58, 94-95, 198

Bolivia 79

Boudon, Raymond 57

Brahmins 35, 59, 66

Branti v *Finkel* (1980) 149

Brennan, William 176

Broder, David 188

Brown, Jerry 148

Brownlow Commission (President's Commission on Administrative Management) 131

Buchanan, James 141

Budget 130, 131, 132, 198

Budget and Impoundment Control Act (1974) 131, 134

Bureau of the Budget 132, 134

Bureau of Indian Affairs 85

Bureau of Labor Statistics 186
Bureau of Weights and Measures 33
Bureaucratic elite systems 78
"Bureautics" 159, 160
Burnham, James 32
Butz v *Economou* (1978) 177, 178

Cabinet, in United States 126, 127, 128, 190
Caesar 112
Caiden, Gerald 179
Califano, Joseph 135
California 11, 12, 154
Campaign Reform Act (1974) 172
Canada 60, 61
Canon, Brad 142
Carlson v *Green* (1980) 178
Carter, Jimmy 64, 114, 117, 120, 121, 123, 148, 191
Census Bureau, U.S. 186
Chapman, Brian 36, 60, 80, 89
China 38; civil service examinations 35, 41, 54, 116, 117
Chou En-lai 121
Churchill, Winston 36
Citizenship 11, 15, 17, 19, 21, 26, 175, 176, 180
Civil Aeronautics Board 87
Civil rights 139, 175, 176, 177, 178, 179, 181
Civil Rights Act 140
Civil rights movement 46, 140, 189
Civil service 40, 45, 46
Civil Service Commission 22, 86, 173
Civil service examinations 35, 41, 42, 43, 49, 50–52, 54, 116, 117
Clientela relationships 99–100, 102
Clientele agencies 64
Clients 14, 20, 37, 81, 91, 99, 159, 161, 162, 163, 170, 179, 191, 192
  minorities as, 85, 86, 89, 105
Coalition formation 32
"Colonisation" 60
Commerce, U.S. Department of 85
Commission on Civil Rights 86
Common Cause 139, 171, 172, 174
Communist political systems 32, 78, 89
Community Action Agencies 168
Congress, U.S. 8, 13, 15, 25, 141, 148; Budget Office 133, 134; control of bureaucracy 125, 131, 132, 133, 136; reform 133, 134; staff 134
Congress Party (India) 100
Constituents 13, 14, 26, 32, 83, 86, 87, 104, 164, 173, 197
Constitutional Convention 152
Contracting out 135
Consumers Union 172
"Corporatist" system 63, 192
Corwin, Edward 186
Courts 136–42, 144–46
Cronin, Thomas 85, 89, 190

Cox, Archibald 119
Crichel, Downs 124
Crossman, Richard 125

Dairy producers 100
Davidson, Roger 25
Davis, Kenneth 138
Davis v *Passman* (1979) 178
Defense, U.S. Department of 95, 126, 145
democracy 1, 3, 10–15, 17, 21, 24, 32
democratic balance 17–21
Democratic Party 100, 147
Deng Xiaoping 121
desegregation 139
Dicey, A. V. 136, 137
Diem, Ngo Dinh 114
Downs, Anthony 3, 6, 9, 14
Dresang, Dennis 69
Duncan, Otis Dudley 52
Dye, Thomas 164

East India Company 39, 41
Economic Opportunity Act (1964) 167
Education, U.S. Department of 84
Education, Ministry of 36
Egypt 35, 79, 112
Ehrlich, Stanislaw 65
Ehrmann, Henry 94, 97
Eisenhower, Dwight D. 46, 147, 148
Eisenstadt, S. N. 158, 161, 179
Elder, S. 170
Eldersveld, Samuel 19
Elected officials, 163 (*see also* Congress)
Elrod v *Burns* (1976) 148
Energy, U.S. Department of 11
Equal Employment Opportunity Commission 86
Europe, Eastern 56, 195, 197

Farm Credit Administration 86
Featherstonhaugh, J. 69
Federal Advisory Committee Act (1971) 94
Federal Aviation Agency 85, 145
Federal Communications Commission 87
Federal Deposit Insurance Corporation 89
Federal Elections Commission 172
Federal Power Commission 96
Federal Reserve Board 147, 148, 193
Fiorina, Morris 12, 13, 163
Fischer, John 46
Food and Drug Administration 129
Forest Service, U.S. 119, 120
Fortas, Abe 34
Forward, John 77
Freedom of Information Act 11, 150, 173–74
French civil service 40, 60, 97, 126, 187, 188, 189, 195

Gardener, John 174
Garfield, James 40
Garrity, Arthur, Jr. 143
General Accounting Office 134, 135, 198
General Services Administration 86
Germany, West 31, 98
Gerrymandering 133
Gibbons v *Ogden* (1824) 131
Gini coefficient 68
Gini index 67
Gladstone, William 41
Goering, Hermann 114
Goodnow, Frank 136
Gouldner, Alvin 159
Grades, academic 53, 54
Granick, David 100, 101
Great Britain 35, 36, 41–42, 56, 60, 94; civil service 37, 40, 118, 187, 188, 189, 194, 195; empire 35, 36, 39, 114; examinations 41–43
Greenwald, Carol 88, 90, 91, 92, 93, 95, 96, 100

Harris, Louis 16, 163
Haynsworth, Clement 144
Heady, Ferrel 77–80
Health, Education and Welfare, U.S. Department of 84
Heclo, Hugh 46, 115, 125, 126, 129, 187
Heidenheimer, Arnold 179
Heydrich, Rheinhard 114
hierarchy 3, 11, 15, 80
Himmler, Heinrich 114
Hiss, Alger 143
Hitler, Adolf 114, 115
Home, Lord 57
Hoogenboom, Ari 40
Hoover, J. Edgar 9, 190
Horowitz, Donald 143, 144
housing 84, 110
Housing and Home Finance Agency 86
Hummel, Ralph 2, 8, 179
Humphrey, Hubert H. 117
Humphrey's Executor v *United States* (1935) 86

implementation 85
impoundment 132, 134
incompetence 38
independent regulatory commissions 186
India 18, 19, 21, 22, 35, 36, 60, 66, 78, 100
Indian National Trade Union Congress 100
Indians, American 83
initiative 152–54
intelligence testing 43–44
interest groups 9, 18, 26, 90–93, 141, 170–75
Interior, U.S. Department of the 82, 83, 84, 172, 173
Internal Revenue Service 37, 145, 146
Interstate Commerce Commission 86, 145
interviewing 48

Islam 58
Israel 14, 19, 21, 80, 84, 158, 159, 160, 161, 179
Italy 60, 97, 195

Jackson, Andrew 22, 125
Jackson, Henry 21
Janowitz, Morris 16, 17, 18
Japan 61
Jefferson, Thomas 22
Jencks, Christopher 52
Johnson, Frank 139
Johnson, Lyndon B. 46, 84, 114, 148
Justice, U.S. Department of 33, 145

Katz, Daniel 20, 162
Katz, Elihu 158, 161, 179
Kaufman, Herbert 119, 151, 193
Kennan, George 34
Kennedy, John F. 46, 128, 148
Kennedy, Robert 148
Khrushchev, Nikita 114, 115
Kingsley, J. Donald 23, 36, 39, 59, 60, 195, 196
Kranz, Harry 24
Kraus, Eliot 169

Labor, U.S. Department of 64, 65, 84, 147
Labor Party, British 56
LaPalombara, Joseph 99, 100, 101
Laski, Harold 59, 130
Leahy, Patrick 95, 97
Lebanon 61, 69
Lipset, Seymour Martin 179
Lipsky, Michael 161
litigation 283–89
lobbying 89, 90, 92, 93, 172
Long, Norton 25, 66, 67
Lowi, Theodore 8, 14, 88, 90, 91, 105, 106, 129, 142, 166, 191
loyalty 32, 114, 115, 116, 118, 129

Macauley, T. H. 41, 42, 44
McConnell, Grant 14, 87, 102, 103, 104, 105, 106, 180
McFarland, Andrew 171, 172, 174
Mamelukes 35
Mannheim, Karl 66
Mao Zedong 121, 127
Maritime Commission 145
Meier, Kenneth 24, 66, 67, 68, 69, 70
meritocratic system 54, 55
Metcalf, Lee 96
Mexico 78
Meyer, Alfred 158
Michels, Roberto 104, 141
Mill, John Stuart 165
Miller, Warren 164
ministerial responsibility 123
ministries 83, 84, 85
Model Cities Act (1966) 167
Model Cities program 168, 179
Monell v *New York City* (1978) 177
Morrison, Herbert 124, 125

Morrow, William 26, 96, 166, 167, 169
Mosher, Frederick 17, 24, 65, 66
Moynihan, Daniel Patrick 168
Mussolini, Benito 64, 114

NAACP 139
Nachmias, David 68, 69, 84, 159, 161
Nader, Ralph 172, 173, 175
National Aeronautics and Space Administration 85
National Association of Manufacturers 92
National Education Association 191
National Environmental Policy Act 174
National Institute for Mental Health 186
National Labor Relations Board 147
National Society of Legislative Lobbyists 91
National Transportation Safety Board 145
Nazis 32
New York State 12, 175
New York Times 135, 163, 173
Nigro, Lloyd 66
Niskanen, William 115
Nixon, Richard 46, 114, 115, 128, 132, 147, 148, 152, 169, 186
norms 119–20
Northcote-Trevelyan Report 41
North Korea 56
Norway 98
Nuclear Regulatory Commission 186

Office of Economic Opportunity 167
Office of Management and Budget 96, 128, 131, 132
"old boy" networks 56
Olsen, Mancur 141
ombudsman 151–52
organization 1, 4, 5, 6, 14, 18, 25, 75, 83, 84
Ornstein, Norman 170
Ottoman Empire 35, 114
Owen v *City of Independence* (1980) 178

Packer, Herbert 143
Palme, Olaf 32
parantela relationships 100, 102
Park Chung Hee 114
Parkinson, C. Northcote 38–39, 111
"Parkinson's Law" 111, 151
Parrington, Vernon 40
participation, individual 163–70, 180
Pendleton Act (1883) 40
Peters, B. Guy 85, 98, 99, 100
"Peter Principle" 143
Petersen, Henry 115, 119
Philadelphia Convention 76, 152
Pitkin, Hannah 22, 65, 66
Plato 31, 71

Postal Service, U.S. 89, 111-112
political parties 147-49
polyarchal competitive systems 79
Powell, Lewis 178
Presidential control of bureaucracy 125, 132; Executive Office of the President 8, 14, 89, 121
productivity 111
Proposition 13 12, 154
Prussian civil service 39, 40, 118, 126, 188-89
Public Health Service 197
punishment 122-23
Putnam, Robert 69

quotas 56

Reagan, Ronald 148
recall petition 152
Reedy, George 121
referendum 152, 153
regulatory commissions 86
Reich, Charles 157
Reissman, Leonard 161
remiss petition 98
Republican Party 100, 133, 147
Reuss Amendment 153
Rickover, Hyman 190
riots, urban 169
Rivlin, Alice 133
Robeson, William 59
Robinson, Aubrey 144-45
Romania 56
Rommel, Erwin 36
Roosevelt, Franklin D. 137
Rosenbloom, David H. 68, 69, 84, 159-61
Ruckelshaus, William 119
Rousseau, Jean-Jacques 164
Russia 40, 63

Schattschneider, E. E. 141
Schmidt, Helmut 32
Schmitter, Phillipe 63
Securities and Exchange Commission 113
segregation 46, 143
Seidman, Harold 76-77, 85, 87, 94, 97, 101
Selznick, Philip 119
Serov, Ivan 115
Shah of Iran 32, 114
Shelepin, Dmitri 114, 115
Sirica, John 115
Sjoberg, Gideon 160
Small Business Administration 85-86
Smith, Adam 117
socialization 118-19
Social Security 147, 197
Spalding v *Vilas* (1896) 176
specialization 21, 153
Stalin, Josef 118
State, U.S. Department of 186
Stimson, Henry 130
Stokes, Donald 164
Stone, Christopher 140
Storing, Herbert 158

Subramaniam, V. 59, 195
"sunset" laws 150–51, 173, 198
"sunshine" laws 11, 149–50, 173
"supergrade" positions 115
Supreme Court, U.S. 133, 142, 176–78, 188
Sweden 98–99
Syria 60

Taft, William Howard 130
Taney, Roger 125
Taylor Grazing Act (1934) 102
technicians 33, 153
Tennessee Valley Authority 89, 197
Thayer, Frederick 165
Theroux, Paul 34
Thompson, Victor 159
Thorndike, Ernest 44
Three Mile Island 135
Transportation, U.S. Department of 84–85
Trudeau, Pierre 32
Tugwell, Rexford 130
Tullock, Gordon 141
Turkey 38, 40

United States v *42 Kegs of Whiskey* 140
United States v *The Schooner* 140

Veblen, Thorstein 33
Verba, Sidney 120
Veterans Administration 86
veterans, as clients 85, 89
Vietnam War 169
Volker, Paul 148

Wagner, Adolf 5
"Wagner's Law" 5, 112, 151
Waldo, Dwight 76
Wallace, Sayre 9
Walloon 36
War on Poverty 167, 169, 179
Warwick, Donald 5–6
Watergate 115, 116, 119, 128
Weber, Max 2, 3–5, 7, 71, 110
Weeks, Sinclair 97
Weimar Republic 31
Wen, Emperor 116
White, Leonard 125
Whittaker, 154
Wilensky, Harold 52
Wilson, Woodrow 46, 130, 147
Wodehouse, P. G. 193
women 94, 95, 140–41; in bureaucracy 58, 61, 69; as clients 85, 86, 89
World War I 35
Wood v *Strickland* (1975) 177
Wright, Skelly 139
Wu, Emperor 116

Young, Michael 197
Yugoslavia 60

Zeigler, L. Harmon 164

ABOUT THE AUTHORS

SAMUEL KRISLOV is professor of political science at the University of Minnesota; he also has taught at Columbia, Brandeis, the University of Wisconsin, and Tel-Aviv University. From 1974 to 1979 he was chairman of the Committee on Research on Law Enforcement and Criminal Justice of the National Academy of Sciences. A past president of the Law and Society Association and the Midwest Political Science Association, he has been a Guggenheim fellow, a Ford Foundation faculty fellow, and a Russell Sage scholar. Among his books are *The Negro in the Federal Bureaucracy* (1967), *The Supreme Court and Political Freedom* (1968), and *Forecasting the Impact of Legislation on Courts* (1980).

DAVID H. ROSENBLOOM is professor of public administration at the Maxwell School, Syracuse University. He specializes in research on the politics, personnel, and legal aspects of public bureaucracy. Before joining Syracuse University, Professor Rosenbloom taught at the universities of Vermont, Tel-Aviv, and Kansas. He was also an American Society for Public Administration fellow with the Office of Federal Equal Employment Opportunity of the U.S. Civil Service Commission.

Professor Rosenbloom received the Ph.D from the University of Chicago. Among his published works are *Federal Service and the Constitution* (1971) and *Federal Equal Employment Opportunity* (1977). He is coauthor of *Personnel Management in Government* (1978), *Bureaucratic Culture: Citizens and Administrators in Israel* (1978), and *Bureaucratic Government, USA* (1980).